Ivan Lendl, Sergi Bruguera, Guy Forget and Andre Agassi
arriving in Frankfurt on a Lufthansa Airbus for
the IBM/ATP World Championship.

Opposite page: Autographs of the eight Frankfurt finalists
(top to bottom) Pete Sampras, Guy Forget,
Boris Becker, Ivan Lendl, Karel Novacek, Andre Agassi,
tournament director Zeljko Franulovic,
Michael Stich, Jim Courier.

The ATP Tour

Year Two – 1991

The ATP Tour
Year Two - 1991

EDITED BY RICHARD EVANS

The official illustrated
guide to the 78 tournaments
in the ATP Tour –
with the full results

Acknowledgments

My thanks once again to everyone at Toucan who are fast
becoming experts in the intricate workings of the ATP Tour and,
of course, to Kathy Rooney, our editor at Bloomsbury.
Caroline Freud, whose name has changed since last year but not her
attention to detail, has helped enormously in gathering text and pictures
from all over the world and my thanks, too, must go to all our international
cast of contributors, the leading writers and photographers of the game,
whose talents make this book what it is.

First published 1992 by Bloomsbury Publishing Limited,
2 Soho Square, London W1V 5DE

Text copyright © 1992 Association of Tennis Professionals
Design and layout copyright © Bloomsbury Publishing Limited

British Library Cataloguing in Publication Data

A CIP record for this book is available from the British Library

ISBN 0 7475 11284

10 9 8 7 6 5 4 3 2 1

Edited and designed by Toucan Books Limited, London

Originated by J Film, Bangkok, Thailand

Printed by Butler and Tanner Limited,
Frome and London

Dear Reader,

Like the IBM/ATP Tour itself, this second edition of the ATP Yearbook is a bigger and, we hope, a better version of that produced for our inaugural year.

Through the talents of many of the world's leading tennis writers and photographers, once again we have tried to bring you a chronological yet panoramic view of eleven months non-stop action on the men's circuit.

All the indications are that our second year helped to consolidate the success of the first and offered the players and tournament directors, in partnership with our loyal sponsors, a platform from which to build an even more attractive game for you, the tennis supporter.

In the meantime, I hope this book enables you to enjoy another exciting journey around the great courts of the world.

Yours sincerely,

Mark Miles
CEO, ATP Tour

Dear Reader,

It has been another exciting year for all of us involved in the IBM/ATP Tour and, once again it has been a privilege for me to act as President of the Players Council, the body, made up entirely of elected players, which advises the Tour Board on rules and policy matters.

We like to think that some of these rules have a direct bearing on the quality of play and behaviour that spectators and television viewers around the world see on court. And we hope that the improvements are meeting with everyone's appproval.

I hope you enjoy this pictorial record of our world-wide efforts in 1991 and that you will continue to derive pleasure from the great sport of professional tennis in the months to come.

Yours sincerely,

Vijay Amritraj
President, ATP Tour Players Council

Dear Reader,

Once again, the IBM/ATP Tour World Championship in Frankfurt brought down the curtain on another successful year for the Tour – a journey through many cities and countries that you will be able to follow through the pages of this beautiful book.

The fantastic week in Frankfurt provides the world-wide family of Tournament representatives, with all their differing accents, backgrounds and traditions, the chance to mingle and enjoy a mutual pride in being part of a Tour that has changed the world of tennis.

Let us hope that the reward of success that we enjoyed in 1991 will inspire us to even greater commitment.

Yours sincerely,

Franco Bartoni
Chairman, ATP Tour Tournament Council

Contents

IBM/ATP Tour Tennis Goes High Tech in 1992

If the will to win in competitive sport is measured in true grit and undaunted spirit, the human heart clearly becomes the barometer for success. And as philosophical formulas go, there is no more simple nor universally accepted standard of the ages. But on a more practical and realistic plane, athletes' performance levels today are exhaustively examined, analysed and surveyed through a series of sophisticated, state-of-the-art scientific systems which produce an illuminating – if not intriguing – flood of priceless information.

MatchFacts, a front-runner in this field of systemised statistical sports services, marched onto the world's tennis stage at the start of the 1991 IBM/ATP Tour, and its immediate impact has altered the landscape of the sport. While keeping the media – and thus the public – informed with a steady stream of cumulative and comparative statistics, MatchFacts also provide players with an instant and thorough analysis of not only their game, but also their opponents' game.

'IBM has brought to tennis a commitment both financially and as an innovator in improving the quality of information available to the public about the game,' said Mark Miles, CEO of the ATP Tour. 'This technologically advanced statistical service has improved and expanded the horizons of the sport. MatchFacts has had a positive and dramatic impact on the players, media and fans,' Miles said.

MatchFacts paints statistical pictures in two basic categories: performance on serve and return of serve.

Michael Stich, Jim Courier and Guy Forget compare their MatchFacts statistics at the IBM/ATP Tour World Championships in Frankfurt.

In defining serve performance the system provides player stats for aces served, first-serve percentage, percentage of first and second serve points won, percentage of service games won and break points saved. Return of serve statistics consist of percentage of points won against an opponent's first and second serves, percentage of break points converted and percentage of return games won. Using a specially designed scorecard, match umpires record every single point scored during the estimated 3000 matches played annually on the IBM/ATP Tour. These statistics are cumulated weekly and added to the IBM/ATP Tour database to provide updated and invaluable information on the overall leaders for the year.

While the players, media and general public benefit from the statistical flow flashed by MatchFacts, tennis fans attending tournaments have been the recipients of some further IBM high-tech treats thanks to PlayerFacts.

Whether seeking the correct answer to settle a family feud or searching for a favourite player's biographical sketch, tournament ticket holders can now see some 100 of their Tour heroes by simply touching one of three symbols on the screen on an IBM Personal System/2 computer. Housed in kiosks, the PlayerFacts screen offers three basic choices for the on-site viewer. The selection of biographies is always popular as many of the vignettes are accompanied by a full-colour sound video of the star in action, along with career highlights including player rankings and lifetime and annual earnings. For those who wish to recall who beat whom in past tournaments, the PlayerFacts system allows a viewer to select one competitor from column 'A' and one from column 'B' whose head-to-head comparison is packaged on the screen. Previous winners of the tournament currently being played can be screened by touching a third PlayerFacts option.

Keeping in step with adding yet another dramatic dimension to the game, IBM has introduced the PS/2 based radar gun system that measures the speed of each serve and prominently displays the results on a large electronic scoreboard in the court area. An IBM PS/2 tracks service speeds throughout a match and provides analysis to determine where service speeds were most effective.

Such are the high-tech gifts of innovation and wizardry which IBM has presented to the ATP Tour. Advanced technology has made a tremendous contribution to the game of tennis, where its impact has enhanced the flow of information to the media, has immensely increased fan excitement and has served to raise to new heights the players' insight and awareness of their game.

Lufthansa and the ATP Tour – a High Flying Partnership

Lufthansa – a worldwide airline with routes to 190 cities, professional tennis players – worldwide travelers competing in all parts of the globe – a natural combination waiting to be matched.

Lufthansa is an airline whose history dates back to 1926 from the union of two German airlines: the history of tennis is 'somewhat' older. Lufthansa is an airline whose growth really took off at the beginning of the 1970s with the introduction of the jumbo jet: the popularity of tennis can also be said to have begun its boom at that time.

But Lufthansa began its involvement with sports sponsorship with another sport in 1974 – soccer. The airline sponsored the World Soccer Championships that year; tennis and other sports followed. Over the years, sport sponsorships have become an important part of the communications mix at Lufthansa and have been integrated into the company's overall corporate marketing strategy.

In recent years, Lufthansa has increased its emphasis on tennis. In January 1989, the German carrier formed a partnership with the ATP Tour, the governing body of men's professional tennis, and signed on as its official international airline. For Lufthansa, the ATP Tour seemed one very good way to increase awareness among the millions of tennis fans and players of the scope of the airline's services. Lufthansa has become a visible player in both men's and women's professional tennis; it is also the official international airline of the Davis Cup and the Federation Cup.

The ATP Tour provides Lufthansa with its most comprehensive tennis association as tournaments are played in 59 of the cities to which Lufthansa flies. This far-reaching relationship is beneficial both to the airline and to the players. Players who participate in the cooperative programme receive special travel privileges on Lufthansa's worldwide routes. In return, these players wear the airline's logo and serve as its ambassadors at tournaments and special events around the world. Lufthansa's tennis partnership with the ATP Tour includes being a founding member of the ATP headquarters in Ponte Vedra Beach, Florida.

A total of 70 players participated in the first year – 1989 – of the Lufthansa/ATP programme. The programme is open to the top 300 singles and top 50 doubles players. Those who sign up with Lufthansa can move up the Lufthansa ladder as they compete in tournaments and improve their ATP rankings.

Jaime Yzaga of Peru won a close race in 1989 for the top spot in singles closely followed by Christo van Rensberg of South Africa, and Jan Gunnarsson of Sweden. Others in the top ten that first year were Jim Grabb, Kelly Evernden, Paul Chamberlin, Petr Korda, Paul Annacone, David Wheaton and Dan Goldie.

ATP rankings determine players rankings in the Lufthansa ladder. The top ten players in singles and doubles are awarded Lufthansa flights. During the 1990 season, 104 players signed up to be Lufthansa ambassadors and compete in the airline's travel bonus programme. Players from the U.S. and Czechoslovakia led the 1990 Lufthansa singles rankings. Richey Reneberg took the number one prize followed by Karel Novacek and Derrick Rostagno. Danie Visser and Pieter Aldrich were both number one in doubles on the IBM/ATP Tour computer and in the Lufthansa standings.

Leading this year's rankings in singles is Karel Novacek, who ranks number 8 on the computer (the first time a Lufthansa player has broken into the top ten in singles). Number two is Petr Korda, who currently ranks number 9 in the world. Danie Visser is once again leading in doubles.

This year, Lufthansa also played a role in the first IBM/ATP Tour Grass Roots Challenge which brought together eight inner-city junior teams from tennis development programmes for a two-day, round robin competition in late August in Harlem. The carrier provided transportation for ten young players from London, Madras and Melbourne who were invited to the New York City event organised by IBM/ATP Tour Charities.

Lufthansa believes it is an ideal partner for the ATP Tour on an international level, and professional tennis is an ideal sport for a quality international airline to sponsor. The German national airline is proud of its worldwide reputation for service, reliability and punctuality. It is proud to be named, year after year, as one of the three top airlines in the world by readers of Conde Nast Traveler, a leading travel magazine, and by business and investor magazines. Top tennis players are those who strive for quality; top airlines do the same.

Tennis is a sport played by nearly 45 million people around the world. Last year, Lufthansa flew 22.4 million passengers. Professional tennis matches draw tennis fans everywhere, many of whom are also Lufthansa passengers. Joining forces with the ATP Tour provides a 'perfect partner' for the airline with a 'passion for perfection'.

Lucille Hoshabjian

1991 – Advancing into the Nineties

By Richard Evans

While the world economy reeled from war in the Gulf and deepening recession, the professional tennis circuit, epitomised in greater part by the global spread of the IBM/ATP Tour, proved remarkably resilient and virtually immune from the general economic downturn.

The Tour's sponsors remained steadfast and loyal; only one tournament – Casablanca – was temporarily suspended because of the Gulf War and the queue to join the Challenger circuit or the Tour itself remained as long as ever. Prize money was up; crowds were up; player commitment increased and so did television exposure. The innate attraction of a wonderful game was proving, once again, to be irresistible.

If part of the secret for this success lay in the increasingly streamlined organisation of a Tour entering its second year of operation, the prime factor was, of course, the excitement, variety and standard of competition produced on court by the players themselves.

The much prized position of No. 1 on the ATP computer changed hands four times during the year between Stefan Edberg, the final encumbent, and Boris Becker, who exploded into the top spot at the Australian Open in January only to fall to third behind the year's most consistent performer, Jim Courier, by November.

As early season titles were swept up by the likes of Courier, Guy Forget, Karel Novacek and Sergi Bruguera, those critics who prefer the certainty of the status quo were predicting that the Edberg-Becker-Lendl triumvirate would re-assert its authority once the summer's Grand Slams came round.

But Courier won the French Open and, in an even bigger surprise, Michael Stich beat Becker in Wimbledon's first-ever all German final to claim the game's most coveted crown. The locker room was, perhaps, less amazed than the public at Stich's success and the pedigree that his peers had recognised for some time was born out when he went on to win the Mercedes Cup in Stuttgart on clay, the OTB International at Schenectady on hard court and the CA Trophy in Vienna on indoor carpet.

Edberg, triumphing as is his custom in Tokyo where he won both the Suntory and Seiko titles, succeeded where Bjorn Borg had always failed by winning the U.S. Open but was sadly absent through injury from the IBM/ATP Tour's grand finale in Frankfurt.

There was, however, nothing sad about the way Pete Sampras re-asserted himself as a class act after a troubled start to the year, by beating the durable Courier in the World Championship final. Sampras's success brought down the curtain on a week of high quality play on the new Greenset Trophy court at Frankfurt's Festhalle – an arena of character and charm that is beginning to give the ATP Tour's showpiece ending to the year an atmosphere all of its own.

The ATP Tour World Doubles Final was special for a very different reason. After weeks of negotiation between the various tennis bodies in South Africa, unification was achieved in time for ATP Tour CEO Mark Miles to authorise a switch of venue from Sanctuary Cove in Australia to Johannesburg. Despite an opening day demonstration by a small group that felt change was happening too fast, the World Doubles Finals were played in front of increasingly large and appreciative crowds and the players rose to the occasion, visiting townships for coaching sessions as well as playing some superb tennis. Fittingly for a team that had dominated the year with three Grand Slam victories, Anders Jarryd and John Fitzgerald won the title with a hard fought four-set triumph over Ken Flach and Robert Seguso.

'I've never won this title before,' Fitzgerald said afterwards. 'But the most important thing is the advancement of tennis in South Africa. There will be some good players coming out of here in the next few years.'

Those thoughts, selflessly expressed by one of the game's best ambassadors, was a fine way to bring down the curtain on another year of improbably high achievement.

Pete Sampras and the Lambert Crystal Crown in Frankfurt. *(Gianni Ciaccia)*

Michael Stich – Man of Destiny

By John Barrett

Sitting on the members' balcony at the All England Lawn Tennis and Croquet Club that sunny Sunday afternoon with her middle son Torsten, the mother of the Club's newest member could hardly believe it. Gertrud Stich gazed down at the crowd of expectant fans thronging six deep against the barriers outside the Royal entrance below and, with a puzzled look, asked innocently:

'Who are they waiting for, the Duchess?'.

'No, Mrs Stich,' I smiled, 'They are waiting for a glimpse of the new Champion.'

Laughing quietly, she said, 'What a pity Detlef and Andreas have had to fly home – they would have been amused by all this fuss over Michael.'

It was apparent that the Stich family do not like fuss. They cherish their privacy. Yet, at that moment, Gertrud Stich realised that life would never be quite the same again. Overnight Michael, the baby of the family, had become a world figure – not yet as recognisable as Germany's most famous son, Boris Becker, the man whom Michael had just annihilated in straight sets that momentous afternoon of the first ever all-German men's final – but sufficiently famous for privacy to become an increasingly rare commodity.

It all seemed such a long time ago that Gertrud and Detlef Stich used to take the three young boys down to the local tennis club near their home in Elmshorn, some 20 kilometres from Hamburg. Like so many other families they enjoyed playing tennis with their friends simply for the fun and exercise it provided.

'They never pushed me,' remembers Michael. 'Andreas helped me quite a bit but he is eight years older and had his own friends so I used to play with Torsten. None of it was very serious though.'

When Michael started to win local junior tournaments it became a little more serious. 'At that age I used to enjoy playing football at school as much as tennis. It was frustrating at times to lose to people I thought I should beat and I was not always able to accept calls that went against me. I may look cool out there today but I wasn't always as well behaved – it has taken me a long time to develop a philosophical attitude.' Michael is in good company. Bjorn Borg, the epitome of controlled beaviour, was once suspended as a junior for his outrageous behaviour.

Michael was 16 when Becker won Wimbledon for the first time. 'I remember watching on television and thinking what a great achievement it was – for Boris and for Germany – but it did not really affect my attitude to life. I never dreamed of becoming a professional tennis player myself – not then.'

Two years later Michael followed Boris as the national junior champion. He was nearly 18 and had completed his 13 years of schooling by passing his Abitur with distinction. In 1988, like every other young German, he had to present himself for National Service.

'That made a difference. I began to realise that it might be a good idea to turn professional. It would mean giving up football, of course, but you couldn't expect to have everything.'

Michael was maturing, and by this time, surveying the world from a height of 6'4" (1.92m), his beanpole body projected around the court on matchstick legs that gave him the appearance of an underfed stork. But he had also developed a beautifully timed serve, flashing groundstrokes that were spectacular but erratic, and an ability to caress the ball with sweet touch on the volley where his wide wingspan made him a difficult man to pass. The raw material of his greatness was already there – a fact recognised by the Iphitos Club in Munich who recruited Michael to represent them in the prestigious Bundesleague.

It was there, a year later, that Michael began one of those successful partnerships that are so often found in the background of future champions. Coaching at Iphitos was a quiet New Zealander, Mark Lewis, whose brother Chris had been the Wimbledon finalist of 1983. Like his brother, Chris was a fitness fanatic with a knack of recognising talent in others. He was also a great motivator. 'I owe a great deal to Mark', acknowledges Michael. 'As I got to know him I came to respect his judgement. More than that – I trusted him, and that is not an easy thing in the modern game when so many are only out for themselves.'

Michael had repaid the Iphitos invesment by helping them to become the German champions in 1990. It was typical of him that within days of his Wimbledon triumph he turned out for them again, as promised. 'I had made a bargain and I kept to it. It was as simple as that,' he says.

The speed of Michael's advance to a top ten ranking has surprised some, but the potential had been apparent early. Success in the German satellite in 1989 was followed by his arrival in the quarter-finals at Queen's Club where, despite carrying an injury, he took a set off Ivan Lendl and prompted the great man to suggest that '....his serve could give us all a lot of trouble'. Just how much, even Ivan could not have guessed.

A study of Stich by Serge Philippot

The first title came at Memphis in 1990. The following January he surged to two finals in Australia. His progress to the final again in Memphis was the prelude to a significant performance at the French Open. By now fully fit and well-motivated, he showed us the basic quality of his all-court game by going through to the semi-finals where the eventual champion, Courier, spent a long, hot afternoon subduing him in four sets.

All this was as preparation for the glorious deeds to come at Wimbledon. Somehow, there was an air of inevitability about Michael's serene progress. Had he perhaps read his Omar Khayyam?

> *'Tis' all a Chequer-board of Nights and Days*
> *Where Destiny with Men for Pieces plays:*
> *Hither and thither moves, and mates, and slays*
> *And one by one back in the closet lays.'*

Dan Goldie was the first to be slain and the bodies of Diego Nargiso and Omar Camporese quickly joined him in the closet.

Then, in the fourth round, an unmistakable air of destiny. The Russian left-hander Alexander Volkov, ahead by 3-1 in the fifth set, led 30-40 on the Stich serve. A blazing ace saved the day. The Gods smiled again four games later when, with Volkov serving for the match at 5-3, 30-15, Michael, running wide, hit a forehand pass that landed on the line for 30-30. On the very next point a desperate backhand pass clipped the top of the net and was deflected for a winner. Instead of match point to Volkov, it was break point for Stich. Two games later the match was over. Miraculously, Michael had survived and you began to understand who was writing the script.

To his credit Michael had no problem in reading it. In succession Courier, the No. 4 seed and Stefan Edberg, the defending champion were humbled by some of the finest serving and opportunist returning ever seen on Wimbledon's hallowed lawns. By now Michael knew he was striding with destiny. 'For sure, I'll have a good chance in the final,' he had said, without bravado. The victory, in straight sets, was absolutely stunning. Two strokes won it for him – his second serve, which was awesome in its power and penetration, and his backhand returns and passes which continually thwarted Becker's attempts to impose himself on the match and even threatened to undermine the former champion's sanity.

Success will not change this level-headed champion. 'Remember, it is just a game,' he says. 'I can still improve in lots of ways and I shall go on playing for as long as I enjoy it. But there are other things in life. Love means a lot to me, as does my family. And I need time to myself, time to reflect on who I am and what I'm doing.'

We all know what he will be doing on Monday 22 June this year – walking out to the cheers of the centre court crowd as he opens the 1992 Wimbeldon programme in defence of his title. This time though, his mother will know what all the fuss is about.

Jin Courier sets his year in motion at the Newsweek Cup in Indian Wells. *(Michael Baz)*

Jim Courier Jumps to No. 2

By Peter Bodo

Your local postman may be a day late with your mail, Federal Express may guarantee next day delivery, but when the Courier is Jim, the delivery is *always* early.

For instance, take the 1991 year in tennis. At the onset, the dewy-cheeked, deliberate 21-year-old from Dade City, Florida, was considered a solid Top Ten prospect, a foot soldier in the United States' growing campaign to re-establish itself among the world tennis powers. He was ranked No. 25 on the IBM/ATP computer, and overshadowed by promising David Wheaton, flamboyant Andre Agassi and the surprise 1990 U.S. Open Champion, Pete Sampras.

But when the smoke cleared after the 1991 ATP championships in Frankfurt, only Stefan Edberg stood between Courier and the summit of the game. Such an ascent is never easy, but Courier negotiated the slopes with precision, intelligence and confidence, drawing liberally on the advice of his Spanish coach, Jose Higueras.

'I'm a much different player than I was a year ago,' Courier confessed at the end of '91. 'My emotions used to be all over the place. I was always excited, living on a roller-coaster in my matches. But through the year I became a much more controlled payer. I now *pick* my time to get excited, which is much more productive. I owe that, along with developing a better all-round game, to Jose. He's brought it all to me.'

Courier's ascent began with a torrid three-week run that bagged him two tournament titles (the Newsweek Champions Cup at Indian Wells, where he defeated Guy Forget in the final, and the Lipton at Key Biscayne, where his victim was Wheaton), a 12-match winning streak, and his first top ten ranking, at No. 9. The most striking feature of Courier's mental game in those tournaments was his maturity, while his technical game was enhanced by a new willingness to attack behind his most punishing groundstrokes. Although he still played a baseline game, Courier began to do so with greater aggression – thereby putting that decisive, extra bit of pressure on his opponents.

After an inauspicious Davis Cup debut Courier created the centrepiece of his charmed year. At the French Open, he vanquished Edberg, the imminent Wimbledon champion Michael Stich, and Agassi in successive rounds.

Two years earlier at the very same tournament, Courier won a bitter four-set struggle with Agassi. Afterwards, Courier freely criticised their mutual 'coach', Nick Bollettieri, for obviously and insensitively supporting Agassi in the battle between his proteges. Ironically, the key element in Courier's win over Agassi in the '91 final was provided by Courier's new coach, Higueras. During a rain delay early in the match, after a strong start by Agassi, Higueras managed to calm and steel Courier. It was a different match when they returned from the break. Courier outplayed Agassi and Higueras had clearly outcoached Bollettieri to turn the tide in the rivalry between America's top young players.

Courier lost to Stich at Wimbeldon, but then, so did everybody else. Although Courier played consistently in the summer, he showed a window of vulnerability in his loss to the Czech Peter Korda at Montreal and two losses to Sampras (Cincinatti and Indianapolis). Like some other aggressive baseliners, Courier's game can be smothered by serve-and-volley tennis – not by any helter-skelter power player, but by the kind who can take away the pace and force Courier into having to stretch and dig out the ball for his passing shots.

The object lesson in this exercise was provided by Edberg in the final of the U.S. Open, after Courier had another bracing run with a quarter-final win over Sampras and a semi-final drubbing of renascent Jimmy Connors. The brilliant and idiosyncratic Swede dominated Courier with his plethora of off-speed kick serves, skidding approaches and viciously sliced volleys.

Prosperous and tired, Courier helped the U.S. advance to the Davis Cup final round and then, after a good rest, he played up to standard and reached the final of the IBM/ATP World Championship in Frankfurt, where he ended his official season with a loss to Sampras.

The blueprint for Courier's off-season was drawn up by Edberg in the U.S. Open final, and by the mercurial Sampras. He can hold his own with pure power players, either baseliners or serve-and-volley practitioners. He primarily needs to solve the 'passive-aggressive' opponents who can neutralize his pinpoint passing shots and avoid engaging Courier in rallies.

'This year had been kind of a whirlwind for me, and a quick year,' Courer said. 'I'm not concerned with my Number Two ranking. Sure it brings pressure but it's still awfully nice to have. I was talking about this with Jose, and the good thing is that we still feel I'm two, three years away from my best tennis. So far, my best has only been my best to date.'

Considering this Courier's record for early delivery, those words will surely put his rivals on alert.

BP Nationals

By Joseph Romanos

Wellington, 31 December-6 January
Tournament Director: Ian Wells

It was a case of all's well that ends well for BP National's tournament director, Ian Wells, at the Renouf Centre in Wellington. Watching over the traditional first tournament of the year's ATP tour, Wells saw his three wild card entries – New Zealanders Kelly Evernden, Brett Steven and Bruce Derlin – and his top two seeds – Soviets Andrei Cherkasov and Alexander Volkov – bundled out in the first round. Worse was to follow when Patrick McEnroe, younger brother of Big John and therefore the most recognisable name in the draw, was hustled out of the tournament 6-2, 6-3 in a second round clash with Christian Bergstrom. By the weekend though, Wells was smiling again as two stirring semi-final duels, both of which were decided by a third-set tie-breaker, set up a final between Tasmanian 20-year-old, Richard Fromberg the third seed, and Swedish newcomer Lars Jonsson, played in front of the largest crowd that the tournament has yet drawn.

The stringbean Fromberg, in the middle of a hot spell which had seen his ranking rise to 32nd after two tournament victories in 1990, was far too

Ian Wells was smiling again as two stunning semi-finals drew record crowds.

good in a lop-sided final which lasted 106 minutes. It almost goes without saying that the final was played in swirling winds and Fromberg, with his economical stroking and big serving, handled the conditions far better. 'It was rough to play consistently out there,' said the Australian. 'But I took my chances. My serve was working well, so I was able to get into the net and bustle him.' Fromberg impressed with his calm temperament and seemed to flow through the final.

He came up well after two gruelling preliminary matches. In his quarter-final he was given a torrid time by smooth-stroking Indian Ramesh Krishnan, a particular favourite in Wellington. As are most of Krishnan's matches, this was a contest of placement against power and this time it was the power of Fromberg which just got there, 5-7, 6-4, 7-5.

Perhaps fortified by this narrow escape, Fromberg fronted up confidently against Bergstrom in the semi-final. It was even closer – 6-3, 5-7, 7-6. The tie-breaker was a thriller which Fromberg finally clinched 8-6.

On the other side of the draw Jonsson, in the Swedish manner, progressed almost unnoticed to the semi-final (without dropping a set) and then faced big-hitting Italian Omar Camporese.

For a while it appeared the volatile Italian would simply overpower the more clinical, but less powerful Swede. Gradually Jonsson, playing in his trademark long bike shorts and reversed cap, climbed back into the match, but he never looked comfortable and was a relieved man when he squeaked home 5-7, 6-3, 7-6, though the tie-breaker, 7-3, was not quite so desperate as in the first semi-final.

Jonsson, two months younger than Fromberg, did not play well in the final. He appeared affected by the pressure of his first ATP singles final. Fromberg, to his credit, never relented and by the end it was a frustrated and harried Jonsson on view. 'I was not that concentrated,' said the Swede. 'I was a little sore from the semi-final and did not move well. Also my concentration was not good. Perhaps I was too confident after yesterday's match. I will learn from this for the next time I'm in a final.'

The doubles was a strange event in which the South American pairing of Luiz Mattar (Brazil) and Nicolas Pereira (Venezuela), the third seeds, fought back to win a see-sawing three-setter over the scratch pairing of Jaime Oncins (Brazil) and John Letts (USA) 4-6, 7-6, 6-2. For quite a while Letts and Oncins, who had to qualify to get into the doubles draw, seemed to have the match for the taking, but two or three crucial volleying errors in the heart of the second set cost them dearly. After losing the tie-breaker 7-3, they were blown away in the third.

Pereira, though he has not had a happy time of it in singles in Wellington – he lost in the first round qualifying this time – must have some

Fromberg in action en route to the title. *(Courtesy of the BP Nationals)*

affinity with the Renouf Centre courts, for it was his second straight doubles title. In 1990 he had teamed with Evernden to claim the doubles crown. The clear doubles favourites were Spaniards Sergio Casal and Javier Sanchez, but they were strangely off form in their quarter-final against the last remaining local hopes, Steve Guy and Brett Steven, and lost 6-1, 7-6.

Australian Men's Hardcourt Championships

By Craig Gabriel

Adelaide, 31 December-6 January
Tournament Director: Ron Green

Just 90 minutes from the Barossa Valley, one of the superb wine producing regions of Australia, the City of Churches rang out its bells on the first Sunday of the new year and a young Swede, Nicklas Kulti won his first career title, the West End Australian Hardcourt Championships, and then said: 'Adelaide will always be in my heart.'

Kulti, 19 years of age and hailing from Vaxjo, Mats Wilander's hometown, withstood a strong mid-match challenge from Michael Stich to hold out for the title 6-3, 1-6, 6-2 in 89 minutes. 'I don't know the right words to describe how I feel, but I know that happy is not big enough,' said Kulti after receiving the $21,600 cheque and trophy from Ron Green, President of the South Australian Tennis Association, and co-tournament director with Colin Stubs.

The tournament was quite a buzz as Boris Becker was the top seed, but Adelaide sporting fans, who in recent years have become tuned to the speed of Formula One cars racing through their city streets in the season's final grand prix, had to move even faster to catch a glimpse of the German. Kulti's best friend Magnus Larsson used his 6-foot 3-inch frame to power down cannonball serves and deflate any hopes Becker might have

entertained. The German was stunned by the ferocity of the Swede's serve and more times than he would care to remember Becker was left standing in amazement as small yellow blurs whizzed past his face, just like the multi-coloured machines. The top seed managed to take the match to a third set tie-breaker but at this crucial stage his own serve, a staple part of Becker's game, deserted him and he double faulted and watched the match slip through his fingers.

The second and sixth seeds certainly provided tennis fans with a glimpse of what was to come through the year. Jim Courier at No. 2 went to the semifinals where he ran into Michael Stich and once again it was a battle of the respective arms as big serving ruled the day. Stich finally prevailed 6-4, 7-6 (8-6).

The climatic conditions experienced during the week were erratic to say the least and players really had to take things one day at a time as the mercury jumped around between 43° and 23° Celsius. And it was amid misty rain that the doubles title was claimed by Stefan Kruger (for the second time in three years) and Wayne Ferreira of South Africa with a 6-4, 4-6, 6-4 result over the Dutch tandem of Paul Haarhuis and Mark Koevermans.

Few noticed when Niklas Kulti beat a young German in the final at Memorial Drive. But then Michael Stich started winning things... *(Norman Lomax)*

Holden N.S.W. Open Tournament of Champions

By Craig Gabriel

Sydney, 7-13 January
Tournament Directors: Barry K. Masters & Rod Read

Guy Forget had taken his shaven head and equally bald doubles partner Jakob Hlasek to Hawaii for a Christmas holiday after the pair had claimed the ATP Tour World Doubles Championship at Sanctuary Cove. By the time Forget returned for the Holden New South Wales Open at White City, a little fuzz of protection from the summer sun had started to appear on the Frenchman's pate but, in his racket arm at least, the strength of Samson remained.

Striking a rich vein of form that would soon lift him into the world's top ten for the first time in his ten-year career, Forget won this famous title with a blistering defeat of Michael Stich, another man destined for big things in 1991, in just 73 minutes by a score of 6-3, 6-4. His serve, producing 28 aces for the week and timed as fast as 201 km/h, decimated all who faced him across the net. The victory made Forget the third Frenchman in seven years to win at White City. Henri Leconte won in 1985 when the tournament was still played on grass and then Yannick Noah added to the Gallic flavour on Rebound Ace in 1990.

I was satisfied,' said Forget, who earned $32,400 for his premier victory outside France. 'I didn't play [in the final] as good as the other days, but it was good for my confidence to win five matches

Michael Stich gave fans a glimpse of what was to come in 1991... he was playing in his second consecutive final of the year. *(Courtesy N.S.W. Open)*

Guy Forget was like a tornado through the tournament, never dropping more than four games in any one set. The Frenchman's hair had just started to grow back after he shaved it off with Hlasek just two months before, but still he needed head protection. *(Courtesy N.S.W. Open)*

in a row.' He then added, kissing his wife Isabelle and infant son Mathiou: 'It is important to win elsewhere and I am happy about this win. This is one of the good ones and I hope there is more to come.' The final was played with great spirit, respect and sportsmanship as Stich, who needed treatment on his right elbow from trainer Rob Hanna during the match, and Forget extended points to each other over doubtful calls in the second set.

The top seed Ivan Lendl lost valuable match practice in the lead up to the Australian Open. The year before the Czech had reached the quarter-finals losing to the acrobatic Yannick Noah, but this time it was his own stomach muscles and the persistent Australian Wally Masur who caused the problems in the first round. After winning the first set 6-2, Lendl's serving power decreased markedly, and Masur, sensing a problem produced better returns and levelled the match with a tiebreaker 7-5. Lendl then retired to save himself for Melbourne.

By the quarter-final stage the tournament had just one seed left in the field: Forget. To watch the Frenchman in action was a sheer delight as the racket flowed through points. So dominant was Forget that, until the final, he did not lose more than three games in any one set with the total number of games lost being just 12.

The doubles title went to the affectionately known 'Beastie Boys' Scott Davis and David Pate, rallying back from a set down to defeat Darren Cahill and Mark Kratzmann 3-6, 6-3, 6-2.

The top seed Ivan Lendl lost valuable match practice in the lead up to the Australian Open.

Glorious weather made for a very enjoyable week in Sydney while out on the fabulous harbour, Tournament Directors Barry Masters and Rod Read had put together what was being billed as the 'Battle of the Sexes'. David Wheaton and his brother John sailed in a yacht race against Pam Shriver and Anne Smith ... the end result was a couple of bruised male egos.

Benson & Hedges New Zealand Open

By Charlie Risso-Gill

Auckland, 7-13 January
Tournament Director: Tom Kiely

Auckland is known as the 'city of sails' because those New Zealanders who are not knocking lumps off each other in the name of a sport called rugger are pursuing the more gentle aspects of sailing. The Benson & Hedges New Zealand Open offered the players involved in the tournament the chance of some competitive sailing, a chance which they seized eagerly. Eric Jelen, Alex Antonitsch and Luis Mattar were amongst those who crewed three 50-foot ocean racing yachts on a day around the harbour. It was a special experience with the lads proving they can jib the mainbrace without being seasick over the portside. 'Ah harr, me matey!'

Once the seadogs had reached *terra firma* a job was in hand for Brazilian Luis Mattar and Jean-Philippe Fleurian in the semi-final. Fleurian, a rugged Frenchman who is no stranger to the Pacific, having spent much of his childhood in New Caledonia, had created the one of the two major upsets to hit the Benson & Hedges in the early rounds by beating top seed Emilio Sanchez 6-2, 7-6. Now, the power of his serving and months of practise on hardcourts in Florida paid off as he overpowered Mattar in three tough sets. In the bottom half of the draw Marian Vajda had been responsible for the removal of the No. 2 seed, Andrei Chesnokov in the second round and had

Big crowds turned out for the Novacek – Fleurian final. *(Norman Smith)*

Lars Jonsson of Sweden earned a tough three set victory over Italy's Omar Camporese in the second round at Stanley Street. *(Serge Philippot)*

then gone on to overcome Germany's Patrik Kuhnen in the quarters. That set up a semi-final between Vajda, a Slovak from Bratisdlava and Karel Novacek, a Czech from Prague.

Novacek, the fourth seed, was more aggressive throughout and, although he conceded the second set, he stormed through the third without losing a game. At 25, Karel was through to the seventh Tour final of his career and, had he but known it, on the threshold of the most successful year he would enjoy since his first appearance at the senior level in 1983.

In contrast Jean-Philippe's only previous appearance in a final was at Itaparica in 1986. They had met just once before in Nice in 1988. Novacek was the winner then and the odds-on favourite to win again.

In a tight match where both sets went to tie-breaks Novacek showed he had the slight edge, grabbing the first by seven points to five and the

second by seven-four. Winning the points that mattered in the crunch enabled Novacek to become the 1991 winner of the John Redwood Trophy and earn 90 ATP computer ranking points – points that, by autumn, would help this powerful professional to move into the world's top ten.

The doubles final was a class act with the Spanish pair of Sergio Casal and Emilio Sanchez just edging out Grant Connell and Glen Michibata of Canada.

The tournament was a great success for Auckland Director, Tom Kiely. 'The players are much happier than they were a few years ago,' he said. 'New Zealand has four international events whereas years ago we had only one.' Kelly Evernden who left Auckland for a spot of 'bungey jumping' on South Island agreed. 'I'd heard that tennis is the third largest participant sport in New Zealand which surprised me quite a lot, because when I was growing up it was about 9 or 10. It's looking very positive'.

Ford Australian Open

By Richard Yallop

Melbourne, 14-27 January
Tournament Director: Colin Stubs

Boris Becker had spent most of his tennis career trying to forget Melbourne, but the 1991 Australian Open ensured he would never forget it. Not only did he win the title for the first time, at the sixth attempt, but the victory sent him to the No. 1 ranking for the first time.

We've got used to all sorts of victory celebrations: Borg sinking to his knees on the Wimbledon grass; fists pumped in the air; racquets tossed into the stands; but Becker gave us something completely new – the disappearing act. At the moment of triumph, when the last point had been won in his 1-6, 6-4, 6-4, 6-4 victory over Ivan Lendl, he leapt deliriously in the air, disappeared down the players' tunnel, and set off for a run round the park outside the National Tennis Centre. A security man followed in hot pursuit.

Perhaps Becker was doing his version of the Garbo routine; he wanted to be left alone with his emotions. The same theme came through in his victory press conference, when he let the reporters know that one of the penances of being a famed tennis player was having to talk to the media all the time. He hoped, having reached his target, he could stay committed for

'Just as you thought – Becker, Edberg, Lendl and McEnroe in the semi-finals!' Patrick McEnroe enjoys his little joke with the press. *(Serge Philippot)*

Having ousted Guy Forget in straight sets in the quarters, there were more alarms in his semi-final against Patrick McEnroe, when he found himself a set down, and 0-30 down on his service at 2-all in the second. He responded with the 'Boris stomp', a stream of incredulous, self-directed ravings, and it seemed to exorcise the demon within. Rolling in the heavy artillery, he served 23 aces, and swept to a 6-7, 6-4, 6-1, 6-4 win.

In the other semi-final Ivan Lendl checked the majestic progress of the current No.1 Stefan Edberg. Edberg double-faulted on his second match point, and Lendl jumped at his reprieve,

another two years and (by implication, though he did not mention the player directly) not do a Mats Wilander: lose motivation as soon as the goal of No. 1 had been attained.

Becker was barely coherent at the on-court ceremony ('It's unbelievable. I can't say anything. I'm sorry') and in the interview room he said: 'It's difficult to explain. I've trained for so long, and I didn't expect to do it here.'

Melbourne had previously been a recurring nightmare for Becker: in 1985, when he was reigning Wimbledon champion, he lost in the early rounds on Kooyong's grass to Michiel Schapers; in 1987 he had another Kooyong brainstorm, losing to Wally Masur, being fined $2,000 for unsportsmanlike conduct, and splitting with his coach Gunter Bosch.

The omens were not good for a 1991 victory, especially when Becker found himself two sets all and reeling on his heels midway through the fifth in a third-round marathon with the Italian Omar Camporese. Camporese hit a volley long when he had the German at his mercy, and Becker did not look back. It took him five hours and 11 minutes to beat Camporese by 7-6, 7-6, 0-6, 4-6, 14-12 – the longest match in the tournament's history – and he took it as a sign that the local gods were at last smiling on him.

Becker in full voice as he wins the Australian Open and jumps to No 1 in the world. *(Brunskill)*

23

Patrick McEnroe needs assistance from ATP trainer Todd Snyden on his way to the semi-finals. *(Serge Philippot)*

Not a cuddly pair, normally, but David Pate and Scott Davis seem happy enough with their koala bears after winning the Australian Open doubles. *(Serge Philippot)*

progress to the semi-finals. He had never been past the second round of a Grand Slam in singles, and early on in Melbourne, when the name 'P. McEnroe' kept being written on the draw sheet, it drew the press response, 'Oh, he's McEnroe's brother; he's a doubles player.' But by the quarter-final, when McEnroe had a plucky five-set win over Christiano Caratti, finishing the five-set match in a brace after straining his back in the second set, he had emerged as a character in his own right.

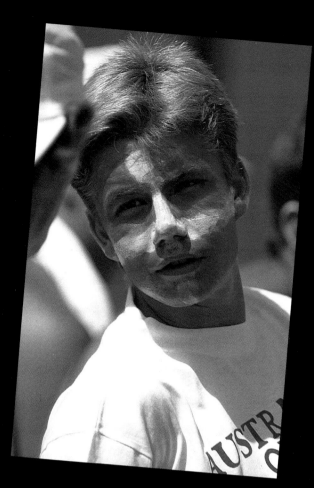

Swedish players never lack support at Flinders Park. *(Serge Philippot)*

winning 6-4, 5-7, 3-6, 7-6, 6-4. In the final, after losing the opening set, Becker moved into his Wimbledon mode, suddenly unleashing a forehand winner down the line on break point, or diving acrobatically to put away a volley. The decisive strikes happened so quickly that Lendl, striving methodically as ever, barely had time to realise he was the victim of a court mugging. Two or three such flashes of the racquet head were enough to give Becker his first Australian title.

If it was Becker's title, it was Patrick McEnroe's tournament. He made headlines because he made no headlines. A year earlier, elder brother John had emblazoned himself across the back pages by being disqualified from the Open by Supervisor Ken Farrar. Now Patrick, baby-faced and looking in need of mothering, charmed his way into Melbourne hearts with his self-effacing but spirited

He had a deceptively plain-looking game (looking all the more so when compared to John's scintillating patterns) but when he swung that forehand it was mighty effective. If you watched him play the double-handed backhand you would never have known it was a McEnroe on the court.

Yet once he opened his mouth, you knew. The intonation was the same; and the wit. He patiently soldiered on through all the questions about being 'Junior'. He was playing because he loved the game. 'I didn't want to play because of John, and I didn't want not to play because of him.'

Humility was also his strong shot. 'I've never had the talent or speed, so I knew I had to work harder,' he said. 'It's nice to know the dedication I've had this past year has paid off.'

If, with a brother of John's genius, he was brave ever to take the court, the same determination showed through in his two opening five set wins, against Thomas Hogstedt and Johan Anderson. By the time he had taken the first set against Becker in the semi-final, playing with outrageous nerve in the tie-break, he had proved conclusively that he was not just a doubles player. He did, though, reach the doubles final, with David Wheaton, but lost to Scott Davis and David Pate, in four sets. It ensured that he left Melbourne remembered as Patrick McEnroe, singles player, and brother of nobody.

25

Muratti Time Indoor Championships

By Anna Legnani

Milan, 4-10 February
Tournament Director: Fabio Sapori

The tennis fans who had braved the snow to reach the Forum Assago, the new site of the Muratti Time Indoor Championship, were rewarded with a week of fine tennis and intense emotions. Though the top four seeds all fell in the first two rounds, the Milanese spectators were not entirely disappointed, as the protagonist of the biggest upset was rising star Cristiano Caratti, who took out none other than Ivan Lendl, ranked number three in the IBM/ATP Tour computer and 1990 title holder. The third set tie-breaker that sealed the young Italian's victory and proved the solidity of his nerves saw all the players on site flocking to the stands to witness the event live. Caratti, who had earned a wild card after his quarter-final performance in the Australian Open, became the hero of the week, and the tournament was soon re-baptised 'Caratti Time Indoor Championships', while newspaper headlines declared that this was '18-Caratti tennis'.

Alexander Volkov (left) and the man who kept the crowds cheering all the way to the final, Cristiano Caratti.
(Gianni Ciaccia)

A wintery start for tennis at the newly-built Forum Assago. *(Gianni Ciaccia)*

The young Italian then confirmed his stunning success by taking out Nicklas Kulti and Carl-Uwe Steeb, coming back from 2-5 down to take the first set in the tie-breaker against the German to make his first career final. By this time, however, Caratti was mentally exhausted, not being used to playing at such a level for five matches in a row, and was thus an easy prey for Alexander Volkov, who had swept past Pat Cash and Jakob Hlasek to reach his fourth career final, his second in Milan. The Soviet rapidly dispatched the first set, setting a pace that a worn-out Caratti could not hold, and his accelerations often found his opponent off timing. The local idol managed to return from two breaks down in the second set to equal Volkov on 5-5, but his energy was spent, and Caratti couldn't avoid a 6-3 7-5 defeat.

Volkov's success allowed him to break into the top twenty, the goal that he had set for himself in the past season and had been just short of reaching. Caratti made another leap in the rankings, improving by thirty-two places to break the top fifty. This was the start of a fascinating battle between him and Omar Camporese for the supremacy in Italian tennis.

In the doubles final, Omar Camporese and Goran Ivanisevic made up for their first round losses in singles by taking the title over Tom Nijssen and Cyril Suk. Camporese was the 1990 doubles champion with compatriot Diego Nargiso, while Ivanisevic hadn't won in doubles since Frankfurt in 1988.

The Forum is a brand new multi-sports complex that will hold facilities for twenty-five sports once completed. Not all these were available yet, but the doubles winners did test the bowling allies with Proserv's Sergio Palmieri and IMG's Fabio della Vida, and also proved their varied talents in several hotly contested matches of pitching pennies along with Italian 1972 Davis Cup winner Paolo Bertolucci.

Volvo Tennis/ San Francisco

By Paul Settles

San Francisco, 4-10 February
Tournament Director: Barry MacKay

Kicking off the North American segment of the IBM/ATP Tour at the Volvo Tennis/San Francisco has certainly had its rewards for the long-time promoter and tournament director, Barry MacKay. For the past two years, a great sense of excitement and anticipation has surrounded the tournament, as some of the world's top players have made their IBM/ATP Tour debuts for Bay area tennis fans. In 1991 the list included three of the world's top ten players: fourth ranked and defending champion, Andre Agassi, ninth ranked Andres Gomez and tenth ranked local favourite Brad Gilbert as well as former champion John McEnroe.

Prior to the start of play, local journalists and tennis fans buzzed with questions about the exciting week of tennis that lay ahead. Could Agassi defend his title as easily as he had won it in 1990? Would Gilbert rebound from his 1990 first round loss to play his best tennis in front of a home town crowd? Could Gomez stop a losing slide from the second half of 1990 and regain the form that had taken him to the French Open title earlier that year? Would Mayotte's newly formed partnership with coach Billie Jean King help him in his quest to re-enter the top ten? And finally, could McEnroe recapture the San Francisco crown after a two year absence from the tournament?

One look at the doubles draw provided similar intrigue. Top seeds Scott Davis and David Pate came to San Francisco as the IBM/ATP Tour's newest No. 1 team, riding a 10 match winning streak and two consecutive titles (Sydney and the Australian Open). Their competition would come from the former No. 1 pair Rick Leach and Jim Pugh, who only two days earlier had extended their unbeaten Davis Cup streak with a victory in Mexico. But perhaps the most surprising and potentially dangerous team in the doubles draw was the first-time combination of Agassi and McEnroe, a last minute wild-card innovation from tournament director MacKay.

The action of the first few days of the tournament foreshadowed the excitement of the following weekend. An opening night Civic Auditorium crowd of 6000-plus fans saw the Agassi-McEnroe show cut short as the fluorescent duo succumbed to the fourth seeded Neil Broad and Kevin Curren 1-6, 7-6, 7-5. Northern California native Gilbert managed to salvage the crowd's spirits however with a hard-fought three-set victory over Germany's Patrik Kuhnen.

In other singles action, veterans Mayotte and second-seeded Gomez struggled past unheralded opponents before faltering in the second round:

Mayotte to fellow Stanford University alum, Dan Goldie, and Gomez to the hard serving David Pate. Although Agassi and McEnroe fared better in advancing to the quarter-finals, both received scares in the second round. Agassi, the consummate on-court entertainer was atypically business-like in a 3-6, 6-4, 6-3 win over Udo Riglewski. A similarly focused McEnroe had to save two set points in the second set in order to silence the feisty Australian Mark Kratzmann 6-5, 7-6.

If, with a few exceptions, both the singles and doubles draws had held true to form through Thursday's action, Friday's quarter-finals results saw some unlikely heroes emerging. While Agassi and Gilbert advanced as expected in one half, the other semi-final pitted Australian Wally Masur, victorious in a thrilling third set tie-break against David Pate, against the winner of the featured Cahill-McEnroe match. To the chagrin of a boisterous pro-McEnroe crowd, Darren 'Killer' Cahill killed any chance of Mac regaining the San Francisco title by out serving and volleying the master server and volleyer in a come from behind 7-6, 3-6, 6-3 victory to set up an all-Aussie showdown in the bottom half.

Meanwhile, in the doubles, three of the top four seeds had been knocked out by the semi-finals. Davis and Pate's winning streak was halted at 11 in the quarter-finals by Jonathan Canter and Tobias Svantesson, while Leach and Pugh were upset by Brian Garrow and Brad Pearce in the first round.

If there had been any doubt about Gilbert's chances to win the title before the tournament, they were certainly laid to rest by the 6200 Civic Auditorium fans who watched him easily dispose of Agassi 6-1, 6-2 in the first semi-final. Gilbert's no-nonsense style and counter punching strategy effectively neutralised the 'show biz' in Agassi's groundstrokes. In the final, he would meet Cahill, who had once again come from a break down in the third set to defeat fellow countryman Masur 4-6, 6-4, 7-5. For Cahill, the match-up with Gilbert proved to be perfect. Gilbert's methodical no-pace approach was a welcome change to the chip-and-

charging opponents he had faced in his three previous matches. Hitting well over 60 per cent of his first serves and using his quickness around the net, Cahill forced Gilbert to change gears and play shorter, faster points. The result was a 6-2, 3-6, 6-4 victory for his first title since 1988. His efforts for the week also earned him $32,400 first prize and a twelve spot jump to 36 on the IBM/ATP Tour rankings.

By the week's end, the Volvo Tennis/San Francisco was truly Darren Cahill's tournament. More accurately though the tournament really belonged to Australia as Wally Masur and Jason Stoltenberg defeated Ronnie Bathman and Rikard Bergh in the doubles final 4-6, 7-6, 6-4 to complete the sweep. Australia had quietly and unassumingly conquered San Francisco.

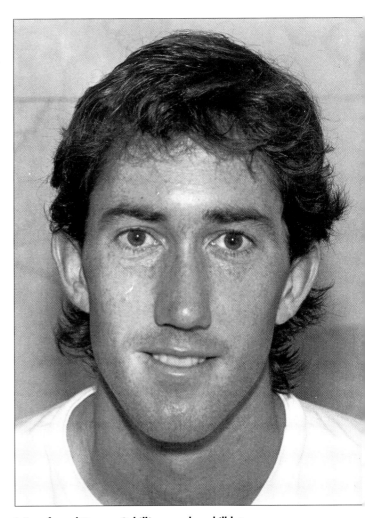

Injury forced Darren Cahill's year downhill later on but at least he could harbour fond memories of the city by the Bay. *(Russ Adams)*

Chevrolet Classic

By Lauren Goldenberg

Guaruja, Brazil, 4-10 February
Tournament Directors: Marco Bismarchi & Ricardo Bernd

Sydney, Tokyo, Stuttgart ... now the cosy beachtown resort of Guaruja, Brazil, just a few hours drive from the hustling metropolis of São Paolo, joins the ranks with these elite cities in hosting two events on the 1991 IBM/ATP Tour. In early February, part one of the Guaruja story unfolded. First played as a challenger and as a Tour stop since 1987, the 1991 Chevrolet Classic was contended on the courts of the Hotel Jequitemar and Spa, which is located alongside the serene and secluded Pernambuco Beach. First round losses of the top four seeds opened up the draw with the casualty list including Brazil's highest ranked player and the tournament's top seed Luiz Mattar, who had dominated the event by capturing the title for three consecutive years (1987-1989) and finishing as the runner-up in 1990.

Losing the top seeds was not the only damper of the tournament. Several severe rainstorms out of the north fell on the lush Brazilian tropics, indicating an end to the summer season and forcing play to be delayed. Included in one of the delays was a thrilling semi-final match against a determined Patrick Baur of Germany and the gentleman from Japan, Shuzo Matsuoka. Matsuoka was leading 5-4 in the third and decisive set when the skies opened up and suspended play until the following day. The throngs of bikini-clad beachgoers returned to watch Baur, who had been down 4-1 in the third set, fight back with his aggressive all-round play to win the match in a tie-breaker which propelled him into a final showdown with Brazilian Fernando Roese. Baur, who came into the tournament ranked 135, triumphed over the wild card entrant 6-2, 6-3. 'This is the most important win of my career,' an elated Baur expressed after the match. In regard to playing a Brazilian in the final, he jested, 'I knew I'd have to fight not just Roese, but the spectators too. I kept my mind on winning. I think this was my best match all week.'

Throngs of bikini-clad beachgoers returned to watch Patrick Baur fight back.

Surfacing from behind the shadows of his fellow countryman, Baur demonstrated to the tennis world his ability to compete with the best, as he earned his first career singles victory to add to his two doubles titles. A stellar year had been launched which would include a second singles title win a few months later at Seoul and a surge into the top

About 10 years ago, a teenage Mats Wilander mused on where his career might lead him while life continued on the beaches of Brazil. Now, as Wilander's great career winds down, the seaside resort of Guaruja has become one of only four cities to host two tournaments on the IBM/ATP Tour.

100 for the first time in Baur's six-year career. Roese's year was also off to a good start. Recently crowned as Brazil's national singles champion, the gentle giant from Novo Hamburgo in the southern part of the country, came into the tournament ranked 252 and managed to ease through the tournament without dropping a set until the final match. 'I didn't have a chance to win,' the 25-year-old explained. 'Baur was almost perfect. He served and volleyed very well. He surprised me with his return of serve. I didn't expect him to play this way, but this is still the best result of my career.' The 'career best' theme followed into the doubles competition as well when, in a rain-delayed final, the first-time, all-French pairing of Olivier Delaitre and Rodolphe Gilbert won their first career doubles title over the American team and No.2 seeds, Shelby Cannon and Greg Van Emburgh 6-2, 6-4.

Patrick Baur, a surprise winner on the South American circuit. (Schittini)

U.S. Pro Indoor Tennis Championships

By Diane Pucin

Philadelphia, 11-17 February
Tournament Director: Marilyn Fernberger

It was fitting that the championship match of the 1990 U.S. Pro Indoor Championships should go five sets and last 3 hours and 20 minutes. Because the $1 million event, held at the Spectrum where a blue tennis court took the place of a basketball court or a sheet of ice, was marked by matches that lasted late into the night.

Winner of that five-setter was iron man Ivan Lendl, the No. 1 seed. In an enthralling final played before 15,724 appreciative fans, Lendl served 23 aces and handed No. 2 seed Pete Sampras a 5-7, 6-4, 6-4, 3-6, 6-3 defeat. A year earlier, Sampras had first made a mark in professional tennis on the same court. As a shy 18-

More sell-out crowds at the Spectrum. *(Russ Adams)*

All smiles as Derrick Rostagno shows some Philadelphia children about grips and things. *(Russ Adams)*

year-old, Sampras had crept through the tournament virtually unnoticed until he beat Andres Gomez in the final and won his first-ever pro tournament.

But in 1991 Sampras was a star. He had won the U.S. Open in a shocker. He had upset Lendl in an intense five-set quarter-final in the process. So when Lendl and Sampras met again in Philadelphia, there was a little more at stake than another mid-winter title. 'Yes,' Lendl said afterwards, 'that U.S. Open match was on my mind.'

Lendl had never been a fan of the U.S. Pro Indoor. It's not that he didn't like Philadelphia. It's not that he didn't appreciated the keen attention that tournament directors Ed and Marilyn Fernberger pay to every detail. It's just that Lendl, who finds imperfection intolerable, is driven to distraction in the early rounds because the set up entails two courts set down side by side. He grumbled about not finding his rhythm, about spending more time returning balls to another court than to his opponent. But he also had his mind on

business. He knew he was playing Philadelphia, playing one more week, then taking five weeks off. 'I want to play many matches,' Lendl had said early in the week. 'I need the work.'

He got it. So did most of the players. Lendl played a three-and-a-half-hour semi-final that lasted almost until 11.30 pm and trailed No. 3 seed Brad Gilbert 6-4, 3-0, 40-15. Then, serving to go 4-0, Gilbert double-faulted. 'That was rather important,' Lendl said. 'It would have been hard to come back from 4-0 down.' Lendl had to be back at the Spectrum for his championship match in less than 24 hours. He handled the schedule better than No. 4 seed John McEnroe had.

McEnroe finished his quarter-final wipe-up of 19-year-old Finn Aki Rahunen around midnight on Friday, then was scheduled to play Sampras in the 12.30 pm semi-final on Saturday. 'This makes no sense,' McEnroe railed. And, indeed, McEnroe was a listless loser to Sampras 6-2, 6-4, on what happened to be his 32nd birthday. Still, McEnroe played a fine tournament. A year earlier, he had lost his first match here, talked of

How do you get Ivan Lendl to smile on court? Tournament director Marilyn Fernberger found the solution. She struck up the band. *(Russ Adams)*

retirement and withdrew from a series of tournaments. This year, McEnroe seemed refreshed and eager for the upcoming season. 'I'm looking forward to this year,' McEnroe said after his loss to Sampras. 'I'm in good shape for a change.'

While the top four seeds made it to the semi-finals, the tournament certainly didn't start out according to form.

Six seeds lost their first matches. Most surprising was No. 6 seed Jim Courier's lacklustre effort, a 6-2, 6-4 defeat to doubles specialist Jim Grabb. The most disappointing was the quick exit of No. 16 seed Patrick McEnroe. He was playing his first ever tournament as a singles seed and making his first tournament appearance since a stunning run to the semi-finals of the Australian Open. But admittedly rusty and a little nervous, Pat McEnroe put up little resistance to

There were some excellent early-round affairs. Sampras, playing in his first tournament of the year, needed to be at his best to escape Washington with a 6-3, 7-6 (9-7) fourth-round win. In the quarters, Lendl had a tense second set with future Wimbledon champion Michael Stich before pulling out a 6-2, 7-6 (9-7) win. Stich and his partner, Udo Riglewski, did play on the final Sunday, though. The two Germans lost to Rick Leach and Jim Pugh in the doubles final.

The singles final was most special, though. After losing the first set, Lendl trailed Sampras 4-1 in the second set. Sampras admitted afterwards that he might have gotten a little complacent at that point. 'I was surprised at how hard Ivan fought. I didn't think he would put up quite so good a battle.'

But Lendl did. Just three weeks from his 31st birthday and Lendl taught the teenager a lesson. 'If I'm in a tournament,' Lendl said afterwards, 'I will fight my best to win. That's what I'm here for. To win.'

another talented young American, Mailivai Washington, and lost 6-0, 6-3. 'I've never had to wait until Wednesday to play before,' the younger McEnroe said. 'I don't think I handled it well. Next time I will.'

The other seeds to lose their first matches were: No. 5 Jay Berger to Kevin Curren; No. 8 Tim Mayotte to qualifier Wayne Ferreira; No. 10 Derrick Rostagno to another qualifier, Chuck Adams; and No. 12 Mark Koevermans to Rahunen.

They tied a yellow ribbon for the troops in the Gulf at the U.S. Pro Indoor. (Russ Adams)

Donnay Indoor Championship

By Richard Evans

Brussels, 11-17 February
Tournament Director: Jean-Noel Bioul

Guy Forget triumphs for the second time on the 1991 ATP Tour in mid-February. *(Serge Philippot)*

With the echoes of distant gunfire in the Gulf and snow clogging the roads to the Forest National Stadium on the outskirts of town, tennis did not seem the likeliest of occupations in Brussels in the second week of February. But if conditions and circumstance hurt attendances early in the week, the players still enjoyed the hospitality of the Brussels Hilton and the efforts of Jean-Noel Bioul's team to keep them focused on the points and prize-money on offer at this $600,000 event.

As always, some focused better than others and it was Guy Forget who laid claim to the $77,500 first prize in singles by beating the unseeded Andrei Cherkasov 6-3, 7-5, 3-6, 7-6 in a well-fought final. It was quite an effort for the amiable Frenchman to be celebrating his second ATP Tour title of a year only six weeks old. His triumph in the New South Wales Open the previous month had suggested that Forget's days as a classy but frequently disappointing member of the Tour's supporting cast were over. And his performance in the Donnay Indoor Championship confirmed it.

This was an event that contained the top two players in the world but neither the new No. 1 Boris Becker nor Stefan Edberg could halt the left-hander's impressive progress through the draw. Becker, already feeling the added weight of expectation on his shoulders as the world's top ranked player, was forced to relinquish his brief tenure on that demanding pedestal when he pulled a muscle during his semi-final against Cherkasov and was forced to retire at 2-2 in the third set.

Forget, however, needed no assistance from fortune in removing the Edberg threat. He did it himself. After losing the first set, Forget started ripping his service returns to such good effect that he snatched the second 6-0 off the startled Swede. Edberg struggled to recapture the dominance he had enjoyed earlier in the match but the Frenchman is now a far meaner fighting machine and, with those southpaw serves still piercing the Swedish defences at nearly 200 km/h, Edberg eventually realised he was fighting for a lost cause. Forget took the final set 6-3.

Cherkasov, who had defeated his fellow Russian, Andrei Chesnokov 7-5, 6-1 in the quarters, used his solid ground game to keep Forget on court a long time in the final but Guy's nerve held at the end of a tight fourth set and he clinched the tie-break, and with it the title, by seven points to five.

Forget and his Swiss partner Jakob Hlasek may have won the ATP Tour World Doubles title at Sanctuary Cove only two and a half months before but the first round loss they suffered here at the hands of Libor Pimek and Michiel Schapers proved, sadly, to be symptomatic of the form they would experience in the months that followed. By the time the World Doubles was switched to Johannesburg, Forget and Hlasek had lost all hope of being able to defend their crown. The giant pairing of Pimek and Schapers capitalised on that early success by going all the way to the final where they crashed 6-3, 6-0 to Todd Woodbridge and Mark Woodforde, a couple of Aussies whose trek through the snow in Brussels would, indeed, lead all the way to a plateau in the Transvaal the following November.

Eurocard Classics

By Andrew Longmore

Stuttgart, 18-24 February
Tournament Director: Markus Gunthardt

The Eurocard Classics in Stuttgart should have featured the next episode of one of the longest-running sagas in tennis. Stefan Edberg and Boris Becker had two-stepped their way through the indoor season, from Sydney to Tokyo to Stockholm to Paris, and then tangoed to Australia in the New Year, where the music stopped for the Swede and the German became number one. Now, like one of those marathon dances so popular in fifties America, the pair had returned to Europe for a February fling. They shoot horses don't they? Becker, his body battered by the relentless pace, must have wondered if tennis players might suffer the same fate.

Desperate to protect his ranking, Becker took a wild card into Brussels earlier in the month, only to break down with a thigh injury, losing his top position to Edberg again. Sadly, for those who had cheered their champion to the title just 12 months before, Becker had to miss the next rendezvous with his regular partner in Stuttgart. It was a bitter blow to Ion Tiriac, Becker's manager and the founder of the Stuttgart event, as well as for the spectators.

Edberg, of course, needed no second invitation, profiting from his rival's absence to beat fellow Swede Jonas Svensson in four tight sets and to win his first title of the year and a cheque for $137,500. 'This was a very important win for me,' said the champion. Important, partly because it increased his lead over Becker on the IBM/ATP computer to 400 points; partly because it restored some of the confidence which had drained away during his defeat by Ivan Lendl in the semi-final of the Australian Open.

Computer tennis? Edberg trys his hand against a different kind of opponent. *(Paul Zimmer)*

Swedes united – all smiles after Edberg defeated Svensson in the final. *(Gianni Ciaccia)*

Without ever quite revealing his elegant best, Edberg did not drop a set in reaching the final with wins over Markus Zoecke, Omar Camporese, Magnus Gustafsson and Jan Siemerink, a 20-year-old Dutch qualifier whose fresh face, gentle manner and aggressive serve-and-volley tennis helped fill the void left by Becker's withdrawal.

Even in his absence, Becker dominated the early headlines by announcing that he had parted company 'amicably' with his long-time coach, Bob

Brett. On the face of it, the timing of the split was strange. Just a few weeks before, on the centre court at Flinders Park in Brett's home town of Melbourne, the pair had reached the climax of a relationship which had always been more professional than personal. There was surely more work to be done.

Yet, both men clearly saw that triumph as the end of an era. The phlegmatic Australian had brought discipline to Becker's game and guided him to three grand slam titles – Wimbledon, the US

Ion Tiriac, mastermind behind the Stuttgart event, gave Italy's best known tennis journalist Rino Tommasi a cake for his birthday. And then cut his tie off! *(Serge Philippot)*

Open and the Australian – during their three-and-a half-year partnership. 'They have had a great run, but it was time for a change,' said Tiriac simply. Brett went to coach the wayward but supremely gifted Goran Ivanisevic, and Becker turned for help to his old friend and Davis Cup captain Nikki Pilic. 'I would have said "no" to anyone but Boris, but, with him, I have no choice,' said Pilic.

Going into the week, the hottest player on the tour was that elegant left-hander Guy Forget, who had capped a remarkable run by winning his second title of the year in the Donnay Indoor Championships at Brussels the previous week and entering the top 10 for the first time in his nine-year career. One of the best athletes on the tour, the Frenchman can jump his own height of 6 foot 3 inches and run 400 metres in 53 seconds, but he has always been the third musketeer of French tennis, the quiet Athos to Noah's Aramis and Leconte's Porthos. Though he would deny the

> *The pair had spent the New Year surfing in Hawaii, but it was Forget who rode the waves best this time.*

charge of inferiority, Forget's emergence at the age of 25 has coincided with the near-retirement of Noah and the decline of Leconte.

Seeded six, Forget had to set aside personal feelings to beat his best friend and doubles partner, Jakob Hlasek, in the second round. The pair had spent the New Year surfing in Hawaii, but it was Forget who rode the waves best this time, winning in two tie-breaks. Another tie-break sealed victory over Ivanisevic in the quarter-finals, but, having had a match point in the second-set tie-break against Svensson, he finally broke against the rock of the Swede's growing assurance, losing 2-6, 7-6, 6-2 in the semi-final.

In the other semi-final, Edberg ended a fine run by the left-hander, Siemerink, ranked 98, who reached the last 16 at the Australian Open and upheld Holland's growing reputation as a nursery for tennis talent by disposing of Horst Skoff, Sergi Bruguera and Andrei Cherkasov without losing a set. Edberg, though, knew too much for the Dutchman and too much about Svensson, who had progressed quietly through the gap where Becker should have been.

Svensson had never beaten his Davis Cup colleague and only briefly looked like doing so in the final when he served for a two sets to one lead at 5-4 in the third set. A double-fault and three further errors effectively ended his chances. Edberg broke again immediately to take the third

set and quickly opened up a 3-0 lead in the fourth to reassert the laws of probability. 'I think Jonas played the best he's played against me,' said Edberg. It was still not good enough.

In the doubles final, the Spanish pair of Sergio Casal and Emilio Sanchez took their first title of the year, beating Nick Brown and Jeremy Bates 6-3, 7-5 in the final. The unseeded British team had knocked out top seeds Forget and Hlasek in the first round and the Mexican Davis Cup pair of Leo Lavalle and Jorge Lozano on the way to their first major doubles final.

Sergio Casal and Emilio Sanchez collect their second doubles title in as many months on the 1991 tour and look suitably pleased with their rewards. (Paul Zimmer)

Volvo Tennis Indoor

By Linda Pentz

Memphis, 18-24 February
Tournament Director: Tom Buford

If you look carefully in Michael Stich's closet, behind the grass-stained sneakers – they of both historical and sentimental significance – you will probably find a pair of blue suede shoes. Metaphorical or real? What is certain is that

Memphis and Michael Stich have a strange kind of affinity. It happens that way; a player wins a tournament, then wins it again. Kelly Jones has his Singapore, Aaron Krickstein has Tel Aviv. Michael Stich has Memphis. Well, almost.

Ivan Lendl being interviewed by Leif Shiras, still an active player on the Tour but already an accomplished broadcaster. *(Michael Baz)*

Derrick Rostagno, all action, upset Jim Courier in the third round. (*Serge Philippot*)

Ah, what the Memphians could have told you about Michael Stich, had you asked in February of 1990. A young man who will go far! He won the tournament, his first career title. In the ATP Tour player guide that year, some brief notes mentioned that 'grass was his favourite surface'. Not indoor hard courts, the surface used in Memphis. He won there unseeded, but the Memphians knew. This guy can really play.

But a year later, nothing had happened. Stich returned to the Racquet Club in the city where the Blues were born, and Memphis was still his first and only title. All the same, the magic was still there in 1991. He would have won again, easily, but someone told Ivan Lendl that the Memphis tournament, now known as the $750,000 Volvo Tennis Indoor, was such a lot of fun. Very hospitable. Intimate. Southern friendly. The arena inside the Memphis Racquet Club seats only 5000 people. Lendl brought Samantha and little daughter Marika. He played the role of smiling Ivan Lendl the family man, Ivan the Not Terrible At All, and he played terrific tennis all week and won the tournament, breaking the Stich spell on finals Sunday with a 7-5, 6-3 victory.

Bill Mergler of Volvo and the champion. *(Michael Baz)*

The Memphis tournament has upgraded this year to Championship Series stature, but it didn't matter. The event remained the same cosy week of down-home old fashioned Southern hospitality, a cliché maybe, but a true one in Memphis. Rumours abounded that the tournament would have to move next year to surroundings more appropriate for the tournament's expansion, a vast multi-media arena for sports and entertainment. But not for tennis. At least, not for Tommy Buford's brand of tennis. No one wanted the tournament to move there, not even Buford, the tournament director himself, who should have been tempted by the challenge of filling close to 12,000 seats. He kept an open mind, but he knows that it is the intimacy, the proximity of players to fans and volunteers, that makes Memphis. For 1992, the tournament will remain at the Racquet Club.

Lendl beat Stich in the final, but Memphis was also kind to those on the comeback trail – Mats Wilander and Tim Mayotte. Wilander said he was just warming up for his music tour in Sweden where he would be promoting his new album. David Wheaton, Wilander's second round opponent and 6-4, 6-3 victim, probably hoped Wilander was ready for a career change. Gentleman Tim, soon to become the Laughing Cavalier of Wimbledon, enthused over his new coach, Billie Jean King, who had taught him to think and understand. It was hard to imagine cerebral Mayotte, surely one of the tour's intellectuals, being taught to think.

Jim Courier has received the same lesson from his coach, Jose Higueras, but it was early days yet for this soon-to-be Grand Slam winner, and he fell prey to the ever unpredictable talents of Derrick

Rostagno in the third round. Gilad Bloom fell prey to the nightmares that had haunted him ever since he visited his hometown Tel Aviv in January, exchanging the plop of tennis balls for the crash of Scuds. The experience brought a new kind of reality to his life, Bloom said, making the luxury hotels and gorgeous tennis resorts of his daily existence seem somehow unimportant. Bloom won a round in Memphis and began to sleep more peacefully.

Jeff Tarango flew home to Los Angeles after losing in the final round of qualifying, then received an unexpected phone call. Fourth seeded Brad Gilbert, who had received a Wednesday start and a first round bye, had pulled out lame. Tarango was in. Dropping $1000 on a short-notice air fare, Tarango returned to Memphis. He defeated Aki Ranunen and Wally Masur (the 1990 finalist), then lost in straight sets to Michael Chang, reaping $15,400 for his quarter-final finish. His original qualifying earnings had been $480.

Chang, whose coach at the time, Australian Phil Dent, had improved the young American's serve and volley game, took advantage of that new asset to advance to the semi-finals where Stich overwhelmed him 7-2, 6-2. Rostagno was equally over-matched by Lendl in the other semi-final, 6-3, 6-2. Pete Sampras, who at two was seeded to be in the final, also pulled up short, sustaining an injury that forced a mid-match retirement in his third-round encounter with Dutchman, Mark Koevermans. The nature of the problem was never fully explained.

Lendl needed no explanation for his performance in the final. He simply played brilliantly, carving up Stich in straight sets to reinforce his pleasant memories of Memphis. All was not lost for Stich either. He had reached the final again and confirmed what Memphians already knew. This boy was going places. All the way to Wimbledon.

Michael Stich, a finalist in singles, went one better with Udo Riglewski in doubles. *(Michael Baz)*

ABN/AMRO Wereld Tennis Tournament

By Patricia Jolly

Rotterdam, 25 February-3 March
Tournament Director: Wim Buitendijk

I knew I could do it,' Italy's Omar Camporese said in his post-match press conference after an emotional victory in the final of the ABN/AMRO Wereld Tennis Toernooi in Rotterdam. However, when he actually finished off the last point, he got down on his knees in disbelief at what he had just accomplished: he had captured the second singles title of his career at the expense of number one seed Ivan Lendl.

Despite an inauspicious start in the first set, the tenacious 22-year-old Italian proved wrong those who point out his inconsistency. He persisted and recovered to win the two following sets although he was forced into two tie-breaks. 'I think I am still dreaming, I can't wait to see my parents' faces,' he said all smiles. Camporese explained that he felt he had been close to defeating some great players on various occasions during the weeks

Tournament Director Wim Buitendijk is led to the press room by ATP Tour's Patricia Jolly for Omar Camporese's press conference. *(Henk Koster)*

preceding Rotterdam, but that 'something was always missing to achieve it.' Indeed, he had lost to Boris Becker 6-7, 6-7, 6-0, 6-4, 12-14 in the third round of the Australian Open, and in another five-set match in the Davis Cup. At the Stuttgart Eurocard Classics, he had been defeated by Stefan Edberg.

Ivan Lendl was one of the only three seeds to reach the quarter-final round in which he had a rough time eliminating seventh seed, Swiss Jakob Hlasek. If his semi-final against Anders Jarryd was easier, he found out for the second time in a few weeks that the Italian fighting spirit shouldn't be taken lightly. Before Camporese, 19-year-old Cristiano Caratti had defeated him in the second round of the Muratti Time Indoor Championships in Milan.

Although Lendl complained that the crowd was outrageously loud throughout the week, and particularly during the final, he didn't fail to acknowledge Camporese's value. 'After all I have won many matches after my opponent had match point...' he noted. This time, the situation was reversed; Lendl didn't take the chance he had to win the final.

The enthusiasm of the crowd was a source of joy for the tournament's organisers since the record attendance for the week was broken by about 11,000. The ABN/AMRO Wereld Tennis Tournament presented a quality field that might not have lived up to the public's original expectations. Great hopes had been placed on the six Dutchmen featured in the singles main draw, but only two of them got through the first round. However, the event took an interesting turn since a Dutchman, Paul Haarhuis, reached the semis, along with the unexpected Camporese, the number one see and multi-champion Ivan Lendl, and the solid and reliable Anders Jarryd.

The Rotterdam Ahoy stadium crowd which always cheers for the Dutchmen saw Haarhuis whip off the singles draw a Swedish coalition that attempted to bar his way to the top of the draw. He defeated sixth-seeded Jonas Svensson, Magnus Gustafsson, and Christian Bergstrom to reach the

semi-final where he put up a gutsy fight against the eventual champion, Camporese. After winning a promising first set, Haarhuis conceded the second 6-2. He seemed to recover in the third as he struggled in the final tie-breaker, but he eventually bowed out. Another homeboy, Jan Siemerink, who later in the year confirmed his capabilities by capturing the title in Singapore, made it to the quarter-final round.

In the doubles, American Pat Galbraith and Swede Anders Jarryd had teamed up to grab what was to be Jarryd's first title in an impressive series including Wimbledon and the U.S. Open. Seeded number four, the pair managed not to drop a single set on their way to the victory.

Sprightly Ivan Lendl heads for the final – and a surprise defeat. *(Henk Koster)*

Volvo Tennis/ Chicago

By Patrick McEnroe

Chicago, 25 February-3 March
Tournament Director: Kari Volk Mutscheller

I suppose it had to happen as it did. Going into the final of the Volvo Tennis Chicago ATP Tour event, I had exactly 0 singles titles to my name. In fact, I had never played in a championship match. My opponent, however, had reached 115 singles finals in his illustrious career, winning 76 of them. He had three Wimbledon titles and four U.S. Open titles to his name. All in a name you ask? Well, sort of. Our names are the same; our records, well, not quite.

So it was; the final match in Chicago an all-McEnroe affair. John McEnroe, playing in his first final since his 1990 ATP Tour victory in

Basel, against me, his little brother Patrick. I was certainly feeling confident about my game at this point having improved my ranking dramatically by virtue of my semi-final appearance in this year's Australian Open in January. Having begun the year ranked 120 on the ATP Tour computer, I entered the week of Chicago with a ranking of 51.

My path to the final began a bit unsteadily as I escaped the first round by defeating Brad Pearce in a deciding tie-breaker. With two comfortable straight-set wins over Nicolas Pereira, and second-seeded Richey Reneberg, I advanced to the semi-finals to face Canadian Grant Connell.

A family reunion – John McEnroe Snr celebrates every tennis father's ambition, having two sons in the final of an ATP Tour event.
(Michael Baz)

Brotherly love after the battle. (Michael Baz)

It was a tense struggle all the way as we both fought to reach our first final. With solid returning I was finally able to thwart Grant's aggressive play 4-6, 6-4, 6-4.

John's route to the semi-final was smooth. In the first round he defeated the Israeli Gilan Bloom 6-2, 6-1, then followed with another straight-set victory over the stylish Indian Ramesh Krishnan 7-5, 6-3. John was given a walkover through to the semi-final when Alexander Mronz was forced to withdraw because of injury. In a compelling semi-final, John fought for almost three hours to defeat Malivai Washington. Washington is a hard-hitting, all around player who moves very quickly about the court. The youngster from Michigan matched John stroke for stroke as they split two tie-breakers in the opening two sets. John's solid serving and experience came through in the decisive third set 6-4.

Thus the scene was set for the all-McEnroe final, the first meeting between brothers in a championship final since Emilio Sanchez defeated Javier in Madrid in 1987. My father, who had just flown in that morning from New York, watched as I broke John early in the first set and hung on to clinch it 6-3. John picked up his game right from

the start in the second set, serving with conviction and keeping pressure on me in my service games. Before I knew it the set was over 6-2.

We were both certainly feeling very different emotions than we would normally experience in such a match. John obviously felt proud to see me in my first final and playing quite well, but maybe not too delighted that it was happening against him. He certainly did not want to lose to his kid brother. As for me, I looked across the net and saw not only a tennis legend and someone whose tennis game I'd admired for years, but also my big brother who had really helped me reach the position I was currently in. When I was struggling with my tennis career, John always had confidence in me and encouraged me.

All these thoughts went through my head, even as I broke his serve straightaway to open the deciding set. But he broke right back and then again at 3-all, and went on to wrap up the title in Chicago 3-6, 6-2, 6-4. Thus John picked up his 77th career singles title and I gained some valuable experience along with a place in the tennis history books. And as John held aloft the trophy I could not help thinking that if it could not be me with the trophy, I could not think of anyone else I'd prefer to see in that position.

Newsweek Champions Cup

By Bridget Byrne

Indian Wells, 4-10 March
Tournament Director: Charlie Pasarell

On 4 March, as the sun broke through the rain-cleared Southern California skies to gleam on the unspoilt Santa Rosa mountains, the order of play on the Hyatt Grand Champions' Stadium court reflected the sensibility of the tournament director, Charlie Pasarell – memories mingled with modern times as great names of yesterday and today showcased their wares. Down at this plush desert resort in Indian Wells, Pasarell drew on his nostalgia for the past and enthusiasm for the present to create a two-week bonanza, 'The World's Festival of Tennis'. This was highlighted by the $1 million Newsweek Champions Cup but also buoyed and embellished by such sidebar events as the ATP Challenger Series, which offered competitors $50,000 in prize money and wildcards for the finalists into the major league draw, and the premiere ATP $100,000 Senior Championships, which featured 16 famous names, top heavy with trophies, in a sudden death, shoot-out singles and a round robin doubles.

Amid an instant oasis of luxury, Pasarell has concocted myriad additional pleasures to satisfy all types and temperaments of tennis fans – there's always an annual dinner honouring a past champion at which the tart-tongued camaraderie speaks of eras when players really knew who their friends were; there's the sight of Pancho Gonzales

teaching clinics on the hotel's multisurface courts, tagged along by his kid Skyler who seems already to have the body his uncle Andre Agassi has been working overtime to develop; there's always a

Victory for Jim Courier in the desert – the first of a series of triumphs that would lift him to No. 2 in the world. *(Cynthia Lum)*

Mark Miles, CEO of the ATP Tour (left), Charlie Pasarell and Grand Champions Director of Tennis Ray Moore (right) congratulate challenger winner Cristiano Caratti (next to Miles) and Jimmy Arias.

showbiz celebrity or two drifting through the 'good life' crowd, togged out in the sort of tennis gear which costs almost as much as their jewellery. But it's the tennis game, the game itself that, despite all the fun-in-the-sun hoopla, is clearly the focus of the event, the now-and-then, the 'as it is, was and always will be' essence of the sport which stands strong at the heart of Charlie's tournament.

The ever-welcoming Assistant Tournament Director Julie Copeland and TV magnate Merv Griffin. (Michael Baz)

The rain delays which had pushed part of the first week's schedule into the top of the second helped to emphasise this fact as Stadium court play that Monday featured both 56-year-old Ken Rosewall, forever to be known as 'the best player never to win Wimbledon', and 19-year-old Michael Chang, still holding on to his status as the youngest player to win a Grand Slam event. Although ultimately the cheers, the cup and the cheque would go to a big, blunt, redhead in a baseball cap, there was a real touch of class to the

juxtaposition of Rosewall and Chang, two small, darkhaired, little men who play the game for all their worth to the very best of their abilities. Rosewall's deceptively soft, smooth style and Chang's run-into-the ground dedication which has made many a true champion and has brought honour to the profession, however prevalent the forces of faddishness and expediency. Rosewall was on court first in the morning, partnering Jaime

There was also a seniors event before the Newsweek Cup – time for old foes
Stan Smith and Ilie Nastase to get re-acquainted.

Fillol in a Senior doubles loss to Bob Lutz and
Marty Riessen, and then in the early afternoon
Chang the tournament's 9th seed, easily beat
Uruguay's Marcelo Filippini to start his advance to
the quarters where he would lose in three sets to
the number one seed, Stefan Edberg.

The absence of names such as Boris Becker and
Pete Sampras, and the second round loss of
John McEnroe to Jim Grabb, might have
disappointed some of the less knowledgeable fans,
but the sellout crowd for the final days were quick
to learn about and appreciate the talents of the
three players who joined Edberg in the semis – all

fast-rising names who would prove their
continuing worth as the year continued. There was
France's sleek Guy Forget, Germany's even
sleeker Michael Stich and the decidedly unsmooth
American Jim Courier, the small-town boy who
had closed up shop on the glitz merchandiser and
number two seed Andre Agassi 2-6, 6-3, 6-4 in the
third round.

Courier had beaten Emilio Sanchez in the
quarters, causing some confusion in the less
well informed press ranks, who thought Sanchez
was his doubles partner when in fact it was baby
brother Javier who partnered Courier to the doubles

final against the chic French duo of Forget and Henri Leconte. But with only one American left in the singles in the company of three Europeans, the national press pulled out all their best Americana cliches to depict Courier's hometown qualities, finding Floridan symbolism in his orange hair, orange sweatshirt and flamingo-pink-from-the-desert-sun complexion and dwelling at length on his fondness for baseball. But Courier stayed cooler than he looked, referring to upcoming matches as 'just another day at the office' and benefiting from the sensible advice of his Palm Springs based coach Jose Higueras (winner of the tournament in 1983) who had himself taken to the courts to top one of the Senior Shoot-outs, the other going to a very less-than-sleek looking John Newcombe. Higueras had not only worked in the winter to give Courier a backhand slice but more significantly he had instilled in the 20-year-old ex-Bollettierite the benefits of staying clam, the worth of patience and the importance as Courier put it of 'working my way through matches, instead of banging my way through.'

It was the number 3 seed Forget whom Courier met in the final, a player who had continued to blaze with the attack which had already won him two IBM/ATP events in 1991 as he wiped aside the world number one, Edberg, 6-4, 6-4 in the semis, while the Dade City dweller himself got rid of Stich 6-3, 6-2. The final was a grinder, lasting three hours and 30 minutes, and culminated in a win for Courier, 4-6, 6-3, 4-6, 6-3, 7-6. The tie-breaker was 7-4, including a disputed line call, but earned on the third match point when Forget hit a forehand volley long after a good smash by the Frenchman had saved one and a bad smash by the American lost another. At the end of it all, Forget concluded 'It just wasn't my day today' and Courier theorised 'Ever since the second set against Agassi something inside of me just clicked, like all the adrenalin wasn't going to my brain. I wasn't as hyper as I used to be.' So having won his second ever tournament title, he also went out to win the doubles, bringing his earnings for the week to $150,000. Such are the perks of staying cool in the tennis oasis Charlie built.

The Santa Rosa Mountains rise above the spacious suites overlooking the Centre Court. *(Michael Baz)*

Copenhagen Open

By Meg Donovan

Copenhagen, 4-10 March
Tournament Director: Soeren T. Hjorth

The city of Copenhagen is often referred to as the 'Paris of Scandinavia', but the continental influence was decidedly lacking as Swedes Jonas Svensson and Anders Jarryd slugged it out in an all-Scandinavian final at the 1991 Copenhagen Open. In vivid testimony to a resurgent Swedish presence on the tour, Svensson's victory over Jarryd at the Copenhagen Ballclub marked the second all-Swedish final in the space of just three weeks after Svensson's runner up finish to Edberg at the Eurocard Classics. Prior to that, the last all Swedish affair had been at Palermo in October of 1988 when Mats Wilander defeated Kent Carlsson in the title match.

In a way it was poetic justice that the final of the Copenhagen Open should be an all Scandinavian affair, for the event celebrated the return of professional tennis to Denmark after an absence of almost 20 years. Not that tennis talent had been lacking in the small staging post between Europe and the countries of the north. In the 1970s, Denmark boasted not only one of the leading players, but also one of the most exotic personalities on the tour in the form of bearded, jazz playing Torben Ulrich. At home as much with a clarinet as with a racket, Ulrich moonlighted as a host of jazz programmes on Copenhagen radio, and showed an unusual proclivity to improve with age on the tour, recording his most impressive results late in his

career. Kurt Nielsen, another leading figure in Danish tennis who returned as referee of the 1991 Copenhagen Open, still enjoys the distinction of being the only two-time unseeded Wimbledon finalist. But until the start of the 1991 Copenhagen Open, tournament tennis had not been played in Denmark since the last WCT stop there in 1973.

One might never have noticed its absence if the state of the field this year was any indication. Under the steadying hand of tournament director and former Danish Davis Cupper Soeren Hjorth and his volunteer force, the tournament kicked off at KB (Copenhagen Ballclub), with an impressive array of world-class players. All eight seeds won their opening round match and six went on to the quarter-finals. Jarryd, playing what most of his opponents termed 'Top 10 tennis', was at the peak of his game, losing only 18 games en route to the final, four in his semi-final match against Aussie Todd Woodbridge.

Svensson, as during most of his tennis career, was making few waves but much progress in the other half of the draw. Possessing an elegant game which at times looks almost effortless, Svensson has twice reached the semi-finals of Roland Garros, and seems poised to make the transition from simply good to bona fide Top 10. His week in

Copenhagen, which catapulted him to Number 11 in the world rankings, was the first step in effecting that transition. Two weeks later he would crack the Top 10 barrier for the first time in his career.

Jarryd over the course of his 11-year career has reached 80 finals, collecting 7 singles wins and an astounding 40 doubles titles. Accompanied by girlfriend Lotta Sundren and son Nicklas, who warmed him up in the hallway of the Palace Hotel prior to the Sunday final, Jarryd was probably the odds on favourite to win the event. In five previous meetings, Jarryd had a four match edge, with Svensson's only victory coming almost five years earlier at Key Biscayne.

But Svensson had had to struggle a bit more in early round contests with Martin Strelba, Frederik Fetterlein, teammate Christian Bergstrom and finally Jakob Hlasek in the semi-finals. The testing probably helped hone his game to peak form by the finals. Jarryd opened the first set of the final with blistering returns and an aggressive net game, breaking Svensson at love in the second game. But Svensson showed patience in waiting

out his opportunity, maintaining his composure despite a close loss in the first set tie-break. 'I started to convert on break point opportunities and didn't feel so pressured on my own serve,' he noted in his post-match press conference.

February and March showed the tennis world all the promise of Swede Jonas Svensson, who was later to suffer through two months of a debilitating back problem. The injury forced him out of the French Open and slowed his play during the course of the year. But for a brief spell in Copenhagen, with the famous Tivoli Gardens bolted shut for the winter, local fans found magic in the heroics of Jonas Svensson.

In doubles, Todd Woodbridge and fellow Aussie Mark Woodforde fulfilled their billing as Number 1 seeds when they defeated unseeded Mansour Bahrami and Andrei Olhovskiy in the finals 6-3, 6-1. Titlists earlier in the year at Brussels, the Aussies' win moved them to Number 3 on the world ranking list, placing them in the thick of the hunt for a spot at the year end ATP Tour World Doubles Championship in Johannesburg.

Jonas Svensson toasts his success as winner of the first Copenhagen Open with tournament director Soeren Hjorth.

Lipton International Players Championships

By Linda Pentz

Key Biscayne, 15-24 March
Tournament Director: Cliff Buchholz

Youth was served, while 'age' served notice at the 1991 Lipton International Players' Championships, better and generically known as 'The Lipton'.

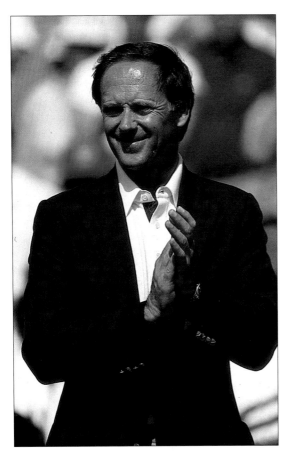

Tournament director Cliff Buchholz. *(Serge Philippot)*

Jim Courier, in the midst of an odyssey that would take him to two Grand Slam finals – he won in Paris but was thwarted in New York – claimed the men's singles title, his second in as many consecutive tournaments. In the final, Courier, then 20, defeated 21-year-old fellow American David Wheaton. How recently it seemed that the United States was decrying its dearth of emerging talent. How patently redundant such a concern seems now. And those once unable to pass the torch are unready to let go, as Jimmy Connors first indicated at the Lipton, and went on to prove in such a blaze of glory at the U.S. Open.

Accompanying Connors in the 'old tennis players never die' category was Harold Solomon, who returned to the game at Key Biscayne, at 38, with more determination, perhaps, than realism. It was not altogether clear to his listeners why Solomon had chosen a comeback after a five year hiatus, and it was even less clear when he played – losing in the first round to Bruce Derlin after a wild card gained him direct entry.

Less of a veteran but almost as winless was 30-year-old Tim Mayotte, who restored confidence and willpower by winning two tough rounds before the flashy Derrick Rostagno defeated him. Mayotte was working at the time with Billie Jean King, a decision that had accorded him a fair amount of publicity. In the second round at the Lipton, Mayotte beat one of the few other players also coached by a woman – Andrei Cherkasov, the 11th seed.

Courier was coming off his second big career win and first in 18 months – at the Indian Wells event where he defeated Guy Forget of France in a five-set final. Courier needed to beat Forget again in Florida, as well as Rostagno and Richey Reneberg to reach the final, but it was really Wheaton, his opponent there, who had the more impressive tournament.

Having been winless all year, Wheaton was perhaps relieved to get past Jim Grabb in the first round. It was the spark his confidence needed. By the fourth round he was ready to summarily dispatch third-seeded Andre Agassi with a stunning 6-0, 7-5 win. Wheaton kept pouring on the paraffin until the flames of his confidence roared. In the semi-finals it was top-seeded Stefan Edberg who crashed and burned, beaten by Wheaton 6-3, 6-4.

The final was perhaps more a psychological war than a strategic one. Wheaton had the tournament's bigger wins, but Courier had been a

A study in multi-coloured concentration.
(Serge Philippot)

A new stadium will soon be built at Key Biscayne to complement the three-year-old clubhouse. *(Serge Philippot)*

champion one week earlier. Courier's body-language was aggressive, Wheaton's a touch defensive. Although Wheaton took the first set 6-4, there was an air of inevitability about Courier's fighting spirit that left no doubt that he would turn things around. He did, taking the title 4-6, 6-3, 6-4.

Reneberg, Courier's semi-final round opponent, could justify the title of 'Most Overlooked American Talent,' having laboured in the shadows of his more exuberant rivals. Quiet diligence paid off for Reneberg at the Lipton as well as the departure of Brad Gilbert at the hands of qualifier Jan Siemerink of the Netherlands whom Reneberg might otherwise have faced in the third round.

Also upset was Boris Becker, more with himself than with the defeat handed to him in the third round by Patrick McEnroe – a turnaround from the Australian Open semi-final encounter in January. McEnroe played well, but Becker also played poorly, out of sorts with himself and the world, a malaise that continued well into the summer. Becker complained about the conditions at the Lipton – blustery and unpredictable – but his misery seemed more deep-seated than anything sea

breezes could provoke. Disenchanted with the direction of the game – more money, less fun – Becker retreated to ponder his future. McEnroe, who had enjoyed the company of Ivan Lendl, Becker and Edberg in the Australian Open semi-finals, is beginning to feel more comfortable with singles success. Having made a concerted effort to prioritise singles over his already successful doubles career, the hard work paid off at the start of the year and continued to do so at Key Biscayne. For too long condemned to older brother John's shadow, Patrick blossomed in 1991. After the Becker triumph, he learned a harsh truth when the letdown he had been most hoping to avoid happened. He was defeated 7-6, 6-1 by the hard-serving Swiss player, Marc Rosset, in his next match. But ever pragmatic and thoughtful, he took it with him as a lesson on which to build greater mental strengths.

Pete Sampras, the fifth seed, stirred talk of a sophomore slump as he departed in the second round to another Gilbert – Rodolphe Gilbert of France. After his stunning U.S. Open win in 1990, Sampras found himself and his talents beneath a magnifying glass early in 1991 with the

Jim Courier on his way to victory in a match under the lights. *(Serge Philippot)*

'sophomore jinx' nipping at his heels. Sampras would end the year in triumph, however, earning his first ever appearance as a member of the United States Davis Cup team in time to play in the final. A pair who were once steadfast campaigners in that cause also returned to the scene of former glories. Ken Flach and Robert Seguso had suffered division and decline and been replaced by Rick Leach and Jim Pugh as the Davis Cup doubles team for the United States, but when that team broke up, and Scott Davis and David Pate slipped up in their semi-final round debut, Flach and Seguso were back. Their return to form began at the Lipton when, unseeded, they reached the final. Two young talents from South Africa, Wayne Ferreira and Piet Norval, defeated them there for the title. But the chemistry was working again.

Not so for the doubles favourites in Florida. Top seeds Davis and Pate departed in the fourth round to the eventual champions. Sergio Casal and Emilio Sanchez, the second seeds, lost to Flach and Seguso in the quarter-finals. Leach and Pugh, the third seeds, were bumped by Neil Broad and Kevin Curren in the third round. Udo Riglewski and Michael Stich of Germany were to enjoy a fine year, but at the Lipton, the fourth seeds ran into Ronnie Bathman and Rikard Bergh of Sweden in the second round and could advance no further.

Everyone benefits at the Lipton. *(Serge Philippot)*

Ferreira and Norval were 19 and 20 respectively when they won the Lipton title, joining Courier and 17-year-old women's champion, Monica Seles, on a champions' dais that offered a decidedly youthful slant at this years Lipton Championships.

Estoril Open

By Richard Evans

Estoril, 1-7 April
Tournament Director: Joao Lagos

These are still formative years for professional tennis in Portugal but, thanks to the expertise of Joao Lagos and his dedicated team, the second Estoril Open advanced the cause in splendid fashion. Unlike the previous year, the weather allowed a youthful spring to bathe this picturesque coastline in warm sunshine for much of the week and the crowds, including the President of the

National Assembly Victor Crespo and other Lisbon luminaries, responded heartily to the lavish hospitality laid on by Lagos and his corporate sponsors.

Unlike those sponsors, such as Axe, Air Portugal, Perrier and Marconi – a brave breed in an underdeveloped economy – the top seeds did not manage to maintain as big a profile throughout the week. Andres Gomez was defeated in the first round by Ronald Agenor 6-4, 6-3 while defending champion Emilio Sanchez found it impossible to reproduce the superb form he had displayed on these same clay courts twelve months before and won only two games against Holland's Paul Haarhuis.

Haarhuis could go no further in singles, falling in the next round to the promising Italian Renzo Furlan but he did manage to help his fellow Dutchman Mark Koevermans to the first doubles title of his career when they beat a third Dutch player Tom Nijssen and his Czech partner Cyril Suk 6-3, 6-3 in the final.

But despite all this Dutch success, the singles trophy remained firmly in Spanish hands. Sergi Bruguera made steady rather than spectacular progress through the draw early in the week, needing three sets to get past the veteran Argentinian

Sergi Bruguera and his hard-earned trophy.
(Gianni Ciaccia)

Finalist Karel Novocek being interviewed outside the picturesque stadium court. *(Richard Evans)*

Andrei Chesnokov sets off in vain pursuit of a Bruguera lob in a close fought semi-final clash. *(Richard Evans)*

Eduardo Bengoechea in the second round and another three to wear down the persistent No. 3 seed Andrei Chesnokov in the semis. None of that preparation seemed good enough at the start of the final when Karel Novacek unloaded so many winners that the young Catalan did not win a point in the first three games of the match.

Novacek's heavy hitting had carried him past Omar Camporese, Goran Prpic, Javier Sanchez and Marian Vajda without the loss of a set and had he continued for much longer Bruguera would have been engulfed. But Sergi is blessed with determination as well as talent and he hung on, blunting the power of Novacek's blitzkrieg until the big Czech started to miss. Then, having saved one set point in the tie-break, Bruguera suddenly seized the initiative and, as his opponent tired, went on to claim the first ATP singles title of his young career 7-6, 6-1.

This is just the beginning,' said Lagos as he observed guests filing into the vast hospitality marquee on finals day. 'We have a long-standing tennis tradition in Portugal but not at this level. We need to create the right atmosphere as well as the proper competitive level on court. Then things will start to fall into place.'As the players will confirm, Lagos is making rapid strides in the right direction. The Atlantic coastline between Estoril and the pleasant seaside town of Cascais where the tournament hotel is located is, after all, the logical place to set the European claycourt season in motion as it rolls eastwards across the continent.

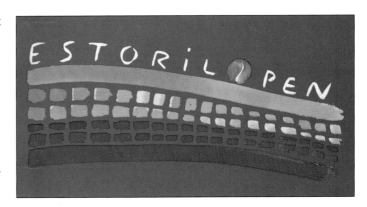

Salem Open '91

By Craig Gabriel

Hong Kong, 1-7 April
Tournament Directors: David Baukol & Lincoln Venancio

The wing tips of the 747 appear almost to touch the buildings on either side as the plane comes into land at Kai Tak airport, on the Kowloon side of Hong Kong. Once again the IBM/ATP Tour touched down in the most exciting continent on earth, Asia, as the colony hosted the first tournament on the four-week mini-swing through the Far East. We have moved into the Year of the Ram in the Chinese calendar, but little changes the lifestyle of the locals, as slow-moving junk boats make way for dragon boats or the Star Ferry shuttle which crosses Hong Kong harbour between the island and Kowloon.

> *When all the dust had settled two unexpected players were competing for the first prize of $33,700.*

Not too far from the frenzied life of the city centre is Victoria Park, home of tennis in the colony, where for the second consecutive year the Salem Open was held. It is the only official tennis tournament in Hong Kong, promoted by Pro Tennis Management which is directed by Lincoln Venancio and David Baukol. In 1991 the $260,000 Salem Open boasted an impressive field headed by the local hero Michael Chang and John McEnroe, but neither made it past the quarter-finals. In fact Chang, as the top seed, was the only seed to venture as far as the last eight. American Todd Witsken cut short Hong Kong's view of McEnroe with a win in the first round, and it was South African Gary Muller who caused plenty of havoc by stopping Tommy Ho, Chang's heir-apparent in Asia, and then Chang himself in a quarter-final which proved to be the match of the tournament. With Chang it could easily have been like going back to the days of Beatlemania. Michaelmania swept Hong Kong as the Chinese American was mobbed by fans who gave security guards plenty of concern. In Hong Kong, Chang is the greatest thing since chopsticks.

However, when all the dust had settled on a bright Sunday afternoon for the singles final, there were two generally unexpected players competing for the first prize cheque of $33,700: Wally Masur, who had won his first professional title in Hong Kong back in 1983, and a lanky 19-year-old Dutchman, Richard Krajicek, playing his first final. In the semis Masur had defeated the 1990 runner-up Alex Antonitsch, and Krajicek had ended Muller's giant-killing run. The final, which lasted one hour and 26 minutes was certainly a battle of serves that saw Krajicek close out the final 6-2, 3-6, 6-3. Masur, according to the new IBM MatchFacts system, ended the week with the highest first serve percentage at 77 per cent, but the cannonballs hit by Krajicek gave him 31 aces for the week (10 in the final) and the number one position in that category.

The doubles event was won by one of the year's new tandems, Patrick Galbraith and Witsken, 6-2, 6-4 over Robert van't Hof and Glenn Michibata. For the winners it was their first title together since grouping at the NSW Open in Sydney just three months before.

Holland's Richard Krajicek beat Wally Mosur to claim his first ATP Tour singles title – surely the first of many.

Prudential Securities Tennis Classic

By Sandra Harwitt

Orlando, 1-7 April
Tournament Director: Richard Adler

It's no secret that many people think 13 is a cursed number. For Andre Agassi, however, 13 was definitely lucky at the 1991 Prudential Securities Classic. Agassi's 6-2, 1-6, 6-3 victory over fourth-seeded Derrick Rostagno gave him his 13th career title - and his first conquest of the year. 'I forgot what Sunday's at a tournament were like,' revealed the top-seeded Agassi, who was sidelined with a stomach injury soon after his crowning performance at the 1990 ATP Championships in December.

Florida normally conjures up visions of picturesque beaches on either the Atlantic Ocean or the Gulf of Mexico. Although Orlando, a landlocked city in the middle of the state, lacks the beach scene, it doesn't lack in abundant offerings. As the players soon found out, this Southern city is a happening spot. Nicknamed 'The City Beautiful', Orlando is one of the world's top tourist destinations.

In between fulfilling their commitments on court, the players dropped their rackets to take in the sites. Among the famed attractions to choose from were Disneyworld, Epcot Center, MGM Studios, Universal Studios and Sea World of Florida. Nightlife included the Hard Rock Cafe/Orlando which hosted a player party during the event.

Despite the copious diversions, tennis managed to remain the focus of the week. The spirited Agassi wasn't the only court star searching for success in Orlando. Second-seeded Pete Sampras attempted to back-up his 1990 U.S. Open triumph by garnering an ATP Tour title. Third-seeded Brad Gilbert hoped for his first win since Brisbane, the previous September. And Rostagno wanted to prove his first ever-victory at the 1990 Volvo International Tennis Tournament was no fluke.

One week away from celebrating his 21st birthday, Agassi showcased his innate talent to end Rostagno's aspirations for a second crown. Agassi's brawny baseline bashing, recently peppered with an increasingly powerful serve, outlasted Rostagno's go-for-broke game. Rostagno's serve-and-volley style has a reputation on tour - it alternates between being brilliant and erratic. 'It seems like he defies all strategic logic,' said Agassi, of Rostagno's flamboyancy. 'He plays crazy tennis, going for things people don't think possible. Derrick plays with very little margin for error and it's tough to do that week after week.' Agassi wasn't anticipating any miracles in Orlando. His stomach ailment at the end of 1990 was making his return to the circuit a slow success story. He was expecting the Florida event to be no more than a building block back to top form. 'I was not expecting myself to play my best

Once again Andre Agassi obliges for the autograph-hunting youngsters.
(Michael Baz)

tennis,' revealed Agassi, accompanied by girlfriend, Wendi Stewart. 'But, I felt extremely clean hitting the ball. I did a lot better than I thought I'd do.'

Rostagno, a laid-back Californian, doesn't take an intense view of his sport. He loves playing, but winning isn't everything. He says what he likes best about Agassi is 'he's brought a little life and more smiles to the game.' Wild abandon wasn't a lucky charm for Rostagno in the final, but it worked wonders in his 7-5, 6-4 semi-final win over Sampras. Rostagno played the reigning Open Champion, who suffered a brief nosebleed on court. Every serve, return-of-serve and volley was an intimidating weapon. Rostagno, half kiddingly, joked that the win over Sampras 'felt good' because he was defending his family's honour. Rostagno said that's important because 'we're a very close family and they're always in my heart.'

The 25-year-old Rostagno and Sampras grew up playing at the same club. Since Rostagno was six years older and a more advanced tennis player, Sampras often relied on Rostagno's father as a hitting partner. The last time the two played the inevitable happened, Sampras beat the elder Rostagno. Now, the son had avenged his father's loss.

Orlando represented another disappointment for Sampras, looking to recapture the magic of his first Grand Slam victory. Unfortunately, he couldn't find any rhythm - his serve was obviously

on vacation against Rostagno's onslaught. Sampras insisted, however, that neither the nosebleed nor the heat and humidity affected his performance. 'I was serving really inconsistently and if I'm not serving well, I'm forced to stay back,' admitted Sampras, who acknowledged he was getting frustrated in the second set. 'You just can't stay back when you play someone like Derrick, who goes for all or nothing.'

Agassi's semi-final foe was unseeded Malivai Washington. Coached by Brian Gottfried, the ATP's Director of Tennis, Washington is a player waiting to happen. He's a talented athlete with a strong mind. Washington has played a lot of close matches with top players but has yet to make his big breakthrough. Agassi's 6-4, 7-6 (8-6) win was another almost, but not quite, appearance by Washington. 'When I play him again, I'll know what he's going to do,' said the confident Washington, who believes improvement and time will bring him to the winner's circle. 'I know what he can do now and I'll know what to expect. I think I'll know what to do to beat him.' Washington was responsible for removing Gilbert from the draw in the quarter-finals. Gilbert, the defending champion here, was not destined for a sterling repeat performance in 1991. He struggled through the first two rounds only to lose to Washington in three sets. For the victor, Orlando was definitely 'The City Beautiful' in April. It became Agassi's first milestone of the year.

Suntory Japan Open Tennis Championship 1991

Tokyo, 8-14 April
Tournament Director: Toshiro Sakai

It could have been likened to something out of Star Wars. The new $25 million retractable roof over the Ariake Colosseum, built in less than a year, was like an inter-galactic object as it slowly opened and shut to allow tennis to continue almost uninterrupted by the elements at the $1 million Suntory Japan Open. 'We are very excited about the new roof and we believe the roof will be of great benefit to tennis,' said Tournament Director Toshiro Sakai, himself a former No. 1 ranked player in Japan. Two giant sectors, each weighing 1,850 tons, slide parallel to the ground in a north-south direction; it takes 20 minutes to cover the court, allowing the tournament to continue in all weathers.

However, for the final that saw Stefan Edberg defeat Ivan Lendl, the giant structure stayed open, as the heavily overcast sky provided a natural ceiling above the stadium. For the first time the final was played over the best of five sets and Edberg took just one hour and 57 minutes to wrap up the match 6-1, 7-5, 6-0 and claim a hat trick of titles at the event. In fact, for the 25-year-old Swede, playing his fifth consecutive final at Ariake, it was his fourth Suntory victory. 'I am very happy because this is the best tennis I have played so far this year and one of the better matches I have ever played,' said Edberg. 'I was doing everything well and I kept the pressure on Ivan.'

Once again Stefan Edberg proved invincible in Tokyo, with backhand volleys like this – his speciality – helping him to his fourth Suntory victory in his fifth Ariake final.

The magnificent Ariake Stadium now has a sliding roof, which takes 20 minutes to cover the court once rain threatens. *(Craig Gabriel)*

Lendl did show some flashes of brilliance early in the second set, but he described his effort on the whole to be 'frustrating'. 'Anything I touched went wrong and I was playing catch up tennis,' said Lendl. 'The third set was a joke. The result was more frustrating than disappointing because nothing would go right ... the third set was really an avalanche.'

Like the roof, the tournament became an open-and-shut case for Edberg as he teamed up with Australian Todd Woodbridge for the first time to win the doubles 6-4, 5-7, 6-4 against John Fitzgerald and Anders Jarryd.

But the tournament had more than just the roof to look up to. The country's number one tennis son, Shuzo Matsuoka continued to be idolised by his screaming fans. Only two players can truly rival him for popularity in Japan, Edberg and Michael Chang. Even members of the Japanese royal family number among Matsuoka's fans; Prince Akishinonomiya, second in line to the Imperial Throne, had played tennis with him when he was 14.

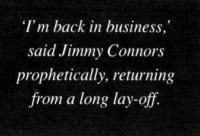

'I'm back in business,' said Jimmy Connors prophetically, returning from a long lay-off.

While Shuzo was busy with one thing, Jimmy Connors had the enthusiasts marvelling at his return. The 38-year-old, still in the early stages of a comeback after wrist surgery in 1990, went to the third round of his fourth event in 1991, took a set off Edberg and exclaimed, 'I'm back in business! The time came when I thought I'd never play again,' he said. 'You don't know how much you like the game till it's taken away from you.'

Trofeo Conde de Godo

By Toni Frieros

Barcelona, 8-14 April
Tournament Director: Sixto Cambra Sanchez

Blue sky, blazing sun, red clay an enthusiastic crowd ... and the best tennis anyone had ever seen in Barcelona. All the ingredients were there to make the 1991 'Trofeo Conde de Godo' – the Open Tennis Championship of Spain – into the best tournament ever played at the enchanting Real Club Tennis Barcelona.

Boris Becker, Andre Agassi, Guy Forget, Goran Ivanisevic, Sergi Bruguera and Emilio Sanchez, among other talented rackets, with their tennis full of inspiration and skill, offered the spectators the best highlights in a long while in the 1992 Olympic City. There were so many favourites to win the event that no one could have guessed that the final would take place among Spaniards Emilio Sanchez and Sergi Bruguera, though this was the final all the Spanish fans had wished for at the start of the week.

Bruguera had just come from the first victory in his professional career in Estoril the week before, and soon proved his strength and confidence by defeating Becker, then ranked two in the world, in straight sets 6-2, 6-4 in the third round. Sanchez, on the other hand, had a doubtful

Czech-mate! Tomas Smid (right) worries his opponent Andrei Chesnokov with some tactical play on the chess board. *(Richard Evans)*

Argentinian Horacio de la Pena and Italian Diego Nargiso won the Godo Cup doubles trophy but split up soon afterwards. *(A. Tonelli)*

Sergi Bruguera heading for a Catalan clash with Emilio Sanchez. In the final, Sanchez outplayed his compatriot 6-4, 7-6, 6-2. *(A. Tonelli)*

beginning, cancelling two match points with Andrei Cherkasov in the second round. Cherkasov was leading 7-5, 5-4, serving for the match, and had two match points, one on 40-30 and the other after the first deuce. Emilio came back to 5-5, won the second set 7-5 and the third 6-3. Who said Emilio doesn't know how to suffer?

Meanwhile, the biggest attraction was Andre Agassi, at his first official appearance in Spain. He was always scheduled for the night session, as everyone wanted to see the 'phosphorescent guy' who appeared at Barcelona airport with pillows under his armpits asking for the nearest McDonald's. Agassi's tennis attracted the best crowd ever at the tournament: for three straight days the crowd on centre court was such that there was no more space to fit a needle.
'I really like the crowd,' said Andre. 'The public here is warm, polite, knows everything about tennis and is very nice.' Argentinian Guillermo Perez Roldan was the man who shattered Agassi's dream in a wonderful, unforgettable match which ended 6-0 6-7, 7-6.

A picturesque view of the famous Centre Court at the Real Club de Barcelona. *(A. Tonelli)*

The tournament had already lost its defending champion in the first round. Andres Gomez had a disappointing defence of his title, losing to Marcelo Filippini. Another big surprise was Jordi Arrese's victory over Frenchman Guy Forget, who occupied at the time the fourth spot in the IBM/ATP Tour rankings. Moreover, Arrese had to play the whole tournament with a special bandage on his injured right hand.

The semi-finals gave the tournament a chance to break a negative streak. Not since 1970 had Spanish players advanced so far. The last ones had been Manolo Santana, who had defeated Yugoslav Zeljko Franulovic, and Juan Gisbert, who had lost to Rod Laver. Bruguera and Sanchez accomplished the feat, and both with superb performances against their respective opponents. Bruguera showed his fair play by correcting a linesman's call to give Guillermo Perez Roldan a point. It would seem only normal, but Sergi did it when he had a match point. Bruguera finally won 6-4, 6-4.

Emilio Sanchez, meanwhile, had to play against two opponents – one on the court, Martin Jaite, and the other in the stands, where some spectators behaved unfairly, booing Emilio after his victory. Why? The issue dates from September 1990, after the Soviet Union-Spain Davis Cup match. On that Occasion there was a confrontation between Emilio, his brother Javier and Sergio Casal, and Manolo Orantes the Spanish Davis Cup captain, who had chosen Bruguera to play instead of Javier Sanchez. Since then, in Spain the rivalry has been intense, and the crowd took part in it, showing its preferences.

TROFEO CONDE DE GODO

GODO 91

V TROFEO WINSTON

However, the most important thing was that two Spaniards went on to play the final. It was the first time since 1969, when two Manolos, Santana and Orantes, had fought for glory in the tournament. Obviously, Bruguera and Sanchez playing each other in this atmosphere created plenty of tension. Would it lead to Emilio's revenge after his defeat in the last Spanish national championship, or the continuation of Sergi's brilliant career. The best man won, and that was Emilio Sanchez, who was better prepared physically, with a score of 6-4, 7-6 (9-7), 6-2. Bruguera was suffering from a little tendinitis on his right knee, and made a lot more mistakes than Sanchez, who played extremely well.

After the match Emilio made a beautiful speech, thanking his coach Pato Alvarez for his support. At this moment, part of the crowd booed Emilio, who continued, 'My relationship with the Barcelona crowd is like that between a boy and a girl, where he is in love with her and she gives him no love in return. But I will always love you.' And then the champion lifted up the brand new silver trophy, which weighs eight kilos and took 1500 hours of hard work at Barcelona's finest jewellers. It will be very difficult to have another tournament like this one. I dare say impossible. But as everybody knows, there is nothing impossible at all.

Some people booed because local rivalry with Bruguera is intense, but Emilio Sanchez had every reason to smile after his fine victory. (A. Tonelli)

Philips Open

By Bruno Cuaz

Nice, 15-21 April
Tournament Directors: Pascal Portes & Dominique Bedel

The Promenade des Anglais, the most famous of Nice's boulevards, had a very British feel about it during the week of the Philips Open. Intermittent rain and temperatures that refused to rise much above a distinctly chilly 5°C on semi-finals day, despite the spring sunshine, made tennis-watching a hardy business for the dedicated Nicois fans. By the Sunday, however, Martin Jaite was helping to warm up the atmosphere during the course of an evenly fought final against the skilful Yugoslav Goran Prpic. Prpic ran and chased everything, despite the customary knee brace he wears, but eventually succumbed to the Argentine 3-6, 7-6, 6-3.

In an event marked by the early fall of seeded players, Jaite displayed the confidence he has derived from adopting a more aggressive style of play on clay and was particularly effective in the

Jaite and Prpic battle for the title on the court Suzanne Lenglen made her own back in 1919 *(G. Ciaccia)*

Martin Jaite and some Argentinian body language try to move the balls. *(Serge Philippot)*

semi-final against the powerful Karel Novacek whom he finally managed to beat 7-6 in the third after two hours and 20 minutes. Jaite's success lifted him back into the top thirty on the ATP computer while another Argentine, Alberto Mancini, was also starting to show the form that had made him a top ten player in 1989 before a slump set in. Now forced to qualify, Alberto did so with gusto and went on to reach the quarter-finals – satisfying progress for his new coach Alejandro Gattiker even though Alberto was unable to outmuscle the hefty Novacek.

Placed at the start of the clay court season, the Nice tournament is frequently the scene of numerous upsets. The 1991 event was no exception with Novacek being the only seeded player to get past the quarter-finals. For French fans, the biggest disappointment was the first round defeat of Guy Forget who lost to Jaite. Forget did, however, have time to win the award for the fastest serve, recording a speed of 194 km/h. This success was doubly welcome as the organiser of the contest was one of Guy's sponsors, ONET, but it still wasn't enough to console him for his elimination.

For the French, the revelation of the tournament was Cedric Pioline who, at 22, reached the semi-finals of an ATP Tour event for the second time in his career. He had been given a wild card on the basis of his semi-final appearance at the strong Parioli Challenger event in Rome the week before and continued with his winning ways on the courts of the Parc Imperial, dominating Fabrice Santoro, Alexander Volkov and Henri Leconte in successive matches. Pioline, whose father and brother both played top level volley ball, only chose to make tennis his career after reaching the final of the French Junior Championships in 1987. A classy attacker and excellent returner, he still seems to have considerable margins for improvement, despite suffering a straight-set defeat at the hands of the experienced Prpic.

The Nice tournament has been organised by former Davis Cup players Pascale Portes and Dominique Bedel since 1988 and although this year's event suffered somewhat from the weather, once again new talent burst to the fore – a sure sign that spring on the Riviera, if not wholly evident, was just around the corner.

KAL Cup Korea Open Tennis Championship

By Craig Gabriel

Seoul, 15-21 April
Tournament Director: Moon-Il Kim

The Olympic Tennis Stadium in Seoul's Olympic Park was once again the site for the KAL Cup, although on occasions the centre court was adapted for sports other than tennis. There were days when the inclement weather forced the cancellation of matches, but tennis players, being the hardy souls that they are, began playing a sort of volleyball with a tennis ball in the rain. Anything to keep themselves on their toes. To the resounding applause of the two spectators who elected to brave the wet conditions and hope for the day's resumption of play, which never came, defending champion Alex Antonitsch teamed up with ATP Tour Manager Paul Settles against Richard Krajicek's coach Rohan Goetzke and Karsten Braasch. The Austro-American combination took the match 4-2.

With no seeds left, Baur and Tarango emerged to fight it out in the final for the first prize of $20,000

When the rain cleared, the top two seeds in the event, Dutchman Jan Siemerink and defending champion Alex Antonitsch, along with Richard Krajicek and Gilad Bloom, the No. 4 and No. 6 seeds respectively, were the only seeded players in the quarter finals. Siemerink, who had performed well in Asia twelve months before, fell to the popular Japanese player Shuzo Matsuoka.

Krajicek, the winner at Hong Kong two weeks before, lost a thrilling match with German Patrick Baur, while American Jeff Tarango dismissed Bloom. So at the semi-final stage no seeds were left in the event. In the final Baur and Tarango had emerged to fight it out for the first prize cheque of $20,160.

In a match lasting two hours and 24 minutes Baur came through as the winner, taking his second event of 1991 after facing two match points in the final set, 6-4, 1-6, 7-6. Tarango played immaculate tennis in the second set and at 5-4 in the third was two points away from the match. Then at 6-5, with the German serving, Tarango held those two match points only to see Baur power down some huge serves and scrape through. 'It feels great to win another tournament,' said Baur. 'The conditions were very good to play in and I just kept trying in the match.'

Antonitsch meanwhile managed to salvage some lost pride when he teamed up with Bloom to clown their way through the draw and win the doubles event 7-6, 6-1 over Kent Kinnear and Sven Salumaa.

Kelly Jones (right) always manages to make an impact in Asia. Having won back to back titles in Singapore in 1989 and 1990, Kelly resorted to merely looking imperious in Korean costume in Seoul. As usual, ATP Trainer Bill Norris can't resist showing a leg.

Volvo Monte Carlo Open

By Richard Evans

Monte Carlo, 23-29 April
Tournament Director: Bernard Noat

In one of the best finals the tournament has seen in years, Sergi Bruguera defeated Boris Becker 5-7, 6-4, 7-6, 7-6 to win the Volvo Monte Carlo Open. But, with due respect to Sergi and Boris, their match is not what will be remembered about this year's event at the fabled Monte Carlo Country Club.

It will be remembered as the tournament in which a great champion tried to cheat the passing years and, in doing so, discovered a few harsh truths about the way professional tennis has changed in the past decade. It will be remembered for the

way tennis's answer to Gary Cooper tried to do his stuff at High Noon again and found that a Colt 45 was no longer enough. It will be remembered as the tournament that saw Bjorn Borg try to be Borg again and fail.

Some found it sad, everyone found it riveting. Alain Delon turned up to make the draw, James Coburn arrived to join the entourage of Bjorn's soon-to-rejected guru Ron Thatcher, a 79-year-old martial arts professor who had got him fit but couldn't tell him what racket to use. And the press turned up in droves.

Boris Becker, ever the gracious loser, listens to Sergi Bruguera's explanation of how he won the Monte Carlo title. *(Serge Philippot)*

Preparing for lunch in the sun on the terrace of the Monte Carlo Country Club. *(Serge Philippot)*

Bjorn Borg and Alain Delon share a joke with Prince Albert as Tournament Director Bernard Noat prepares to tell the world that Borg has drawn Jordi Arrese in the first round. *(Serge Philippot)*

Borg had practised impressively enough against Becker and Goran Ivanisevic in the days leading up to the event. With his quick fire tempo, running after loose balls, trotting back to baseline to serve with minimum preparation, Borg had actually made Ivanisevic pant. But all that was practice. Borg's High Noon arrived near enough on time, at 1.00 pm on the Tuesday when, headband in place and shoulders rolling in familiar style, he descended the long flight of steps from the locker room in the company of a small Spaniard ranked 52 on the ATP computer called Jordi Arrese. The roar echoed back from the craggy rocks that overhang the club and the sporting world held it's breath. The only certainty was that Arrese was about to become famous. Borg, weilding a wood racket specifically crafted in Cambridge to his specifications, hit an authentic Borgian backhand passing shot early on and another roar erupted. But it was cruel deception. Soon it became clear that Borg had no penetration and was unable to get his teeth into the match against as solid a claycourter as the Spaniard. Alain Delon had done him no favours by pulling Arrese's name out of the hat for his first competitive match since he had lost to Henri Leconte in Stuttgart eight years before.

Soon it became evident that Arrese was not going to miss, nor was he going to give Borg a target. The encouragement from the packed stands became muted; the sun hid behind the clouds and it turned cold. By the time Arrese had completed his 6-2, 6-3 victory the first drops of rain were splattering the red clay – teardrops for a fading dream. Relaxed and philosophical at his packed post- match press conference, Borg said, 'My expectations were not as high as some people's. I knew it was going to be tough. A lot of the time I didn't know where to hit the ball. I need more matches.' Dumping the guru, Borg went off to Rome to train with Adriano Panatta and Paolo Bertolucci who at least talked tennis sense to him and put a graphite racket in his hand. But several months later there was no more news from the man who tried to prove that legends live.

Bruguera, meanwhile, was busy capitalising on the fact that a tall young Swede called Magnus Larsson had been disrespectful enough to knock

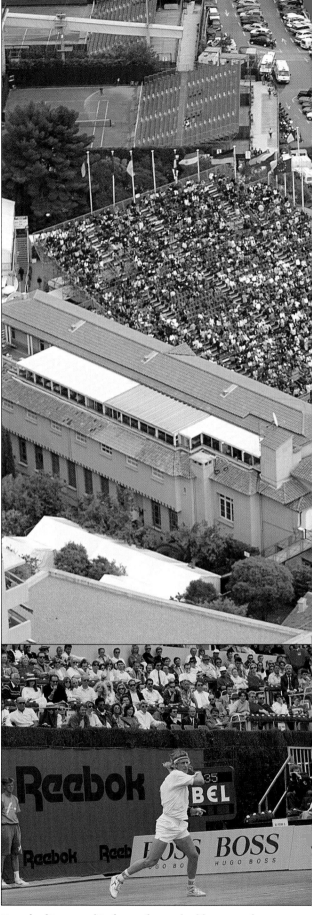

Borg looking good in front of a packed house at the Monte Carlo Country Club – but not good enough to beat Arrese. *(Serge Philippot)*

Views of the world's most spectacular tennis setting. *(Serge Philippot)*

Stefan Edberg out of his way in the top half of the draw. Larsson then lost to another Swede Magnus Gustafsson who in turn was defeated by Bruguera in the quarters.

Becker, who had dropped sets to Javier Sanchez and Alexander Volkov was in dominant form by the time he powered his way past Goran Prpic in the semis. His first clay court title seemed to be there for the taking. But Bruguera, with his sound double-handed backhand and lovely touch, was

bolstered by the confidence of that first ATP Tour title in Estoril and battled brilliantly through the two deciding tie-breaks to win a tight thrilling encounter.

In doubles the Australian Laurie Warder and his ambidextrous American partner Luke Jenson won a title that would help propel them towards the ATP Tour World Doubles Championships by beating the Dutch pair Mark Koevermans and Paul Haarhuis in another close struggle 5-7, 7-6, 6-4.

Epson Singapore Super Tennis

By Craig Gabriel

Singapore, 22-28 April
Tournament Director: Graeme Plum

The most amazing island in the world once again ended the four-week Asian mini-circuit with the $250,000 Epson Singapore Super Tennis and for the second time in a month a Dutch player, also appearing in his first final, proved to be the major benefactor, just as Richard Krajicek had been in Hong Kong. In the year's first all left-handed final, Jan Siemerink defeated Israeli Gilad Bloom 6-4, 6-3 in one hour and 24 minutes to claim the $30,960 first prize, the biggest of his career.

Meanwhile, for Grant Connell and Glenn Michibata, it was third time lucky. This was their third time in Singapore and their third final of 1991. All that just had to pay dividends and, in a superb and thrilling final, the Canadians won the title 6-4, 5-7, 7-6 against Stefan Kruger and Christo van Rensburg, a pair of South Africans who, happily, were to find themselves persona grata all over the world before the year was out.

Indian junior Leander Paes, wild-carded into the event, scored the first upset of the week when he dismissed the third seed Wally Masur 6-2, 5-7, 7-5. It was a tough loss for the veteran Australian but he would have been aware that Paes' pedigree marked him as a young player on the threshold of greater things. Paes had been the first major success story to emerge from the six-year-old Britannia /Amritraj Tennis School, set up in Madras by Vijay and his brothers under the supervision of Peter Burwash coaches. Paes surpassed expectations by winning Junior Wimbledon in 1990 and much of the determination and skill he displayed on the grass courts of the All England Club was in evidence as he battled through a tough third set to beat Masur.

At the quarter-final stage the top two seeds, Todd Woodbridge and Jan Siemerink were left and in the next round three of the four players were southpaws; Jason Stoltenberg, enjoying a return to form, was the exception.

The days in Singapore were leisurely as the heat and humidity did not usually allow play to begin until 4pm. So it was a case of lazing around the pool of the world's tallest hotel or wandering through the streets of Little India or spending time, and money, at the shops down tree-lined Orchard Road. Nothing was hurried, whether it was a ride on a 'bum boat' or a tricycle, during what definitely has to be the 'escape week' of the IBM/ATP Tour. The daily mid-afternoon thundershower was a welcome respite for most; the only problem was that once the clouds had cleared the humidity went back up and it was back to square one.

A first ATP Tour title in Singapore for another of those rising Dutchmen, Jan Siemerink. *(Henk Koster)*

Tournament director Graeme Plum had gone out of his way to allow the players a most enjoyable time in Singapore which is such a crossroads for east and west. There was breakfast with an Orang utan at Singapore's beautiful zoo where Kelly Jones, a local favourite with sports fans (having won the first two events played on the island in 1989 and 1990), Thomas Hogstedt and Kent Kinnear joined in the monkeying around with the day's most important meal. And there was a day out at the famed Tiger Balm Gardens, as Jones, this time with ATP Tour trainer Bill Norris decided to adorn the robes from the period of Genghis Khan, with both men being more than thankful that tennis was not played in such a bygone era.

Unlike the doubles champions who seemed to like doing things in threes, it would have been too much to ask Jones to win his third consecutive singles title in Singapore, especially as he had never won one anywhere else! Unhappily for his fans, the former Pepperdine University star could not survive the first round this time, going down in straight sets to another man who plays well in the Far East, the 1990 Seoul champion, Alex Antonitsch. The Austrian could not capitalise on that victory, however, and went out in the next round to Connell who was also active in the singles at the Epson, going all the way to the semis before Siemerink served him off court, 6-2, 6-2, thus setting the tone for another outstanding performance against Bloom in the final.

XX Trofeo Grupo Zeta Villa de Madrid

By Ramon Sanchez

Madrid, 29 April-5 May
Tournament Director: Jose Edison Mandarino

It was like coming back home. After being away for nineteen years, the Villa de Madrid was held in the Club de Tenis Chamartín, the scene of the inaugural event and the venue where it will be held until at least 1993. The tournament was a great success. The organisers had set up a Centre Court with capacity for 4700 people, and the public gave their full support. On Wednesday, with Bruguera's debut, all the tickets were sold out and there were so many people waiting in the street that the police had to be called.

Anyone who had bet at the beginning that the finalists would be Jordi Arrese and Marcelo Filippini would have been considered crazy. A lot of players in the draw were in better shape and the credentials of these two were not exactly positive: the best that either had achieved in the year was to have made the last 16 in Barcelona.

Sergio Bruguera and Emilio Sanchez looked like the best competitors in the field. The day that the tournament began, Bruguera reached his second triumph of the season in Monte Carlo, while the eldest of the Sanchez Vicario family had won the Godo Cup in Barcelona two weeks before. In spite of this, neither showed their true worth in Madrid. Within two days, the favourite had disappeared. Emilio lost to Renzo Furlan in his

first match and Bruguera could not pass the round of sixteen, losing to Javier Sanchez on a terribly windy day. A similar tale could be told of the third seed, Andres Gomez, winner in 1990. After winning the French Open, the left-hander from Ecuador crashed down the rankings and he had still not recovered. He had to retire with a leg injury when his opponent, the Dutchman Jacco Eltingh, was up in the third set.

Some months before, Arrese and his coach and friend, Roberto Vixcaino, had decided to make some changes in Jordi's game. These changes, focused on the service and on the level of aggression, were decisive and enabled Arrese to win the third title of his career in Madrid, after those of San Remo and Prague last year. Conde, Altur, Champion, Novacek and Filippini were the obstacles passed by Arrese on his way to victory: a trajectory that improved every match till reaching great performances in the semi-final and final. With Novacek, he played a really perfect match. The day before, he had said that in order to beat Karel it was necessary to move him from one side of the court to the other, provoking his mistakes. He then proceeded from theory to reality. Novacek had great trouble in moving his strong body (1m 91 height and 81 kg weight), and Jordi won quite easily.

In the final, he played an equally splendid match although his tactics were different. Arrese was as sure as usual at the back of the court, but he was also very successful at the net, winning sixteen of his seventeen attacks. After picking up the trophy, he said: 'I did not want to delude the spectators. During the last three years I have had it in mind to be in the top twenty of the ATP rankings and now I think I can do it.'

Besides Jordi, one should also remember the performances of the other semi-finalists, Novacek, Filippini and Javier Sanchez, who repeated his 1990 place in the last four. Another outstanding player was the young Spaniard German Lopez, beaten by Javier in the quarter-finals, the fastest server in the tournament (190 km/h), producing 48 aces in his three matches.

The doubles had samba rhythm, because three of the four finalists were Brazilian. The winners were the pair consisting of the Argentinian Gustavo Luza and Cassio Motta, who beat Luiz Mattar and Jaime Oncins in the last match. A nostalgic note was provided by the presence of Mats Wilander and Jimmy Connors, but neither lasted long. The American, who had been for two years without playing on clay, was not lucky in his first match against Motta, and the Swede, lacking in competition rhythm, was beaten in the second round by Franco Davin. For them, the best days are over.

Throughout the tournament, famous people from politics, sport, show business and high society filled the boxes of the Chamartin. And for the whole of that week, Madrid society revolved around the tennis. The future of the Villa de Madrid, Trofeo Grupo Zeta, is optimistic. Next year, the prize money will be increased to $750,000 and everybody hopes that Madrid will soon have the big tennis tournament the city deserves.

By keeping his eye on the ball Javier Sanchez not only defeated number two seed Sergi Bruguera but also outlasted elder brother Emilio by reaching the semi-finals where Marcello Filippini beat him. However, it was fellow-Spaniard Jordi Arrese who got his hands on the trophy after defeating Filippini 6-2, 6-4.

BMW Open

By Meg Donovan

Munich, 29 April-5 May
Tournament Director: Lothar Lanz

Success at the Iphitos Club is no stranger to Guillermo Perez-Roldan. The 21-year-old native of Buenos Aires has played the Munich tournament on five occasions, reaching the finals three times. But, true to the pattern established over the course of the past two years on the IBM/ATP Tour, it was the newcomer who claimed the spoils at the 1991 Munich BMW Open.

Magnus Gustafsson, whose win in retrospect may have been the spark which ignited his meteoric rise to the upper reaches of tennis' elite later in the season, escaped with an injury-interrupted win.

A torn hamstring had put an end to Perez-Roldan's bid to become a triple winner in Munich, and had given Gustafsson his first-ever singles title.

Ironically, it was Gustafsson who missed four months of 1990 after surgery to his left knee, rejoining the Tour at Basle where he reached the quarter-finals. But Perez-Roldan too had been plagued with nagging injuries during the year. At his first event, Lipton, Perez-Roldan twisted an ankle which sidelined him for almost a month. He then came back to play in fits and starts in the

month leading up to Munich, reaching the semi-finals of another historically lucky tournament for him, Barcelona, but suffering second-round losses at both Nice and Monte Carlo. At the BMW's host Iphitos Club, he returned with a vengeance, fairly waltzing through the early rounds before meeting up with Gustafsson in the final.

En route, he lost a total of just 17 games while dropping Number 2 seed Goran Ivanisevic among others. In the semi-finals, Gustafsson's teammate Christian Bergstrom was the victim of a 6-0, 6-0 shellacking by Perez-Roldan which gave the Argentinian a 'bagel' two years running. In 3000 matches recorded in 1990, only two had been bagels, one of them Perez-Roldan's 6-0, 6-0 defeat of Xavier Daufresne in Bologna.

Gustafsson in the role of giant-killer, was advancing through the other half of the draw.

However, Gustafsson in the role of giant-killer was advancing through the other half of the draw with some solid wins to earn the other spot in the finals. In the first round, the 24-year-old Swede ousted crowd favourite Michael Stich, a resident of nearby Elmshorn and already a three-time finalist on the 1991 tour by that point. He then defeated

On his way – Magnus Gustafsson winning the first of the titles that pushed him towards a place in the top ten. (Thomas Exler)

the Austrian Horst Skoff and Stich's doubles partner Udo Riglewski to be rewarded by a semi-final match-up with No.1 seed Ivan Lendl. Lendl had returned to red clay for the first time since Bordeaux 1989 in Munich. Gustafsson took the match in straight sets to set up his championship match with Perez-Roldan which he went on to win 3-6, 6-3, 4-3 Retired.

Gustafsson's win boosted him 11 spots on the world ranking list to No 21, a progression which was to continue throughout the year with the watershed breakthrough into the Top 10 coming after his title win in Hilversum. Only the next week, Gustafsson (who like fellow Swedish Top 10 entrant Jonas Svensson is coached by German-born Tim Klein) would go on to reach the finals of another German tour stop - Hamburg - and in subsequent weeks would add to his collection of titles with wins in his home country at Bastad and Hilversum two weeks later. In a year of resurgent Swedish presence on the IBM/ATP Tour, Gustafsson could look back and say that, for him, the spark was lit in Munich.

In doubles, another Swede, Anders Jarryd, was also catching fire but the flame was not yet strong enough to finish the week with a win. Jarryd and first-time partner Danie Visser, blazed through

the early rounds before stalling in the championship match won by Americans Patrick Galbraith and Todd Witsken 7-5, 6-4. Visser's long-time partner Piet Aldrich had been forced to undergo shoulder surgery following Monte Carlo, and Jarryd's regular partner John Fitzgerald did not make the trip to Munich. So the two talented veterans paired up to reach the finals in their first outing together, defeating Roger Smith and Tobias Svantesson, and Brod Dyke/Laurie Warder after benefitting from a first-round walkover to set up their match with Galbraith and Witsken.

Galbraith and Witsken had played most of the year together, splitting up only for the Stuttgart Indoors and Rotterdam where, ironically, Galbraith had won the title with Jarryd. In the run up to Munich, Galbraith and Witsken had one title, Hong Kong, and reached the semi-finals of Monte Carlo before falling to Jensen and Warder. With one eye on the ATP Tour World Doubles Final in November, as Witsken explained, the pair were tested in the early rounds but came through unscathed. In the semi-finals, a hard-fought 6-3, 6-7, 7-5 victory over local heroes Udo Riglewski and Michael Stich gave them their berth in the finals. Once there, they jumped out to a lead and never looked back, winning easily in straight sets.

USTA Men's Clay Courts of Tampa

By Charlie Risso-Gill

Tampa, 29 April-5 May
Tournament Director: Michael Burns

Tampa, situated on the Gulf of Mexico is one of America's most modern cities and home to America's latest hero, General 'Stormin'' Norman Schwarzkopf, CO Allied Forces, Middle East Command. Known as the 'soldiers' soldier', he

executed a brilliant campaign by dispatching the Iraqis from Kuwait you could say in two sets, love - love. During the week of the first annual USTA Men's Clay Courts of Tampa, the city prepared for the General's homecoming and hosted

Jack Mills, USTA Regional Vice-President, hands the tropy to Richey Reneberg. *(David Wagner)*

the first tournament of the 1991 ATP Tour on the unique American 'green clay'. David Beard of Welch Tennis Courts Inc, a local company, was on hand to explain the differences between the fast dry surface of Tampa and its European cousin, the brick red variant.

Basically the surfaces are the same with the exception of colour. The raw material of fast dry is basalt and is mined from quarries in Pennsylvania whereas red clay is a combination of crushed brick and European clay. The fast dry surface is making a bit of a comeback on the American circuit and is seen as the ideal preparation for the European clay court season. Historically American players were raised on both grass and green clay but the advent of hard 'cement' courts has meant that a generation of American players are accustomed to one surface. A case in point was the number one seed in Tampa Richey Reneburg. 'Any match I can win on clay is a great bonus!' Reneburg, who likes to take the ball on the rise, was able to adjust his game to suit the fast dry clay court surface.

Tampa saw the return of Sweden's Mikael Pernfors who had reached the semi-finals of a challenger event the week prior despite an Achilles tendon problem. His run was ended in the quarter-finals by Czechoslovakia's Petra Korda, a former army reservist. 'I play because I have fun doing it', the former French Open finalist revealed.

The final coincided with General Schwarzkopf's homecoming celebrations. It was Sunday and Tampa was alive with passion, patriotism and victory. As the temperature soared into the 90s Petr Korda and Richey Reneburg battled it out on centre court but the American held his cool to win his first career title with a 4-6, 6-4, 6-2 win in one hour, 48 minutes. Reneburg who didn't drop a set until the final was elated. 'I was very happy to win', the former Southern Methodist University standout exclaimed. Korda, who was recovering from an ankle injury was still pleased with the second final showing of his career: 'At the moment I'm happy just enjoying my tennis'. Reneburg's win in Tampa put the 25-year-old

American at number 20 from 27 on the IBM/ATP Tour, a career high.

In doubles an all-American final between the veteran pairing of Ken Flach and Robert Seguso picked up an amazing 25th doubles title together. They fought back to a win of 6-7, 6-4, 6-1 over former doubles No 1, David Pate and Tampa singles champion, Reneburg.

Meanwhile in Tampa's football stadium, to complete a Sunday that was as American as apple pie, 'Stormin' Norman' thanked a throng of thousands, plus every section of Uncle Sam's armed forces, for the 'mother of all homecomings'.

Eye on the ball but for how long? The popular Mikael Pernfors made an all too rare appearance in Tampa. *(David Wagner)*

Panasonic German Open

By Dieter Koditek

Hamburg, 6-12 May
Tournament Director: Gunter Sanders

This is the history of a foot fault, making a career because it marks the highlight of the tennis professional's career who profited by it. Fortunately it did not harm the other tennis player's career much. The setting of the story is the semi-finals of the German Open in Hamburg Rothenbaum. When he played Karel Novacek, it was everything but hopeless for Michael Stich, on whom were focused the last hopes of the German audience having to celebrate a German title winner

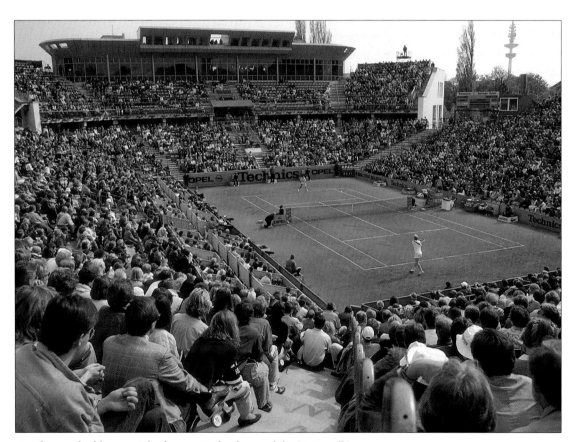

Another packed house at the famous Rothenbaum club. (A. Tonelli)

Eye on the ball – all the power and concentration of Karel Novocek as he battles to the German Open title.
(Metelmann)

Danilo Marcelino shows Brazilian touch as he dummies past an opponent in the player's soccer match. Arms upraised Claudio Pistolesi thinks it's a foul. *(Metelmann)*

after several years at this traditional tournament. He was leading by 5-3 (3-6, 6-2) in the third and decisive set when serving. His game was supremely good and nobody among the 10,000 crowd had a doubt that he was going into the finals on that Centre Court, which had been completely modernised after four years work.

But then it happened: Michael Stich played an ace at 30 all. But only a few seconds later a voice called it a foot fault. It was like a thunder clap. Michael Stich was frozen and the cheering of the crowd stopped immediately; even Karel Novacek did not know what was going on. The crowd began to whistle and the usual unsuccessful discussions started. The judgement of that lonely man at the side was not altered. So what had to happen

occurred: Michael Stich, who obviously lost his concentration and had become very tense played a double fault with his second serve. Instead of having a matchball, he had a break point against him. Like a professional Karel Novacek coldly took advantage of the situation and managed to break him. He saved himself into the tie-break which he finally won 7-5.

In history there are many examples without contradictory decisions in tennis where a player who thought himself the winner left the court as loser. But in this case even Karel Novacek admitted that we would have travelled to the next tournament without that decision. So Michael Stich's anger and disappointment were at least understandable. 'Without intending to reduce

Of course the question remains whether that man had the necessary sensitivity at that moment. But tennis is a game which is decided by faults and not only the players have the right to make mistakes.

There is a continuation to this story which is a happy ending for Karel Novacek. The industrious player from Prague, who plays more than 30 tournaments a year, took advantage of the situation and made the finals the following day the greatest success of his professional career. He won against Swede Magnus Gustafsson in a strange match 6-3, 6-4, 5-7, 0-6, 6-1 and with it a cheque for $125,000 – the highest prize money of his life. Furthermore he had made the decisive step which opened the way into the Top Ten. Gustafsson who after the finals in Kitzbuhel and Prague did not have a chance against Novacek was handicapped by a shoulder injury. In the middle of the second set he even had to get it treated which did not prevent him from getting better after he had already lost two sets. After four sets it was open again. But whatever the decisive factors were – courage, power or power of nerves – at the end they were undoubtedly on Karel Novacek's side. Proudly he presented the trophy to his wife Maya, who accompanies him on every tournament tour.

Although Karel Novacek and Magnus Gustafsson were not the players that the Hamburgers might have expected to see in the final, it was a very good showcase; it was exciting and entertaining. For the greatest players this tournament was just not it: Goran Ivanisevic did not get out of his low, Ivan Lendl failed right in his first performance against outsider Renzo Furlan, Stefan Edberg had to give in to Michael Stich, and the 1990 U.S. Open winner Pete Sampras was beaten by Karel Novacek in the round of sixteen.

Karel's performance, I do not think the better player won this match,' Stich said. 'It was sure that I was going to win that match.' He added that what made him really feel sad was that 'it is strange that this had to happen in my home country. This does not happen in another tournament in the world. Even if it had been a foot fault one would not call it a fault in such a decisive situation.'

Is this really a just argument? Should it really be that way that players are favoured in their home country? One cannot deny that it might happen and Stich's disappointment in such a situation is undoubtedly understandable and comprehensible. But all over the world the rules are similar for all players and it is not written anywhere that in decisive situations they have to be judged differently as for instance at the beginning of a match. If the foot fault judge calls it a foot fault, it is a foot fault.

Regarding Michael Stich who did not get among the Top Ten because of this foot fault, we know by now that it did not beat him entirely. There was a happy ending for him too. Not at the German Open but a few weeks later on the courts of Wimbledon. And surely he would not want to exchange that title for another one. Finally everything evcns up in life!

US Air/U.S. Men's Clay Court Championships

By Susan Schott

Charlotte, 6-12 May
Tournament Director: Michael J. Burns

Spread over 58 acres of grassy fields bordered by pines and dogwoods, the Olde Providence Racquet Club in Charlotte, North Carolina provided an old-fashioned camp setting for the U.S. Men's Clay Court Championships. Yellow and white striped tents, barbecue grills, and children knocking balls against backboards all contributed to the casual, relaxed air of the week. The tournament, long an uprooted event searching for an appropriate venue and time slot, may have found a permanent home in the Charlotte springtime. Held for the first time here, the seventeenth venue over an 80-year history, the national clay championships is now part of a U.S. spring clay court circuit designed to better prepare players for the rigours of the European clay season.

Yet despite the down home, all American ambiance, a name change to the 'South America/U.S. Men's Clay Court Championships' might have been more equitable in terms of billing. In a field heavy with U.S. athletes, outstanding play by tournament winner Jaime Yzaga (Peru), semi-finalist Javier Frana (Argentina) and quarter-finalist Pablo Arraya (Peru) generated excitement in the singles draw. A touch of North American flavour was added in the all-U.S. doubles final, with Rick Leach and Jim Pugh ousting Bret Garnett and Greg Van Emburgh (6-3, 2-6, 6-3) for the doubles crown.

Jimmy Arias, once a member of the world top ten, celebrates reaching the final of the US Air Men's Clay Court Championship. *(Michael Baz Photos)*

American hopes for a singles champion faded quickly as three of the seven seeded Americans fell in the first round. Second seed Derrick Rostagno lost to wily claycourter Pablo Arraya and Scott Davis (No. 6) and David Pate (No. 8), out of their league on clay, both suffered three-set defeats to lower-ranked opponents. Further disaster struck in the quarters, with top seed Michael Chang, third seed and defending champion David Wheaton, and fourth seed Richey Reneberg all bowing out. Chang lost to Yzaga, the only non-U.S. seed at No. 7, in a passive 6-7 (0-7), 1-6 display. 'Jaime just kept slicing and slicing. I couldn't do a whole lot,' the 1989 French Open champion stated simply. 'He played really consistent tennis.'

The memorable battle between fast-rising, all-court players David Wheaton (then ranked 23) and Mailivai Washington (ranked 88) provided a rare bright spot for patriotic fans. Lipton finalist Wheaton, anticipating a strong season on clay after a rocky start in 1991, prevailed in the first set's rapid-fire serve and baseline exchanges by capitalizing on a handful of loose Washington errors in the 7-3 tiebreaker. But Washington, undeterred, continued his relentless attack on Wheaton. The former university of Michigan star broke Wheaton in the very first game of the second set and never looked back. Nailing 13 aces and dominating play from the net and backcourt, Washington roared through the next two sets 6-1, 6-2 to notch his biggest career win. Thus, the semi-finals and finals became a strictly U.S./South American affair. In the semis, fifth-seeded Jimmy Arias, conqueror of fourth seed Richey Reneberg in the quarters, overcame a nervous start to edge battle-worn qualifier Javier Frana 3-6, 6-3, 7-5. By mixing up the pace and playing wide to Washington's weaker forehand, master clay-court tactician Yzaga cooled Washington 7-5, 6-2 in the other semi.

For both Arias and Yzaga, survivors of a long week of gritty matches in thick Southern humidity, the Charlotte finals presented a golden opportunity to regain a winning edge in their careers. The 26-year-old Arias, a feisty contender on clay in the early 80s, had not won a title since

But it was Peru's Jaime Yzaga who took off in the final to capture the fourth singles title of his career. (Michael Baz Photos)

1983 in Palermo; Yzaga, possessor of an elegant all-court game, last won on hardcourts in Itaparica in 1988. In the end, Yzaga felt most at home on the green clay in Olde Providence's setting of rustic simplicity. By attacking Arias' suspect backhand and second serve, and moving the ball around well, Yzaga sailed through the first set and handled Arias' late surge in the second to gain a 6-3, 7-5 victory. 'Winning a tournament does a lot for my confidence, I have been wondering when I was going to win another,' admitted Yzaga, who defeated four Americans en route to his fourth career victory. 'Really, it's a matter of being there, knocking on the door - and having it finally open.'

XLVIII Campionati Internazionali d'Italia

By Ubaldo Scanagatta

Rome, 13-19 May
Tournament Director: Franco Bartoni

There are stars, and then there are stars. Before and after Galileo, and even apart from the science of astronomy, Italians have always believed in 'stars', as evidenced by the great popularity of astrological magazines and the frequent appearance of horoscopes in the news. There is no doubt that on the green hills of Monte Mario, on the timeless silver reflection of the Tiber, on the white marble

Italian Federation officials Michele Brunetti (left) and Luigi Pronchetti join doubles champions Omar Camporese and Goran Ivanisevic for the presentation ceremony. *(Gianni Ciaccia)*

of the Foro Italico, on the salmon-coloured clay courts, on all of the Eternal City in fact, shone an unlucky star in the third week of May.

This is not to slight the efforts of the last King of Rome, Emilio Sanchez, and the runner-up, the assumed 'desaparecido', Alberto Mancini (reborn from the qualies after being refused a wildcard into the main draw by some short-sighted and overly patriotic directors). Sanchez and Mancini, presumably the two of the few who will carry away with them good memories of the 48th Italian Open, except for the treasurer of the Italian Federation.

$ 2.5 million dollars in revenue, a record for the tournament, with tickets the same price as last year, and 200,000 spectators in the two weeks of the men's and women's tournaments, all this represents an outcome much more rosy than that to which we are accustomed to read in Italy.

Nevertheless, even Paolo Galgani, the President of the Italian Federation, who I refer to as 'Palone Happy Heart' because of his tendency to smile and joke and his ability to minimise the unfortunate result, was not happy on this occasion.

The Land of Sun transformed itself into one of umbrellas and, notwithstanding the admirable efforts of the Silver Fox, Cino Marchese, it wasn't exactly La Dolce Vita at the Italian Open this year, even if Anita Ekberg, in addition to Sophia Loren and Ornella Muti showed up at the sponsors village during the tournament. The list of all the

Emilio Sanchez, a finalist in Rome in 1986, on his way to his first Italian title. *(Michael Cole)*

When the skies cleared Michael Cole was able to capture this beautiful portrait of the Foro Italico. *(Michael Cole)*

unfortunate astrological coincidences which occurred at the Foro Italico is much longer than a laundry list after a world tour. And so, I don't even know myself if in this sad Amarcord with overtones of Fellini, I should even mention all of these unfortunate occurrences starting with the depressing withdrawal of the top three players on the entry list – Becker, Lendl and Forget. Perhaps I should start with the first unfinished final in the history of the tournament back in 1955 when

Fausto Gardini won as a result of the retirement of Beppe Merlo in an all-Italian final. Frankly it was probably much more exciting than this year's final between Sanchez and Mancini, a 6-3, 6-0, 3-0 (retired) result.

The match between the big rivals of the 1950s, Gardini and Merlo, provided a great suspense, ultimately becoming the stuff of legends. With Merlo leading two sets to one before becoming too

though in the Argentinian's blood there is a drop of Italian, there was no suspense whatsoever. The match lasted just one set, at which point a betting man would only have had to place money on the exact moment when Mancini would be forced to retire due to a pulled groin muscle.

The best motto for the tournament, the most unlucky of the entire ATP Tour in my opinion, would have been 'when it rains, it pours.' Eight of the top 10 players, or if you prefer three of the best five including Forget, didn't show up, due to their physical problems. Four of the remaining five were already out by the end of the second round. In the first round in fact, Agassi (Number 4 on the ATP rankings) lost. After being offered a wildcard, he repaid the tournament by playing badly against Eric Jelen, eliciting severe criticism. Ivanisevic lost in the first round as well against Paul Haarhuis.

In the second round, Pete Sampras joined the unwilling tourists in Rome, losing to Fabrice Santoro. In the end, only one of the top eight seeds – Bruguera – reached the semi-finals but went no further. The slaughter of the favourites, torn to pieces by the underdogs like the Christians in the Colosseum of old, was not redeemed by the performance of the remaining seeds who also lost in the first two rounds – Stich, Novacek, Gilbert and Perez-Roldan in the first, and Svensson, Gustafsson, Hlasek and Volkov in the second.

Some will remember this unfortunate edition of the Italian Open for its most famous incident – the launch of the sandwich, as they do the tournament in 1978 made famous by the incident where coins were thrown at Borg on court. This time a sandwich landed on centre court during the match between Koevermans and Mancini, thrown by an idiotic spectator at a moment when the Dutchman was one point away from match point, and probably changed the outcome of the match. The chair umpire, Richard Ings, probably surprised by that sandwich at dinnertime, called a let at which point Koevermans came completely unglued and lost control of the match in much the same way that the idiot spectator lost face. Arrivederci

exhausted in the fourth set to convert on two match points, he ultimately fell on the ground overcome by cramps. They say, in fact, that Gardini flew into a rage and in order to avoid allowing the chair umpire to give Merlo the time to recuperate and the match to recommence, cut down the net himself to declare the match finished. In reality, none of this happened even though a lot of people who remember Gardini and his bad behaviour really think it did. Between Emilio and Alberto, two names who could be Italians but are not even

Yugoslav Open-Umag

By Patricia Jolly

Umag, 13-19 May
Tournament Director: Slavko Rasberger

That Monday following the tournament final Dimitri Poliakov still 'couldn't believe it'. The 23-year-old Soviet student in Russian literature was pacing the Ljublana airport, feeling in his pocket the $30,960 cheque awarded for capture his first ever pro title at the second Yugoslav Open.

A qualifier, Poliakov unexpectedly erupted into the main draw final. On his way to the victory he defeated claycourters such as Roberto Azar, Jan Gunnarsson, Francisco Clavet and Jean-Philippe Fleurian, to eventually beat Spaniard Javier Sanchez 6-4, 6-4.

The Spaniards Marco Aurelio Gorriz and Javier Sanchez sample some Croatian cooking.

Jean-Philippe Fleurian couldn't play his semi-final against Poliakov at his full potential because of a back injury that handicapped his serve. Czeck Petr Korda heralded his successful summer season reaching the semi-final, after being runner-up in Tampa a few weeks earlier. Korda inflicted a 6-0 first set on Javier Sanchez before losing the second set in the tie-break and the third 7-5.

Umag was also undoubtedly an inspiring scene for Poliakov's countrymen, since two other qualifiers were from the Soviet Union: the 16-year-old Andrei Medvedev, who soon became the 1991 French Open Junio Champion, and Andrei Merinov. However, neither of them posted a second-round win.

I love tennis, but why don't you ask me about the political and social situation in my country,' Poliakov said to the press in Russian after his victory. 'I am not a politician but when I go back home, I don't notice any change compared to before. It's still difficult to get food, of course, as a tennis player, I suffer less from this situation,' he added. Despite the chaotic times that Yugoslavia was experiencing, tournament director Slavko Rasberger and his team managed to ensure comfort for the players, and warmly welcomed them.

Dmitri Poliakov came through to join the list of qualifiers who end up as champions.

Located on the shore of the Adriatic sea, on the Istria peninsula, Umag was once the Roman dignitaries' favourite summer vacation destinations, and it developed into a busy resort. A natural area for recreational activities, Umag is now famous for its Stella Maris Tennis Centre designed along the same lines as Roland Garros Stadium in Paris. The Italian Open, simultaneously held in Rome, denied Umag the opportunity to repeat last year's all-Yugoslav final between Goran Prpic and Goran Ivanisevic. But the Yugoslav Open still featured two local players: Bruno Oresar and Emanuel Rasberger as well as top level players, and it lived up to the excellent reputation it had made for itself on the IBM/ATP Tour in 1990.

In the doubles Javier Sanchez was back for revenge, and with Israeli teammate Gilad Bloom, he snapped up the crown from the American pair Richey Reneberg and David Wheaton.

Peugeot ATP World Team Cup

By Meg Donovan

Dusseldorf, 20-26 May
Tournament Director: Horst Klosterkemper

Pity the Swedes, who walked into the 1991 Peugeot World Team Cup with a squad which included the Number 1 player in the world and nearly had to leave before the competition had even begun. But don't shed too many tears, for when the clouds had cleared in Dusseldorf, Magnus Gustafsson and Stefan Edberg had become the first duo to win in World Team Cup competition since Monolo Orantes and Jose Higueras led Spain to the title in 1978. Despite a debilitating injury to teammate Jonas Svensson, Edberg and Gustafsson shouldered the burden between them and proved nearly invincible in Cup play. Posting an 8-3 overall record which included one walkover, the Swedes won their second ever World Team Cup trophy with impressive performances by the only two players left in the team.

Sweden entered the only team event on the IBM/ATP Tour with what was indisputably the top-ranked squad on paper and three of the young season's hottest players in Edberg, Svensson and

Brad Gilbert and wife Kim help themselves to the lavish fare at the World Team Cup dinner. (Art Seitz)

Hand in hand, Stefan Edberg and Magnus Gustafsson did it all on their own for Sweden in Dusseldorf, after other members of the team went down with injuries at the start of the week. *(Helmut Müller)*

Gustafsson. All three were ranked among the top 20 players in the world, and all could already claim at least one singles title in 1991. Edberg was the newly restored world's Number 1, reclaiming the spot from Boris Becker in February only three weeks after losing it. He was also 8-3 in five years of singles play in Dusseldorf, although two of those losses had come in a rather dismal performance in 1990. Svensson, winner in Copenhagen over Anders Jarryd, and runner-up to Edberg in the Stuttgart Indoors, was Sweden's newest entrant to the World's Top 10 since Kent Carlsson reached that pinnacle back in June 1987. And Gustafsson was well on his way to becoming an honorary citizen of Germany after reaching

> *Edberg's participation in the final against Yugoslavia was threatened by an injury to his hip.*

back to back finals in Munich (where he won) and Hamburg only two weeks before. For team captain Tony Pickard – a Brit swathed in Swedish colours for the week – it was destined to be a dream week of warm-up for the clay courts of Roland Garros.

But the Scandinavians found themselves with a roster pared down to the minimum of two players after Svensson suffered a back injury in practice the Sunday prior to the start of the event. It was not only a devastating blow to the team, but also to the 24-year-old from Kungsbaka who would also be forced to withdraw from the French Open the following week, a tournament where he had reached the semi-finals the year before.

Tony Pickard, seen here at courtside with Stefan Edberg, created a record in 1991 by captaining two different countries in team competitions – Sweden in the World Team Cup and Britain in the Davis Cup. *(Art Seitz)*

Sweden began its title trek with an opening round Red Group encounter with Argentina, led by Franco Davin, Horacio de la Pena and Javier Frana. The two singles were won by the Swedes, while Argentina copped the doubles. It was the first of only two matches which Sweden lost in round robin play the entire week, although a 6-0, 6-0 forfeit was recorded in the final match against the USSR. Spain, led by Emilio Sanchez, Juan Aguilera and Sergio Casal, were defeated by the Swedes in three straight, and then the USSR (Andrei Cherkasov, Alexander Volkov and Dmitri Poliakov) went down 2-1 and Sweden had earned itself a spot in the finals against Blue Group opponent Yugoslavia, the winner here last year.

Yugoslavia had turned some heads at the Rochusclub in 1990, and returned with the same team in 1991 to defend their title. In the opening match, impressive play from Goran Ivanisevic and Slobodan Zivojinovic produced a

surprising upset over American veterans Rick Leach and Jim Pugh in doubles to cement a 2-1 victory for the Yugoslavs. They had earlier split in singles play when Ivanisevic defeated Brad Gilbert and Aaron Krickstein had knocked off Goran Prpic. Against Germany in the second match, the heroics feel to Prpic who came up with the key singles victory over Eric Jelen, levelling the match at 1-1 after Ivanisevic was defeated by Michael Stich. Ivanisevic and Zivojinovic then pulled off another upset, this time over Riglewski and Stich to earn the winning point for Yugoslavia. In the final round versus Switzerland, Ivanisevic beat Jakob Hlasek and Prpic defeated Marc Rosset to earn the champions the opportunity to defend their crown.

Meanwhile, Sweden suffered another blow when Edberg's participation in the final match was threatened by an injury to his hip. In the final round of play, Edberg's injury had contributed to a straight-set loss to Andrei

Cherkasov. Gustafsson remained the sole healthy member of the squad, with Edberg a large question mark for play on Sunday. It would have been difficult for Gustafsson to play the doubles alone. What might have been disastrous turned historic under cloudy skies on the final day of play when Sweden stole all the thunder. Gustafsson started the Swedes off right, upping his singles record on clay to 21/5 for the year, with a gritty 6-2, 3-6, 6-4 victory over Prpic. That left room for Edberg to breathe, but he wasted little time, closing the door resoundingly on Yugoslavia's aspirations with a 6-4, 7-5 win over Ivanisevic. As Team Captain Tony Pickard later commented, the two singles wins were 'among the best clay court matches I've seen since I began coming to the World Team Cup'. The final doubles was then won by Prpic and Zivojinovic, leaving Sweden with its second World Team Cup title in four years.

Germany's Eric Jelen received the Patriarca Fair Play Trophy from Claus-Peter Doetsch of WDR Radio who hosted the dinner. *(Art Seitz)*

Internazionali di Tennis Cassa di Risparmio

By George Rubenstein

Bologna, 20-26 June
Tournament Director: Franco Bartoni

Mother's Day is normally feted with celebrations of roses and wild flowers. This year it was a special familial day of repentance for Paolo Cane. The Year of the Ram and Sheep took a twist as the Dog chewed and clawed his way back into the spotlight. At the Foro Italico, only a week before, it had appeared that Cane might be practising for his life after tennis as a landscaper. Frustrated and in pain, both mentally and physically after his defeat at the hands of Jakob Hlasek, Cane had rearranged the flower display that lines the walkway between the Pisto Centrale and the men's locker-room in Rome. Now the man the Italian press unkindly call Mad Dog

Night play on hot summer nights in Bologna as the crowds get behind their Italian heroes. *(A.Tonelli)*

The strain shows on the face of Paolo Cane after winning the Bologna title in front of his home crowd. *(A. Tonelli)*

had spent much of the week trying to realign his aching spine as well as his wayward shots in friendlier confines and, under the eye of his coach Fabio Avogadri, Cane found he had less to snarl about in his home town of Bologna.

His week began with a dismissive 6-3, 6-1 victory over Jason Stoltenberg and then overcame Javier Sanchez – the previous week's singles finalist in Umag – and Thomas Muster in impressive style. Cane was particularly pleased with his win over Muster 'I was very happy that I was able to get some sense of revenge for the loss in Davis Cup against Muster last year,' said Cane. 'I was running well and I was very calm. The crowd helped a lot. It was an unbelievable match.'

Calmness is not a state that comes easily to Cane but to Jan Gunnarson it is second nature. The Swedish veteran had been easing his way through the other half of the draw, communicating nightly with his family back home. 'My daughter keeps asking if Daddy is going to bring home a

trophy,' laughed Gunnarson. In the end young Miss Gunnarson had to be content with the runners-up medal. He had played well enough to beat Omar Camporese and so spoil the prospect of an all-Bolognese final and for a while Gunnarson looked as if he might curdle the famous Bolognese cooking for good by taking the first set 7-5 off Cane. But the Italian suddenly hit a rich vein on the return and broke Jan three consecutive times to bounce back into the match, seizing the second set 6-3 and grabbing the decider 7-5 on his eighth match point. The crowd, inevitably, had played its part in sweeping the emotional Cane on to the third title of his career and his first at home. He immediately dedicated the victory to his father, Giancarlo, whom he embraced after the match. 'He was always my top fan and has always suffered watching me. At last I can give him satisfaction.'

In the doubles, Luke Jensen and Laurie Warder continued their fine run, clinching the title with a 6-4, 7-6 victory over the Brazilian duo of Luiz Matar and Jaime Oncins.

Jim Courier – the second American winner in Paris in three years. *(Gianni Ciaccia)*

Hero worship for Frenchman Fabrice Santoro at Roland Garros. *(Art Seitz)*

Since the creation of the French Open Championships, we have seen all kinds of champions in Stade Roland Garros: big ones, small ones, serve and volleyers, baseliners, heavy hitters, artists, left-handers, right-handers, some who were funny, and others who were surly... But never had we seen a baseball player win on the famous Parisian clay. A baseball player? Yes, with his grip, his position and his movements, Jim Courier could weave a baseball bat as easily as he weaves his tennis racket. Which isn't surprising, since he played a lot of baseball before getting fully into tennis when he was 13. From his baseball years, Jim Courier has also retained a fantastic power that had already impressed the French crowd in 1989, when he defeated Andre Agassi in the third round. And this power finally brought him to the top this year, on the famous red clay.

Off-balance but eye still on the ball – not all the skills have deserted John McEnroe. *(Art Seitz)*

Once again Andre Agassi was one step short of the French Open crown. *(Carol Newsom)*

As if in preparation for his US Open heroics, Jimmy Connors kept the adrenalin pumping in Paris, too. *(Art Seitz)*

Round after round, this best representative of the generation of punchers who were brought up with wide-body carbon rackets mercilessly overpowered all his opponents. He only faced one real problem in the third round, when Magnus Larsson was two sets to one up and had three break points in the fourth set. Otherwise, Courier left just one set to Edberg in the quarter-finals and another one to Stich in the semis before reaching the finals against Agassi. For this last match, he was the underdog against his 'old' rival who was also his sparring partner when both of them were hitting millions of balls on Nick Bollettieri's courts in Florida.

At first, Agassi's superiority and his experience of big matches (he had already reached the finals the year before, losing to Andres Gomez) got him to a lead of one set to love and 3-1. At that moment, there was a 20-minute rain delay. When they came back, both players had changed. Agassi had lost some of his concentration and Courier, following Jose Higueras's advice, started standing farther behind the baseline in order to have more time to prepare his shots and to begin 'bombing' his opponent.

This tactic gave him the second set, then he quietly waited while Agassi was producing his maximum effort in the third set, only to come back on top in the fourth and fifth sets, showing he was fitter and had more stamina than Agassi. As clear-minded as ever,

Ion Tiriac had said before the match: 'Agassi will have to win it in three sets. Otherwise he will lose in five.'

Maybe a player like Boris Becker could have fought until the end with as much physical power as Courier; in the semi-finals, however, Becker hadn't been able to weather Agassi's whirlwind game. Agassi played a fantastic match, whereas the German champion was not really at his mental best.

More than Becker, another German player, Michael Stich, surprised the French crowd by reaching the semi-finals.

At that time, who could have guessed that barely one month later, the same Stich would win Wimbledon, beating Becker himself in the finals? Finally, Stefan Edberg, seeded number one, was still bothered by his fragile back and couldn't fully and fearlessly deliver all his shots. And when you meet somebody like Courier in the quarter-finals, you have to be at your physical best in order to stand a chance.

An unexpected and really nice winner, Jim won the singles trophy, and he also scored a victory in doubles: he met Morgane, his girlfriend, in Paris, and hasn't been seen without her since then.

The Stella Artois Grass Court Championships

By Alan Fraser

London, 10-16 June
Tournament Director: Clive Bernstein

The stars turn out for advertising chief Frank Lowe (right) and raincoats can't dim the George Hamilton smile. *(Richard Young)*

When you walk through the narrow gates at Queen's Club in the West Kensington district of London, it is like opening the door of Doctor Who's Tardis. Outside, tight, car-lined streets, where parking can be a survival of the smartest and swiftest, bordered by compact, rather run-down terraced housing; inside, the gleaming red and white marquees, the ivy-clad buildings and the vast expanses of green, green grass that is home to a club steeped in tradition and a spiritual home for every serve and volleyer in the tennis world.

Home for Stefan Edberg is nearby in fashionable South Kensington where the world No. 1 can retain a certain anonymity. He can't hide, though, from the London cabbies who frequently convey him to Heathrow Airport en route to an ATP tour event on whatever continent in whatever hemisphere. 'You're Stefan Edberg,' one said accusingly last year. 'You may well be right,' came the enigmatic reply.

The man standing in the self-service queue for lunch in the grand old red-brick clubhouse, with its famous wrought-iron balcony – an exterior which has scarcely changed in a century – may well be Stefan Edberg. The way he holds his tray offers a clue. He seems about to dispatch a doughnut down the line with the most elegant backhand in the business.

That's young Pete Sampras behind him, isn't it? So young, so athletic, so laid-back, so damned good looking. The U.S. champion at 19, a future Wimbledon champion, it is said, and, therefore, a future winner of the Stella Artois championships. (Boris Becker, Jimmy Connors, John McEnroe and the aforementioned Edberg have won both titles.) But not in 1991. Sampras lasted the week, though only in order to practice, having lost in the second round to Californian Mark Keil, who was playing only his second ATP Tour event and who gleefully informed the first press conference of his career that his previous claim to fame was 'nothing'. He had 'travelled to the ends of the earth' to improve his ranking and was now 'on top of the world'. Some journey.

With Ivan Lendl also losing his first match, to Canadian Grant Connell, attention was even more sharply focussed on Edberg, though a camera lens or two found the Pat Cash comeback of considerable interest. Cash disposed of Kevin Curren and allowed fellow Australian Todd Woodbridge only three games, but missed too many first serves to extend fully Edberg in a quarter-final of considerable quality. David Wheaton, the stars and stripes headbands now a permanent feature of the image, dodged the opposition and the heavy showers, not to mention the persistent rain, to emerge from the other half of the draw. Grass was his kind of surface.

Stars, some wearing stripes, some not, and the Stella have always gone together and, despite the weather, they were to be spotted, as it were, throughout the week. Is that not George Hamilton? Who is that sitting next to Joan Collins? Michael Parkinson has not changed much, has he?

James Bond was a guest for the final. Not Sean, Roger, George, Timothy, or indeed any of the 007s, though. 'My names is Bond, James Bond,' the voice could have said. Because it was. The winner's name was Edberg, Stefan Edberg. The Swede took 86 minutes to defeat Wheaton 6-2, 6-3. His performance was clinical rather than exceptional, though taking the week as a whole, he was well satisfied. 'It is probably the best I have played before Wimbledon,' Edberg was to say after his first, but perhaps not his last, victory at Queen's.

He offered, too, a short list of possible Wimbledon winners. Ivan Lendl, 'if he plays well', Pete Sampras, 'if he puts it together', Pat Cash, 'always tough' and, as an outsider, Michael Stich who is 'playing great tennis this year'. Such prescience, albeit painful prescience. It was Stich, of course, who was to end Edberg's challenge.

Stefan Edberg had wanted to win the Stella Artois Grass Court Championships for a number of years before he triumphed in 1991. The smile says it all.
(Brunskill)

The Continental Grass Court Championships

By Bertold Palthe

Rosmalen, 10-16 June
Tournament Director: Wim Buitendijk

A lot of people would not have grudged Michiel Schapers to win the title in Rosmalen. At 31, the tall Dutchman is one of the tours veterans; this was the fourth Grand Prix final of his long career and this time he was about to make it happen. On the fast grass court he was serving for the match against the Romanian Christian Saceanu, whose best result had been winning the title at

Bristol in 1988, and who does not have the least in common with his idol Ilie Nastase. Schapers, who may not be the most popular player around, gained respect everywhere for his total commitment to the game. He is regarded by national coach Stanley Franker as a vital element in the recent Dutch successes. Schapers did not serve badly and held two match points, but he had to bow to some

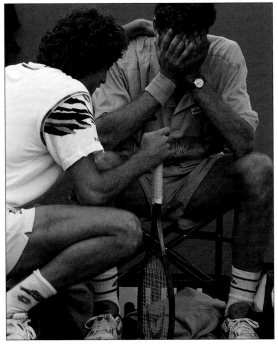

Who said there's no sentiment in pro tennis? Christian Saceanu consoles a distraught Michiel Schapers
(in action above) after the Dutchman had twice been within a point of winning on his own turf. *(Henk Koster)*

When you win a tennis tournament, you gather all kinds of friends. A labrador is only too happy to shake Christian Saceanu by the hand. *(Henk Koster)*

brilliant returns by the Romanian. Schapers, who was ranked as high as 25 in 1988 but at 232 needed a wild card to get into this tournament, was again left empty handed.

The two finalists had a lot in common. Both entered the tournament with low rankings and are better known for hard work than natural talent. In the semis the Romanian caused an upset by beating Jakob Hlasek and Schapers won a hard-fought match against Michael Stich, who was not then regarded as the grass court specialist he proved to be three weeks later. Schapers had also worked with Saceanu's coach Martin Simek for some eight years. The eccentric Czech coach, who is also a well-known journalist and illustrator, has earned himself the nickname 'Rasputin of the tennis courts' with his controversial way of working and provocative statements. He obviously watched the match with mixed feelings but was happy with the result. He described it as being 'like lending you new car to your wife's mother who gets into an accident with it.' The tournament has been adopted by the Dutch Federation which is aiming to develop it

into an 'ABN-Rotterdam-event for the summer'. In spite of a lot of rain and the loss of the top seed in the first round when Guy Forget was ousted by Soviet player Andrei Olkovski, a record 20,000 tennis fans found their way to this small provincial village. The site includes a family fun-park, a sensational car museum with a collection valued at more than $100 million and a magnificent 'House of the Future'. It offers an ideal warm-up for the most important tournament of the year. The grass is very similar to that at Wimbledon (the same Dutch seeds are used at both events) and the players get all the rest they need since the down to earth Dutch fans do not bother their idols in any way.

The recent revival of Dutch tennis was also proven by the doubles final. For the first time in tennis history two complete Dutch teams battled for the title. Paul Haarhuis and Hendrik Jan Davids, who previously had won the Moscow doubles, beat Jan Siemerink and Richard Krajicek. In only its second edition Rosmalen may well prove to be a serious competitor for that other famous Wimbledon warm-up, Queens.

Torneo Internazionale 'Città di Firenze'

By Ubaldo Scanagatta

Florence, 10-16 June
Tournament Director: Fabio Sapori

The cupola of the Duomo designed by Brunelleschi in the background behind the linden trees, and not Saint Stephen's cathedral; the Silver Arno and not the Blue Danube; the Parco delle Cascine, open to the children by day and to the transvestites by night, and not the Prater with its Wheel and Luna Park. The perfume of the stew and bistecca alla Fiorentina and not that of würstel und krauten or of the wienerschnitzl. It was thanks to all these unmistakable signs that distinguish Florence, including the ochre-red villa that hosts the Circolo Tennis Firenze, that the members of the club and the other spectators of the finals between Thomas Muster and Horst Skoff understood that this was the conclusion of the 19th edition of their international tournament and not the final of the Austrian national championships.

And maybe it was, for the promoter whose enthusiasm is dictated by the box office, the best possible final after the Italian players had all once again gloriously left the scene in the first round. These included second seed Camporese (immediately beaten by Thierry Champion who had come to Florence and then Genova to best prepare on red clay for his splendid tournament at Wimbledon!) and No. 7 Renzo Furlan, eliminated by Gabriel Markus. The Florence tournament had made a reputation for itself as 'the easiest event for a qualifier to win' – out of the fourteen times in the history of open tennis that a qualifier had won a tournament, four had been in Florence. The new tournament director Fabio Sapori was very much afraid that it may be one of the four qualifiers, Moine, Carlos Costa, Andres Vysand and Francisco Roig, to inscribe his name on the honours list on which appear the names of Ilie Nastase ('73), Adriano Panatta ('74 and '80) José Luis Clerc ('78 and '81), Raul Ramirez ('79), Vitas Gerulaitis ('82), Andres Gomez ('86) and Andrei Chesnokov ('87). With all the respect due to these four excellent qualifiers, it would not have been a memorable tournament. Costa came closest, reaching the semi-finals where he took a set off Muster.

Instead Fabio Sapori, who succeeded Sergio Palmieri as Tournament Director when IMG replaced ProServ who had problems finding sufficient sponsor funds, was lucky enough to see the final attained by two players who, notoriously, have as much love for each other as dogs for cats and vice versa. Two rivals who would therefore have done anything to prevail. And the fans, tired by too many exhibitions, by too many arranged matches, liked nothing better than a closely fought contest. The result was one of the best finals ever, maybe the best since 1981 when José Luis Clerc defeated Raul Ramirez.

As months and years pass, people remember a tournament by its honours list, and at the most by the final. The 1991 edition of the Kim Top Line Trophy, should therefore leave a good souvenir. I am sure that no one will remember that of the eight seeds, Skoff, Camporese, Koevermans, Arrese, Fromberg, Larsson, Furlan and Santoro, only Skoff had managed to reach the semi-finals against the 'multinational' Eduardo Masso, while Muster and Costa were playing in the other half of the draw. Up to the final, Muster had regularly lost the first set in all his matches (Pedro Rebolledo, Champion, Fabrice Santoro, Costa) to win in the third, while Skoff had defeated Cedric Pioline in two sets, Bart Wuyts and Markus in three and Masso in two. There was no real favourite, since Skoff had beaten Muster five times out of seven, all the last five times, but Muster, winner of the Italian Open, finalist in Monte Carlo and semi-finalist at Roland Garros in 1990, had a much more solid record and was not at all resigned. His former coach Ronald Leitgeb, who had been repudiated a short while before, was back to encourage and support him, on crutches as he had sprained his ankle. It was Leitgeb's management during the Davis Cup match between Austria and Italy that had primed a series of controversies between Skoff's clan and Muster's and exacerbating, if this were possible, their hostility.

Both Muster and Skoff would have paid the $32,000 of winner's prize money out of their own pocket as long as they could humiliate their rival. During the extremely pugnacious match, the two Austrians lost no occasion to mock and even insult each other. Horsti was complaining about the heat, saying he was suffering from a heat stroke, 'My head aches, I'm going to retire...' and Thomas replied 'How can you have a headache if you have no head...' to which Horsti replied 'See who's talking, you microcephal!' and so on. In the end, it was Muster who prevailed, 6-3, 6-7, 6-2, in spite of missing a match point with a very easy smash on 5-4 in the second set. Skoff tried everything to irritate his rival and to counter the asphyxiating heat, inventing all the possible tricks, including two time-out requests, one of which was denied by the supervisor Karlberg, the other

Thomas Muster doing his Ayrton Senna bit after beating arch-rival Horst Skoff. (A. Tonelli)

granted: Skoff returned on court after over five minutes! It ended with Skoff telling the spectators on centre court in my microphone, 'I am happy for Austrian tennis that Thomas is coming back,' but then whispering in my ear, 'If I had been at 100 per cent he would never have won, I am so much more intelligent than he,' and with Thomas toasting on champagne in the lockers with Leitgeb and venting his feeling as follows: 'I hate that guy so much that when I see him in front of me on a court I would like instead to lock him up in a room and thrash him! In any case, it must be Italy that brings me good luck: every time I fall in the rankings I come to Italy, win a tournament and rise back up. Who knows, maybe it is the sun...'

There was a lot more sportsmanship in the doubles final, which was also a foreign affair; Sweden beat Spain: Magnus Larsson and Ola Jonsson defeated Juan Carlos Baguena and Carlos Costa 3-6, 6-1, 6-4.

IP Cup

By Patricia Jolly

Genova, 17-23 June
Tournament Director: Fabio Sapori

Suffering from a minor left-hand injury that had forced him to retire from his first round match in Florence the previous week, German Carl-Uwe 'Charlie' Steeb hesitated to go and play the 1991 Italiana Petroli Cup in Genova. It was only to fulfil his commitment to professional tennis that he dragged himself to the court, and ... captured his second singles career title at Spaniard Jordi Arrese's

Alfonso Mora and Marco Aurelio Gorriz (right) show off their doubles trophies after beating the Italian pair of Massimo Ardinghi and Massimo Boscatto. Fabio Sapori and IP Cup sponsors join in the celebrations. *(A. Tonelli)*

'Charlie' Steeb came through to grab the title after a dubious start. *(A. Tonelli)*

expense. Steeb even showed top form that week since, on his way to grab the singles crown, he ousted last year's finalist Tarik Benhabiles, defending champion Ronald Agenor, and Thomas Muster, who had just won in Florence. Jordi Arrese, more consistent than ever on clay, was appearing in his second final of the year, after winning in Madrid. He fought his way into the final against neighbour Joao Cunha-Silva, countryman and hitting partner Carlos Costa (they share the same coach), and Argentinian friends Roberto Azar and Eduardo Masso.

But on Sunday, his effort to defeat Charlie Steeb was fruitless, and he had to bow out in straight sets 6-3, 6-4. Steeb and Arrese both enjoyed the support of their brothers and friends who had respectively taken special trips from Munich and Barcelona to attend the final event.

Of the six Italians entered in the singles main draw, only Stefano Pescosolido had posted a first-round victory. Therefore, in the doubles final, Gustavo Ardinghi and Massimo Boscatto took up on the heavy duty of hoisting the Italian flag as the only two local representatives remaining in competition. The Italian duo had managed to defeat the number two seeds Shelby Cannon and Greg Van Emburg, but they forgot to take into account Marco Aurelio Gorriz and Alfonso Mora's experience in the doubles field. Gorriz and Mora, seeded number 4, defeated the Italians 5-7, 7-5, 6-3.

Direct Line Insurance Manchester Open

By Reginald Brace

Manchester, 17-23 June
Tournament Director: John Feaver

Goran Ivanisevic did not merely defeat the reigning titleholder Pete Sampras – he routed him 6-4, 6-4 in 44 minutes during which he conceded only six points in 10 service games. Nine aces hoisted his total for the week to 55 against five opponents who all testified to the strength and penetration of the Yugoslav's left-handed thunderbolts. In this form who could stop him from joining Frank Sedgman (1952), Lew Hoad (1957), Jimmy Connors (1974) and Stefan Edberg (1988) as the fifth post-war champion to enhance success at Manchester with Wimbledon's ultimate accolade?

The answer was provided exactly a week later by Britain's Nick Brown who achieved one of the shock results of the year by mastering the serve which nobody came near to taming at the Northern Club at Didsbury. All of which emphasised how transient success can be in a game where there are a lot of accomplished players around but only a few who possess the qualities of technique and temperament to become consistently dominant. Nevertheless it was an impressive glimpse of the potential of Ivanisevic. He battled through three qualifying rounds indoors before playing his first match on grass of the year against the British player Andrew Castle who led 4-1 before succumbing 7-5, 7-6. By the end of the week he had not dropped a set in either the qualifying event or the tournament where he held 98 per cent of his service games against Castle, Jeremy Bates, Arne Thoms, Greg Muller and Sampras.

His most critical moment was when a hurled racket and an Anglo-Saxon expletive in his encounter with Thoms took him to within one step of default by umpire Steve Ulrich. A perilous brush with authority revealed an immature streak of which he is beguilingly aware. 'What I am doing is stupid,' said Goran. 'I play against five players in every match. I play against myself, my opponent, umpires, everybody. Ball boys. Fighting with everybody. It's tough to win.' Manchester was part of the learning process. We will be seeing a lot more of Goran Ivanisevic, particularly when he can harness his enviable resources as impressively as he did here.

We will be seeing a lot more of Ivanisevic particularly when he can harness his enviable resources.

Sadly, unless your name was Cristiano Caratti, the Northern Club did not see a lot of John McEnroe. It had been nine years since the three-

118

In partnership with Omar Camporese (left) Ivanisevic also took the doubles title – beating the English pair Nick Brown and Andrew Castle in the final. *(Tony Smith)*

The end of a lean run – Goran Ivanisevic with his first trophy since Bob Brett became his coach at the start of the year. *(Tony Smith)*

times Wimbledon champion last appeared at Manchester. He won it then, beating Russell Simpson in the final. This time he went down in the first round to Caratti, a 21-year-old Italian playing only his fifth match on grass.

Feeling flat after the euphoria of what he felt was his last Davis Cup tie for America against Spain at Newport, Rhode Island the previous weekend, McEnroe was beaten 7-6, 7-6. He was contrite. 'I would have like to have done better for the people here. But without wanting to take anything away from the tournament or Caratti it's hard to get up for matches like this. You had the build-up for the Davis Cup followed by the build-up for Wimbledon. It was hard to get motivated.'

Moving from a dry, fast court with heavier balls on Rhode Island to slowing Mancunian grass with a faster ball and a lower bounce left his timing awry against a sparky opponent. There were brief cameos of quintessential McEnroe: a vintage snarl at a service linesman; a tart exchange with the umpire after being warned for racket abuse; a withering welcome for a woman spectator who distracted his attention by taking her seat between points - 'Do you need a drink?'. But the talent no longer glowed like lava, and an unusually

philosophical McEnroe talked of preparing to leave the stage where he has played the part of a villain with the strokes of an angel. He thought he would play through 1992 and then retire while keeping his options open about Wimbledon. 'I would like to play there just for the hell of it – a fun experience without the pressure.' Then he was off to London to begin practising for Wimbledon. It was a fleeting visit by the weary maestro. His conqueror, Caratti, was destined to lose in the next round to Todd Witsken. It was left to Ivanisevic to show a champion's class, aided by a typhoon of a service which blew his rivals away.

Snapshots ...

Night time elegance in Dusseldorf as Jonas Svensson and Stefan Edberg air their Boss suits for the World Team Cup Ball. In Stuttgart it was Anand Amritraj and Heidi de la Pena's turn to dress up while in Miami Richard Krajicek danced the night away.

...on the Tour

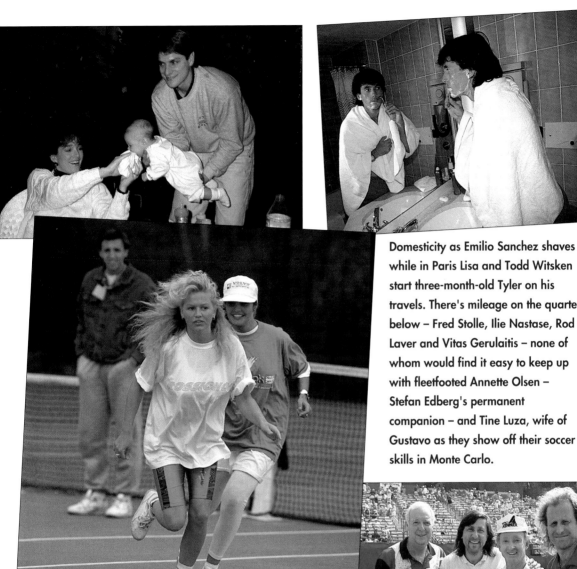

Domesticity as Emilio Sanchez shaves while in Paris Lisa and Todd Witsken start three-month-old Tyler on his travels. There's mileage on the quartet below – Fred Stolle, Ilie Nastase, Rod Laver and Vitas Gerulaitis – none of whom would find it easy to keep up with fleetfooted Annette Olsen – Stefan Edberg's permanent companion – and Tine Luza, wife of Gustavo as they show off their soccer skills in Monte Carlo.

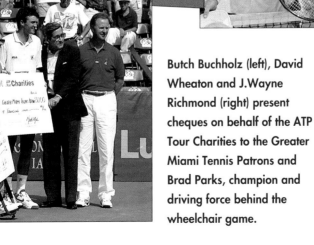

Butch Buchholz (left), David Wheaton and J.Wayne Richmond (right) present cheques on behalf of the ATP Tour Charities to the Greater Miami Tennis Patrons and Brad Parks, champion and driving force behind the wheelchair game.

Wimbledon

By John Parsons

Wimbledon, 24 June-7 July
Tournament Director: Richard Grier

One British sportswriter, though not, I have to admit, a regular tennis writer, placed £50 on Michael Stich to win Wimbledon, two weeks before the Championships, at 66-1. Even on the day Wimbledon began and there was little else to do but review the odds as the rain poured down, the London bookmakers, hardly renowned for their generosity, were still offering 40-1.

Yet 13 days later when, despite the wettest first week in Wimbledon's 114-year history, with only 52 matches completed by the end of the fourth day, the tournament still ended on time, it was Stich, rather than either of the top favourite former champions, Stefan Edberg and Boris Becker, who joyously held up the game's most prized trophy. However unlikely Stich's triumph may have seemed beforehand, there was no doubt that he deserved to join that elite group of only 12 players who have become men's singles champion at Wimbledon in the 24 years of Open tennis.

At the black-tie Champion's Dinner, which has become another unique Wimbledon tradition, the re-instated women's singles winner, Steffi Graf congratulated Stich, not only on making it a double German triumph but on 'becoming a member of the All England Club the hard way – but also the best way.'

How true that was. In his last three matches, having been lucky to survive a match point with a net cord in the final set of his fourth-round clash with Alexander Volkov, Stich first avenged his French Open semi-final defeat by Jim Courier, the Roland Garros champion; then proved himself mentally sterner in an amazing semi-final against Edberg and finally outserved and outplayed fellow countryman, Becker in the first all-German final. 'I had nothing to lose,' said Stich modestly after his 6-4, 7-6 (4), 6-4 victory in the final. 'No-one expected me to beat either Stefan or Boris, especially Boris. 'He was the favourite, the big favourite according to all the papers, so I could go out there and just play my normal game knowing that I had a good chance to beat him.'

Although the 2-hour 31-minute contest was mainly a case of prolonged attrition between two players whose first priority seemed to be to blast one another off the court, if not with their serves, then with their returns, Stich proved superior on both counts. He hit 15 aces, taking his total for the seven rounds to

A very deserving but unlikely champion - Michael Stich receives the Cup from the Duke and Duchess of Kent while Becker still manages a smile. *(Bob Thomas)*

97, two fewer than Becker, though more which really mattered, while his backhand returns could not have been bettered even by Edberg. Looking back, Stich's victory over Edberg, when the London-based Swede suffered the unusual and unnerving experience of losing a match in which he never lost a service game, was probably even more surprising than his defeat of Becker, who had one of those days when too many of his obvious frustrations came to the surface.

Four months earlier after beating Stich at Key Biscayne, Edberg had said of him prophetically, 'He can go a long way' and suggested he was 'likely to be one of the most dangerous players in the draw at Wimbledon.' And that was before he was even high enough in the rankings to think of him being seeded. The last thing Edberg could afford was the folly of two more historic double faults in the second set tie-break, from which he never recovered as Stich went on to win their semi-final, 4-6, 7-6, 7-6, 7-6.

Until then Edberg had advanced serenely, perhaps a shade too comfortably, without losing a set against Marc Rosset, David Pate, Christo Van Rensburg, John McEnroe, whose challenge faded swiftly after a magnificent first set and the year's least likely quarter-finalist, Thierry Champion, who joined Guy Forget in giving France two players in the last eight for the first time since 1946 when Yvon Petra, still in long trousers, went on to win the title. Becker, meanwhile, seldom looked truly confident or consistent. The serve, upon which the rest of his game depends so greatly, wobbled in and out of the proper groove like an old gramophone needle, although he certainly looked the part in his semi-final against David Wheaton, who in turn had once more ruined Ivan Lendl's elusive search for the only Grand Slam tournament title he has never won.

Yet in the final Becker, who wasted come-back chances in the first and second sets, summed it up when he said 'At that stage, tactics alone are not the most important.

'Now what do you think I should be doing about all this?' Becker seems to be asking the lineslady. Neither of them found any answer. *(Brunskill)*

It's who has the strongest mind. He had. My mind was far away.' There was another significant factor. Stich's second serve throughout the fortnight was often even more of a potent weapon than his first.

For months before Wimbledon, the issue which occupied by far the most column inches in many of the British newspapers was the sartorial intentions of Andre Agassi. Thanks to the rain, the fascination lasted an extra 24 hours before the grand unveiling on Centre Court to reveal ... not just predominantly white but all white. Whatever misgivings Agassi might have had about the way he would be received by British crowds were immediately swept away. They responded appreciatively to the mood and the talents of a player more than capable of producing tennis which is as colourful as any rainbow, without the distractive wrappings. Agassi, in his first Wimbledon visit since 1987, took time to settle. He was twice a set down in his first round match with Canadian Grant Connell, which began three days late and did not finish until the first Friday, but in all of the five matches he played, he produced flurries of almost unmatched brilliance before an injury ultimately helped Wheaton beat him in the quarters. Yet both Stich and Agassi's contributions, plus a popular success for Anders Jarryd and the veteran John Fitzgerald in the doubles, were overshadowed by Wimbledon's 'Middle Sunday'. It was an extra day, organised at short notice to tackle the backlog of matches from the first week's rain. Fans were admitted on a first-come, first-served basis, playing a mere £17 for Centre Court seats. More than 12,000 queued all night and then cheered everyone and everything all day, even encouraging the Royal Box, filled mostly by past champions for the occasion, into joining them in regular Mexican waves.

Fittingly Jimmy Connors, who knows better than anyone how to rouse a crowd, was one of those topping the Centre Court bill on a day of non-stop celebration and emotion. The enormous ovation when he left, despite losing to that frequent upset-achiever, Derrick Rostagno, must have made him think he was at Flushing Meadow. Wimbledon had never experienced anything like it. Nor had Jimmy.

By the end of an extraordinary fortnight, there seemed to be no end to Stich's talents. It was a balancing act altogether too clever for Becker. *(Brunskill)*

Rado Swiss Open

By Daniel Fricker

Gstaad, 8-14 July
Tournament Director: Jacques Hermenjat

It was an all Spanish final at the Rado Swiss Open in Gstaad. Emilio Sanchez who had played strongly all week had no problems at all against his countryman, top seed, Sergi Bruguera. Having aggravated an existing pulled stomach muscle he never proved to be too much of a challenge to Sanchez who pocketed the $39,600 prize money after winning three easy sets, 6-1, 6-4, 6-4.

It was not surprising to see these two Spanish rivals on centre court for the final of this ATP tournament. Both players have an impressive record in Switzerland. For Bruguera Gstaad 1991 marked his third Swiss final after Geneva and Gstaad the previous year. But even more impressive is Sanchez' Swiss tournament history. In 1986, the first time he played in Gstaad, he reached the semi-finals, won the tournament the following year, was eliminated in the quarter-finals for the following two years, and this year wins his second Gstaad title. Following his success in Barcelona and Rome, it was the third ATP Tour title for the 26-year-old professional. 'It was not at all easy to keep up my concentration against an injured opponent', Sanchez said.

Just a week after Wimbledon, the Rado Swiss Open presented an extremely strong field with four Top-10 players, all eight seeds ranked within the Top 20 and 26 of 28 main draw players who did not have to qualify having each reached a tournament final at least once in the past two years. The high quality of the field was well illustrated in round 16 when Goran Ivanisevic (ATP-No 12) was drawn against David Wheaton (ATP-No 13).

Wheaton had survived four matchpoints in a first-round-clash against Swiss hero Marc Rosset, and the two other Swiss players in the main draw had done nothing special with Jakob Hlasek eliminated in the first round by Austrian, Horst Skoff, and wild card entry Claudio Mezzadri beaten by Karel Novacek in round 16 having surprisingly beaten Italy's Omar Camporese in the first round.

The only positive headline apart from the new crowd record of 43, 658 fans (3000 more than last year), was Ecuador's Andres Gomez who after a 2 month break entered the ATP Tour with victories over clay court specialists Carl-Uwe Steeb and Goran Prpic before he was ousted by Bruguera in a close 6-7, 6-7 encounter.

Despite the all-Spanish final, the 'Wimbledon of the Alps', which boasted live TV coverage from the first day in 22 countries and 20 million households, was the tournament of Michael Stich. The German was the star of the week, being the first Wimbledon Champion, since John Newcombe in 1974, to visit the Gstaad event in the same year as his win at Wimbledon, and the first to play an event the week following his victory since John McEnroe in 1981.

L̲ocated in the Swiss Alps, Gstaad has a reputation for its famous winter visitors, but during the summer it is a fairly quiet place apart from the week it becomes the centre of the world's tennis attention. The hustle around Wimbledon Champion Michael Stich was similar to that of 1982 when Argentina's Guillermo Vilas attracted the yellow press eager for coverage of his famous romance with Princess Caroline of Monaco. Instead of 140 journalists, within two days 40 more media people had arrived and several foreign TV stations had asked for exclusive pictures of the new German tennis star. Owing to the participation of the fresh Wimbledon Champion, the tournament ran into several unexpected problems, the security had to be tightened and the interview room was expanded for the first post-Wimbledon press conference. But despite all this publicity, Stich was eliminated by Karel Novacek in the quarter-finals.

M̲ichael did not care. 'Gstaad was a very good tournament. It was the best thing to do for me to play on after the big victory in London because I had to concentrate on tennis and therefore had no time to get into trouble off court.'

For Michael Stich, newly crowned Wimbledon Champion, the heavy demand for interviews was eased by the beauty of the Alpine setting. *(Norman Lomax)*

Swedish Open Bastad

By Bjorn Hellberg

Bastad, 8-14 July
Tournament Director: Henrik Odervall

'This is the happiest moment in my tennis life!' Magnus Gustafsson's smile was bathed in glory after beating Argentinian Alberto Mancini with the convincing score of 6-1, 6-2 in the Swedish Open final at Bastad. The blond Swede

Total concentration helped Magnus Gustafsson to his second ATP Tour title of the year when he triumphed on home soil in Bastad. *(Arne Forsell)*

with a hammer in the forehand and a lion in his heart had a remarkable week. Despite dropping sets against his fellow countrymen Niclas Kroon and Christian Bergstrom, he was never in serious trouble at any stage of the tournament.

And in the final, Magnus played magnificent tennis from the first to the last rally. 'Gusten', as he is nicknamed, explained his feelings: 'This is something special which is hard to describe. Of course, I really enjoyed the situation when I reached the semis at Stockholm Open as an underdog in 1987. The same with my very first ATP victory at Munich earlier this season. But this is very different. Ever since my childhood, I have been dreaming of winning at Bastad, in front of an enthusiastic home crowd. And now have I reached that milestone. It's wonderful!'

This was the first Swedish triumph in men's singles at Bastad since 1987 when Joakim Nystrom beat Stefan Edberg in the final. Magnus Gustafsson became the eighth home player to lift the celebrated trophy. Apart from Nystrom and Gustafsson, the following Swedes have been successful in this event, which started back in 1948: Bjorn Borg and Mats Wilander (three wins each), Ulf Schmidt (two victories), Sven Davidson, Jan-Erik Lundqvist and Henrik Sundstrom.

Swedish winners all the way: Rikard Bergh and Ronnie Bathman won the Swedish Open doubles title for the second consecutive year. *(Arne Forsell)*

Alberto Mancini added extra colour to the week. The strong South American showed a lot of guts and spirit when he defeated opponents such as Claudio Pistolesi, Magnus Larsson (a runner-up to Richard Fromberg in 1990) and Alexander Volkov after losing the opening set against all of them. Tall Magnus Larsson caused an early surprise when he showed top-seeded Andrei Cherkasov the exit in the first round 6-3, 6-2. Otherwise, most of the matches followed the expected pattern. In the doubles, the determined pair of Rikard Bergh and Ronnie Bathman defended their title from 1990. Bergh and Bathman won the all-Swedish final against Magnus Gustafsson and Anders Jarryd in straight sets 6-4, 6-4.

And talking of Jarryd: he turned 30 during the week (on 13 July) and the crowd joined in the celebrations. The whole centre court sang to the Swedish veteran, just as the spectators did for Jimmy Connors on 2 September, during the US

Open. Funnily enough, Anders Jarryd is not the only famous Swedish racket star born on 13 July. Sven Davidson entered the world on the same day, but 33 years earlier. And Davidson (who in 1957 became the first Swede to win a men's singles title in a Grand Slam event when he triumphed at Roland Garros) has a firm idea of how the Swedish Open will survive as an ATP-tournament of dignity. He said: 'Many people want to expand the tournament, trying to build bigger hotels, making it more international. Why? My opinion is that we should try to make the opposite! Most of the tournaments are played in big cities where you have problems with transportation and so on. And I suspect the players are a bit tired of the hectic situation in the larger cities. In Bastad we can offer them something different. We have the Ocean a short lob from the centre court. The players can stay in small hotels inside the Stadion area. Everything is picturesque and handy. And I hope it will remain this way ...' Maybe Sven Davidson is right. Who knows?

Miller Lite Hall of Fame Tennis Championships

By George Rubenstein

Newport, 8-14 July
Tournament Director: Mark L. Stenning

Newport had quite an interesting year, both tenniscally and landscapishly. There was a great deal of tennis, including US Davis Cup action in June, and the IBM/ATP Tour Miller Lite Hall of Fame Championships, which featured the introduction of three great male players, Australian Ashley Cooper, Romanian Ilie Nastase, and Argentinian Guillermo Vilas. The Greater New England region suffered some damage due to the exploits of Hurricane Bob, which tried its best to rearrange the geometric parameters of much of the Eastern Seaboard of North America in mid-August.

Another historically noteworthy event took place at this year's Hall of Fame Championships, where Bryan Shelton captured the first title of his career on the IBM/ATP Tour by defeating Javier Frana of Argentina in three sets. The 26-year-old native Alabaman, now residing in Atlanta, Georgia, scene of his collegiate exploits at Georgia Tech, where he secured a degree in industrial engineering, became the first black American to win a singles title since Arthur Ashe defeated Brian Gottfried in Los Angeles on 24 September 1978.

All birthday boys on 8 July – Todd Martin, Joey Rivé and Christian Saceanu. *(Michael Baz)*

Shelton, working with his longtime coach Bill Tym, had first been introduced to the sport by his mother, Regina, at the Huntsville (AL) Athletic Club. Mrs Shelton had joined the Huntsville Women's Tennis League when Bryan was still a child. 'I was aware of the sacrifices that my family had to make for me, but not to the full extent,' related the hard-serving right-hander. 'My coach would give me lessons, and he wouldn't charge me. Fortunately, my family and coach were as accommodating and understanding as they were.'

The year had started off slowly for the youngest of three Shelton sons. He always looks forward to the grasscourt season and was bitterly disappointed when he failed to make the main draw at Wimbledon after reaching the third round in 1990. But he refused to be discouraged and, drawing on memories of good doubles results at Newport the previous year when he reached the final with Todd Nelson, felt that he was due for a good week. The fact that he ended up doing so well was, he felt, a combination of two things. 'Newport itself and the Hall of Fame. A lot of tradition is important. I ran early in the mornings along Cliff Walk. It's a fun town and the people were great.'

The history and tradition of the last black to capture a title wasn't something to be taken lightly, either. Arthur Ashe was a Hall of Famer and Bryan's first racket was an Ashe Composite. He thought it was 'neat' that he became the first black to win a title since Ashe. 'It wasn't something I was conscious of but it distinguishes me from others and that's special,' he said. Proudly Mrs Shelton recalls, 'When people asked him if he was going to be the next Arthur Ashe, Bryan would say, "I'm going to be Bryan Shelton." He was the force...'

Shelton was certainly too much of a force for the powerful Javier Frana in the final, winning a hard-fought scrap 6-4 in the third. But strength of mind and serve had been necessary all week for the Alabaman as he battled his way past a whole succession of tough opponents. Germany's

A first ATP Tour title for Bryan Shelton – an industrial engineering graduate from Georgia Tech. (Michael Baz)

Patrick Baur, already a two-time title winner on the Tour in 1991, pushed him to 7-5 in the third in the first round and that experienced grasscourt performer Christo Van Rensberg also took a set off him in the quarters. Todd Martin, enjoying one of his best weeks that included a victory over top seed Peter Lundgren, ran him close in the semis before going down 7-5, 6-4 and by then Shelton had scented victory.

It was a successful yet frustrating week for Frana who also finished runner-up in the doubles, alongside Bruce Steel. The pair went down to the unlikely combination of New Zealander Brett Steven and Italy's Gianluca Pozzi 6-4, 6-4 in the final.

Mercedes Cup

By Richard Evans

Stuttgart, 15-21 July
Tournament Director: Bernard Nusch

To a certain degree, Michael Stich's performance in winning the Mercedes cup with a 1-6, 7-6, 6-4, 6-2 victory over that rugged clay court specialist Alberto Mancini was almost as impressive as his totally unexpected triumph at Wimbeldon.

Consider the facts. Without belittling the rest of his well-rounded and fluent game, Stich's prime weapon is his serve. Prior to winning Wimbledon his only major title had come indoors on a medium fast carpet in Memphis. In addition, this million dollar stop on the ATP Tour's European summer season had begun just nine days after Michael had held the All England Club's golden cup aloft for the benefit of a stunned centre court.

The intervening week had been taken up with the inevitable round of interviews coupled with an appearance at the Swiss Open at Gstaad where he had reached the quarter-finals. To say

Soccer star Franz Beckenbauer chats with TV commentator Hans-Jurgen Pohmann in the players' lounge. Pavel Slozil, a visitor from the women's tour, can be seen sitting, centre.
(Richard Evans)

Two weeks after winning Wimbledon, Michael Stich comes home to triumph on clay in the Mercedes Cup.
(Paul Zimmer)

that it was a slightly bewildered and very tired young man who arrived back in his native Germany would be putting it mildly.

Yet, even so, this 22-year-old from Elmshorn was quickly proving himself a mature and reliable new superstar. 'I am determined to live up to the commitments I made before Wimbledon,' Stich told the press in a statement that was easier to make than to fulfill.

Stich, however, was as good as his word, as the Bundesliga and Tour events in Schenectady, Berlin, Vienna and elsewhere were to discover. But showing up is one thing – performing at the level expected of a Wimbeldon champion quite another. In Stuttgart, Stich proved he was a champion in more than name.

The switch from grass to clay is never easy and, given the circumstances, Stich should have found it harder than usual. And there were more

than just technical considerations. This was the man who had defeated Boris Becker in a Wimbledon final – the first ever all-German Wimbledon final. This was the man caught firmly in the full glare of the German media spotlight – a glare that Becker himself had frequently found blinding and insufferable.

The potential for Stich to fall flat on his face was clearly evident. Instead this extremely impressive young man progressed through a powerful draw with remarkable ease. Fabrice Santoro, one of Europe's best new claycourters, was handled in straight sets; Javier Sanchez, on the brink of his best season ever, was dismissed 6-3, 6-3, while in the semis another Spaniard Francisco Clavet was also allowed only six games.

It had been in the round before that Stich had come nearest to coming unstuck and ironically it was the only mirror of himself that he faced all week that made him pause. Richard Krajicek is,

Michael Stich in action under blue skies in front of a packed Centre Court in Stuttgart. *(Paul Zimmer)*

like Michael, a big serve and volleyer brought up on clay. Fighting off fatigue on a hot day as well as the venomous power of the young Dutchman's serves, Stich eventually came through in the third set tie-break by seven points to two.

Stich even played doubles, as he continued to do more for Udo Riglewski's sake than his own, and the pair reached the quarters before losing to Paul Haarhuis and Mark Koevermans – the Dutch pair who went down in the next round to the eventual winners – Emilio Sanchez and Wally Masur.

In the bottom half of the singles draw, form was less predictable. Having struggled through a titanic three setter 5-7, 7-6, 7-6 to beat the experienced Masur in the first round, No. 2 seed Guy Forget promptly lost to a qualifier, Lars

Koslowski who had started the year at 314 on the ATP computer and, by virtue of winning the Sevilla Challenger and going on to reach the semi-final here, ended it at 83.

Koslowski, a 20-year-old German with an aggressive clay court game, eventually went down in three sets to Mancini who was the week's other hero. The Argentine's rehabilitation had been growing apace through the summer and this performance, which included fine victories over Andrei Cherkasov and his fellow countryman Guillermo Perez-Roldan, simply provided further confirmation of a talent restored. In the final, however, there was no stopping a Wimbledon champion who became the first of his line since Bjorn Borg to win on clay so soon after walking off the grass, Bjorn having won in Bastad in July 1979.

The week in Stuttgart, which the players always seem to enjoy – possibly because they get to throw Mercedes saloons around the company's test track – was made even more fun this year by the presence of a group of senior players like Fred Stolle, Cliff Drysdale, Vijay and Anand Armitraj and Jose Higueras who not only gave clinics for Mercedes executives but also added greatly to the convivial atmosphere created most evenings in the lobby of the Graf Zeppelin Hotel. It was almost like old times.

The week before, in Gstaad, Emilio Sanchez won the 50th title of his career. So, in Stuttgart, Emilio celebrated, a little dangerously, with the help of Ranald Mjornell of Mercedes and Vijay Amritraj. *(Guido Haug)*

Sovran Bank Classic

By Lauren Goldenberg and Paul Settles

Washington, 15-21 July
Tournament Director: Josh Ripple

The ATP Tour converged on the nation's capital for the start of the summer U.S. hardcourt season riding on the neon shirt-tails of flamboyant crowd favourite and defending champion Andre Agassi who was vying to become the tournament's first repeat winner in its 81-year history. With the summertime heat and humidity still lingering in the air, Agassi, the tournament's top seed, took to the stage almost every evening and entertained the spirited crowds at the William H.G. FitzGerald Tennis Center at Rock Creek Park with his own brand of energized yet flawless tennis. Relying on his powerful backcourt game and improved physical conditioning, Agassi captured his second title of the year without dropping a set.

Agassi's ultimate obstacle en route to the crown was the latest Czech sensation, Petr Korda. Korda, whose ranking had been on a rollercoaster for the previous year and a half, used his success in Washington as a springboard for his runner-up effort in Montreal and his first career title in New Haven. Korda attributed much of his success to his new full-time travelling coach, Vladimir Zednik, who encourages his pupil to enjoy competition as well as life away from tennis. As the tournament's No.12 seed, Korda disposed of Derrick Rostagno and Brad Gilbert on the way to the final. The final, which lasted only 65 minutes, saw Agassi taking the early advantage when he broke Korda's serve in the sixth game of the first set. He capitalized on that lead and never really allowed Korda to make any in-roads during the match. The outcome was 6-3, 6-4 and a check for $77,000 to the winner.

Unlike Korda, the other seeds did not fare as well. John McEnroe, sporting a new cropped haircut for the hot summer season, fell in the third round to Mexico's hopeful, Luis Herrera. Despite the loss, an encouraged McEnroe seemed to have adopted a new attitude towards the game as he reflected on the ways fatherhood had changed his priorities. Unseeded Markus Zoecke awed the crowds on the grandstand and stadium courts all week long with the powerful speed of his serves. The quiet German used every inch of his 6'5" frame to serve his way to the first semi-final showing of his young career.

In the first all-American doubles final of the tournament's history Scott Davis and David Pate captured their fourth title of the year with a 6-4, 6-4 win over Ken Flach and Robert Seguso. The crowds were not the only ones to benefit from the exciting tennis on display throughout the week. Proceeds from the Sovran Bank Classic are used to fund tennis programmes for thousands of local youngsters through the Washington Tennis Foundation.

Back in the groove, Andre Agassi wins his second ATP Tour title of the year. *(Thomas Toohey Brown)*

Player's Ltd. Int'l Canadian Open Championships

By Tom Mayenknecht

Montreal, 22-28 July
Tournament Director: John Beddington

The Player's Ltd. International Canadian Open tennis championships brought to Montreal three former titleholders, the reigning ATP Tour world champion and a total of five players who had Grand Slam crowns to their credit.

Yet in addition to defending champion Michael Chang, former winners Ivan Lendl and John McEnroe and leading men Andre Agassi, Pete Sampras and Jim Courier, the popular hardcourt tournament held at Montreal's Jarry Tennis Stadium also drew a pair of dark horses in 12th-seeded Andrei Chesnokov of the Soviet Union and

unseeded Petr Korda of Czechoslovakia. In the spirit of Canadian Open glasnost, it was the two longshots – better known as clay court specialists – who squared off in the Montreal final and it was Chesnokov who capture the top honours, rallying from the dead to post a dramatic 3-6, 6-4, 6-3 victory before a capacity crowd of over 10,500.

It was a fitting end to a week of upsets that left so many top stars strewn by the wayside. Names like Stefano Pescosolido of Italy, Shuzo Matsuoka of Japan, Jim Grabb and Derrick Rostagno of the United States and, of course, Chesnokov and

This year it was the men's turn to play in Montreal while the women switched to Toronto. The result was the same for tournament director John Beddington – another full house.
(Ted Romer)

Petr Korda and the stylish backhand that took him to the final. *(Ted Romer)*

Korda, took over the event and gave it a new-name feel from start to finish. It was Pescosolido, a clay-courter whose previous career highlight was winning the 1990 Parioli Challenger in Italy, who upset Chang, the former French Open champion who a year earlier came from behind to defeat Agassi, Sampras and Jay Berger en route to the 1990 Canadian Open title. Matsuoka, a member of Japan's Davis Cup team whose career-high ranking was No. 82 in 1988, not only crushed the hopes of 1990 U.S. Open champion Sampras, 2-6, 6-4, 7-6 (8-6)

in the second round, but also ousted Patrick McEnroe, 6-4, 6-3, in the third before running into an inspired Chesnokov in the quarter-final, going down 7-5 in the third. Rostagno, the New Haven champion in 1990, was the blue-eyed knight who knocked off Big Mac in the third round, a controversial, rain-interrupted 6-2, 1-6, 7-6 (7-5) decision. And it was Grabb, better known for his doubles, who eliminated eighth-seeded Gilbert, 4-6, 6-3, 6-4, before pushing Lendl to the limit in a 7-6 (10-8), 6-7 (7-9), 7-5 quarter-final marathon.

139

Andrei Chesnokov looking relaxed with his trophy – the seventh singles title of his career. *(Ted Romer)*

flamboyant Las Vegan. The 23-year-old described the win as a career highlight. 'It was my big personal challenge,' said Korda. 'Maybe I was scared to play him. He beat me three times. He was confident. So it was important to beat him.' The win over Agassi launched Korda on a dream-like path towards a possible final against his childhood idol, Lendl. Korda did his share, beating Raoux, Hlasek and then Courier, but Lendl failed to follow suit.

Despite the string of upsets leading to the semi-finals, Lendl's loss to Chesnokov was a shocker; perhaps the upset of the week when one considered the 31-year-old veteran's career record at the Canadian Open in general and in Montreal in particular. Lendl went into the match with a 28-1 won-lost record at Jarry Tennis Stadium. In 11 years of Canadian Opens, he had reached the finals eight times and won six times. 'I just had trouble opening up the court,' said Lendl. 'My game plan was to create chances and I didn't create them. I have no one to blame but myself.' Lendl broke back after losing his serve in the 11th game of the opening set, only to lose the tie-breaker. With Chesnokov on the brink of victory up 6-5 in the second set, Lendl sealed his fate by double-faulting twice in the 12th game.

With Lendl and Courier out of the picture, the Canadian Open final was disputed for the first time in 12 years between two players whose career credits did not feature Grand Slam honours. In a tournament whose modern tradition has been built on victories by Bjorn Borg in 1979, Lendl in 1980, 1981, 1983, 1987, 1988 and 1989, Vitas Gerulaitis in 1982, McEnroe in 1984 and 1985 and Boris Becker in 1986, it would mark the first time since Eddie Dibbs' triumph in 1978 that a non-Grand Slam champion prevailed at the Canadian Open.

Korda's road to the final was tougher than Chesnokov's, at least on paper. His run included a 7-6 (7-3), 6-2 win over a lethargic Agassi, to whom he had dropped the Sovran Bank Classic final in Washington three days earlier. Korda posted a 6-2, 6-3 triumph over Guillaume Raoux of France; a 7-6 (7-3), 6-4 decision against sixth-seeded Jakob Hlasek of Switzerland before finessing his way to a 3-6, 7-6 (7-1), 6-2 victory over Courier in the semi-finals. Save for the final, Korda's toughest match came in the first round, when he came precariously close to elimination in a 3-6, 6-3, 7-6 (7-5) verdict over Italian Gianluca Pozzi.

Korda, a six-foot-three-inch right-hander, became a factor in Montreal when he aced Agassi on match point of their second-round showdown, ending a 0-for-3 drought against the

For much of the match, it appeared as if Korda would win the title as an unseeded player. He jumped into a 6-3, 3-0 lead and, figuring his first tournament title was only a matter of minutes away, pumped his arms in a case of premature celebration. Korda won just one of the next 12

Canadian favourites Glenn Michibata (left) and Grant Connell – one of the world's top doubles teams – reached the final in Toronto where they lost to Patrick Galbraith and Todd Witsken. *(Joanne Botyanski)*

games as Chesnokov not only forced the third set but took complete control of it by forging a 5-0 lead. Korda struggled to stay alive and rallied to trim the margin to 5-3, but faded in the ninth game. 'I was very tired,' said Korda. 'When I (pumped my arms in the second set) I was just trying to get myself excited but I knew that I was getting tired and that he was taking control.'

Korda's moment would finally come – two weeks later when he defeated Goran Ivanisevic in the final at New Haven, Connecticut – but his disappointment was Chesnokov's joy. 'I'm sure happy that when I was drawing up my schedule with my agent last year, I decided I wanted to play more tournaments on hardcourts,' said Chesnokov. 'This is a great win for me. I'm flying to New York where I will go shopping to Tower Records. Then I'm going to a very nice Italian restaurant for a good meal and, of course, I'm going to get drunk.'

Upsets were also the order of the day in the Player's Ltd. International doubles championships, where top-seeded Americans Scott Davis and David Pate fell in the quarter-finals, losing 3-6, 6-3, 6-4 at the hands of Ken Flach and Robert Seguso. Grant Connell and Glenn Michibata, Canada's Davis Cup doubles tandem, advanced to the finals by outlasting Australia's Wally Masur and Mark Woodforde in the semi-finals, 6-3, 3-6, 6-3. In the quarter-finals Connell and Michibata posted a 6-3, 7-6 (7-5) decision in an interesting all-Canadian showdown against Sebastian Lareau and Sebastien LeBlanc, the under-18 doubles champions at the French Open and Wimbledon in 1990. The doubles final was a roller-coaster ride in which Patrick Galbraith and Todd Witsken ultimately prevailed, 6-4, 3-6, 6-1. By the time the dust had settled on the doubles final, the Player's Ltd. International had drawn 113, 773 spectators, second only to the record of 118,000 set in 1987.

International Championship of the Netherlands

By Carl Houtkamp

Hilversum, 22-28 July
Tournament Director: Peter Van Eijsden

Legend has it that 'Het Melkhuije' (literally, The Little Milkhouse) was once a popular road house for travellers by horse. Tired from their journeys through the Dutch woods, they would

stop there for a glass of milk. 'Het Melkhuisje' in Hilversum is still a gathering place of importance. But today's visitors to the International Championships of the Netherlands drink anything

A suntanned Magnus Gustafsson with the trophy. Jordi Arrese gets the flowers. *(Henk Koster)*

but milk. Diet Coke and beer have replaced this, and big cars drive the players from the courts to their luxurious hotels and back. The spectators watch tennis with a light heart and even enjoy the rain breaks, when they meet with kindred spirits, talk about major players and almost-forgotten tennis days, or simply enjoy a game of bridge.

If tournaments ever get the winners they deserve, then 'Hilversum' couldn't be happier with Magnus Gustafsson as its 1991 Champion. Because of his backboned and merciless performance, the 24-year-old Swede has been nicknamed 'Popeye' or 'Robocop', but off-court the smiling Gustaffson is very genial company. Delighted with the typical Dutch atmosphere as he is, it's no surprise that the down-to-earth Scandinavian asked his fiancée Anne Devries and her mother Marie-Louise to join him in Hilversum.

Jan Siemerink and Richard Krajicek kept the home fires burning by winning the doubles. *(Henk Koster)*

A good time was had by all, mostly because Gustafsson ended up in both finals. He jumped from No.15 into the top ten of the IBM/ATP Tour Singles Ranking for the first time in his career, after beating 1990 Champion Francisco Clavet (his doubles partner!) in the first round, practice partner Lars Jonsson in the second, hard-hitting Marc Rosset in the quarters, 1989 Champion Karel Novacek in the semis and tenacious Jordi Arrese in an exhausting five-set final.

Particularly in his last singles match, Gustafsson was grateful for the cool drinks 'The Little Milkhouse' had to offer: the heat on centre court was cruel and match point occurred only after 3 hours and 37 minutes. By that time, even the 26-year-old Arrese from Barcelona was hallucinating, seeing mirages and Catalonian cows right in the middle of the clay court, and filling containers with cool, cool fluids. After leading two sets to one, the Spaniard lost twelve of the last thirteen games (7-5, 6-7, 6-2, 1-6, 0-6). 'Those clay courts are very slow, you have to work hard for every point. Best-of-five was too much for me,' Arrese explained. This left Gustafsson a bit puzzled, as he was expected to break down first in a fitness test like this. 'I can't believe I did it. I didn't have one day off, because of the rain and my doubles', said the Swede, who in 1990 was kept from the tour for half a year due to a knee injury. 'And still, on a day like this, playing best-of-five, I end up with the winner's cheque. Unbelievable.'

Gustafsson, who lost the doubles final to Dutch youngsters Richard Krajicek and Jan Siemerink, wasn't the only player confronted with some kind of miracle. Mark Koevermans, in his fourth year on the circuit, reached the semi-finals, the first time he had ever made it past the first round of a Grand Prix or ATP event in Holland. The 23-year-old Dutchman expected to lose the first round (he hadn't won a match since the Italian Open) and was planning to go on holiday on the French Riviera. After beating his doubles partner Paul Haarhuis in the first round, first seed Sergi Bruguera in the second and Renzo Furlan in the quarters, Koevermans had to alter his holiday plans. Instead, he chose to have a good time attending the players' party, one of the many attractions at The Little Milkhouse.

Philips Head Cup

By Hermann Fuchs

Kitzbuhel, 29 July-4 August
Tournament Director: Hellmuth Dieter Kuchenmeister

It must have been an inspiration, a foreboding almost, that the ceremonial opening of the new tennis centre court with celebrities from politics, economy and sport had taken place a week before the beginning of the Philips Head Cup. When the first ball was be hit at the traditional stop of the ATP in the Tyrol, it was pouring with rain – and the picturesque mountain chains that make Kitzbuhel one of the most famous ski resorts in Europe were wearing a thick coat of cloud.

Karel Novocek hoists the trophy that evaded him in the 1990 final while runner-up Magnus Gustafsson turns on the charm for a young admirer. *(Duaita Prats)*

It did not lessen the admiration for the new stadium though. The arena holding 6900 people fits into the landscape like an ancient amphitheatre – even the most ardent environmentalists could not find anything to protest about. Of course the new centre court also changed the character of the tournament: since there was not enough time to move all the facilities for sponsors and VIPs, it was almost as though there were two tournaments being played next to each other – one on the new centre court, the other in the old stadium. The fans obviously did not mind. With almost 73,000 tickets sold, the old attendance record was completely pulverised - and that was in spite of possibly the worst weather conditions that the Head Cup in Kitzbuhel has ever been played in.

The rain of course played havoc with the programme. On the fourth day Emilio Sanchez still had not played a point; together with three other players he did not finish his first match until Friday. So they had to be played in 'fast-forward'

A magnificent presentation line up on Kitzbuhel's spectacular new stadium court constructed in just eleven months for this year's Philips Head Cup. *(Richard Evans)*

when it finally stopped raining – two singles plus a doubles match for a player on a single day were not the rule, but not really exceptional either. Almost inevitably, a few of the favoured players got eliminated early: top seed Sergi Bruguera for instance lost in the third round to German qualifier Markus Zillner; Emilio Sanchez, seeded second and a finalist from 1987 to 1989, fell to his long-time rival Martin Jaite in the quarter-finals.

In spite of trying everything, tournament director Dieter Kuchenmeister could not get around extending the games to Monday – but on the extra day at least blue skies and bright sun were laughing upon Karel Novacek and Magnus Gustafsson fighting for the victory. After two hours and 36 minutes of highly dramatic tennis Novacek could dance across the centre court in joy: 'I am extremely happy,' the winner was all smiles, 'because I think that this might have been my best match of the whole season.' By beating the Swede,

Novacek also took revenge for the loss a week earlier at Hilversum. 'I played the big points better this time around,' he explained, 'so my winning was only a question of time.' The final also provided a little consolation for the Austrian fans since their darlings Thomas Muster and Horst Skoff had been eliminated by the two finalists. Gustafsson had beaten Muster in the third round, and Skoff had gone down to Novacek in the quarter-finals – both in three gruelling sets.

The doubles were exciting and sensational up to the end. Last years winners Javier Sanchez and Eric Winogradsky lost in the quarters, top seeds Vojtech Flegl and Cyril Suk and Mansour Bahrami and Daniel Vacekin in the semis. Before the Spaniards Tomas Carbonell and Francisco Roig finally received the winners cheque for $19,800, they had already played six sets that day and the final, against Pablo Arraya and Dimitri Poliakov, a team put together by pure chance, went the full distance too.

Volvo Tennis/ Los Angeles

By Tommy Bonk

Los Angeles, 29 July-4 August
Tournament Director: Robert Kramer

Here is how Pete Sampras got his hard court, pre-U.S. Open season rolling: he began his long journey to defend the Grand Slam tournament he didn't think he could win by winning a tournament he didn't think he could lose. Got that? A year ago, Sampras was some streaky 19-year-old power hitter with bushy eyebrows, a loopy grin and lightning bolts in his racket. Then he won the U.S. Open at 19 years, 28 days, became the youngest men's champion and amused almost everyone by admitting that, yet, it was all a pretty big shock to him, too.

So when Sampras walked on the court for the 1991 Volvo/Los Angeles tournament on the campus of UCLA, he did not walk alone. Actually, he was carrying some fairly hefty emotional baggage with him. Things like ... was he a fluke, was he injury prone, was he really any good? A less-than-spectacular summer, including early exits at both the French Open and Wimbledon, fostered such scepticism. If there were some questions about Sampras's prospects with the U.S. Open coming up, Sampras did not share them.

Sampras insisted he expected to win the Volvo/Los Angeles event, even if Stefan Edberg, Brad Gilbert and Michael Chang stood in his way. The fact that Sampras accomplished just what he expected, knocking out Gilbert, 6-2, 6-7, 6-3, in the final proved that he was just as adept at predicting tennis as he was in playing it. Sampras served nine aces against Gilbert, finished the week with 40 and claimed his first ATP Tour title since his historic victory in the U.S. Open.

For Gilbert, it was still a great week, even though he didn't act like he was having such a rollicking good time against Sampras when Gilbert snatched the cap off his own head and served it into the fence. All it took was a slightly more than routine 7-6, 6-7, 6-4 upset of Edberg in the semi-finals to make this an especially noteworthy event for Gilbert. His father, Barry Gilbert, was in attendance during the week, but one had to look hard to find him. Gilbert didn't allow the elder Gilbert to sit anywhere near the court because he was worried his father would become a distraction. 'I put him in the Bob Uecker seats,' Gilbert said. 'He sits in the top row and yet when I lost my serve against Javier Frana (in the first round) I could still hear him whacking his knee in disgust.'

Edberg, bothered by a sore knee in his match with Gilbert, didn't seem particularly disturbed by failing to defend his Volvo/Los Angeles title. Last year, Edberg felt he peaked too soon during the hard court season and then bombed out in the

Sampras reached the final with Gilbert by ending the upset run of unheralded Italian Stefano Pescosolido, who upended Chang in the second round. Pescosolido, a 20-year-old from Rome, reached his first IBM/ATP Tour semi-final with a victory over Scott Davis, then revealed he had done some sightseeing with coach Tonio Zugarelli. Pescosolido and Zugarelli jumped into a car at their hotel and headed for their favourite place: 'Beverly Hills,' said Pescosolido, who speaks only a little English. The only other words he spoke in English during his post-match interview were 'Michelle Pfeiffer' and 'good tournament'.

No one, not even Michelle Pfeiffer, could have had a better tournament than Sampras and it could not have come at a better time. Although Sampras felt he didn't need to answer any questions about the health of his game or his body, how he played during the week spoke volumes about them both. 'Some people may have questioned me, but I didn't worry,' Sampras said. 'I know I am a good player. And when I'm loose and playing well, I think I'm a pretty tough person to beat.' For a week at UCLA, he was not only tough to beat, he was impossible to beat.

His poor early season form behind him, Pete Sampras regains some of the confidence that earned him the 1990 U.S. Open crown. (Michael Baz)

U.S Open, so the Wimbledon semi-finalist thought he kept himself right on track for where he wanted to be in time for Flushing Meadow. 'Not so bad,' Edberg said in a critique of his tournament. He would proved to be correct in his preparation.

Campionati Internzionali di San Marino

By Anna Legnani
San Marino, 29 July-4 August
Tournament Director: Fabio Sapori

The oldest existing Republic, founded on Mount Titano at the start of the fourth century as a religious community by Dalmatian refugee Marino and which set up its communal organisation during the thirteenth century, now hosts one of the most recent additions to the professional tennis circuit.

The 1991 edition of the Campionati Internazionali di Tennis di San Marino was staged three weeks ahead of the original date to take advantage of a free slot that had unexpectedly become available only two months prior to its initial date. The new site at Parco Montecchio Fabbrica still had to be completed, but the works were accelerated and when the players arrived they found three courts set amidst woods and vineyards just below the historical Rock, and its three guard towers.

Time and location changed, but the main protagonist remained the same as last year: Guillermo Perez Roldan firmly resettled the San Marino crown on his head with a 6-3, 6-1 victory over surprising Frenchman Frederic Fontang.

The Argentinian, who had defeated Omar Camporese, the local hero from nearby Bologna in last year's final, was determined to assert his supremacy after being plagued by ankle and knee injuries at the start of the season.

After scraping through the second round against Dutchman Menno Osting, in a match he only secured in the third-set tie-breaker, and suffering in the first set in the quarter-finals against Spaniard Carlos Costa, Perez Roldan sailed through to the semi-final to meet Renzo Furlan.

If Perez Roldan was a logical finalist, Fontang created a sensation when he took out Arrese.

In the championship round, the Argentinean broke Fontang's serve twice to lead 4-1, but let his opponent return to 4-3. The eighth game was a long battle which the more experienced player finally secured. The young Frenchman's confidence seemed a little shaken and Perez Roldan picked up his game, proceeding to his seventh career title.

If Perez Roldan was one of the logical finalists, Fontang created a sensation when he took out second seed Jordi Arrese in the second round on a score of 6-3, 6-0. He confirmed his startling form by leaving no more than four games to both Claudio Mezzadri and Robert Azar, to reach his first career final. San Marino was in fact the first ATP Tour event where Fontang had been directly accepted into the main draw; he had formerly played almost exclusively on the satellite and challenger level, and his best result so far had been the semi-final in the Zaragosa challenger, which marked the start of a successful two-month spell including a quarter-final appearance in Parioli challenger and qualifications to the main draws in Nice and Rome. Fontang had allowed himself a fortnight off the circuit before the Muratti Time International Championships, and the freshness paid off.

In the doubles final, Jordi Arrese, teaming up with Carlos Costa, partly consoled himself for his early elimination in the singles by taking the title with a 6-3, 3-6, 6-3 win over the experienced South Americans Christian Miniussi and Diego Perez. The Catalans both won their third title, but their first one together after pairing up only for the third time.

The last minute change in date hampered the tournament this year, but the beauty of the ancient Republic, the relaxed atmosphere and the vicinity to Rimini and Riccione, the two most famous holiday resorts on the Italian Adriatic coast, with their mega-discotheques and round the clock night life, ensure a great potential.

Impressive honour guard for the happy champion, Guillermo Perez Roldan. *(Angelo Tonelli)*

Thriftway ATP Championship

By Philip S. Smith

Cincinnati, 5-11 August
Tournament Director: Paul Flory

One of the best draws of the year on the IBM/ATP Tour came together at the Thriftway ATP Championship as late wild card entrants Boris Becker and Ivan Lendl joined Stefan Edberg, Jim Courier, Andre Agassi, Guy Forget, Pete Sampras and David Wheaton at the $1.3 million event played near Cincinnati. The field was explosive and the week's two biggest servers, Sampras and Forget, produced a final full of fireworks. Sampras, who lost his serve only once all week, boomed out 41 aces – to lead the tournament – and reached the final with wins over Edberg and Courier. Forget's serve was as hot as Sampras's as he blasted 38 aces – second highest at the tournament – and lost only one set. The final was more of the same as the pair combined for 28 aces – 14 each – with serves consistently in excess of 110 miles an hour.

In the end it was Forget who ruined birthday plans for Sampras (due to turn 20 the day after the final) by winning 2-6, 7-6 (7-4), 6-4. The Frenchman's third title of the year hardly came easily. Sampras won the first set handily in 20 minutes, prompting for most fans the memory of the 1990 final in which Edberg dismantled Brad Gilbert 6-1, 6-1 in 52 minutes. It was the second-fastest final of 1990 and the most lopsided championship match in the history of the

Agassi may win the bare mid-riff contests but it was Sampras's serve that took him to the Cincinnati final. *(Russ Adams)*

Elegance and precision are the hallmarks of Guy Forget's superb backhand. *(Russ Adams)*

tournament. Forget, however, soon found his rhythm and a way to return Sampras's serves. After winning the second set in a tie-break, Forget outlasted his younger counterpart to pick up his first title in the United States and the $170,200 winner's cheque.

But despite the fire-power on display, the one moment most fans will remember came in the third and decisive set and had more to do with old-fashioned chivalry than high-powered tennis. Forget held a 2-1 lead but was down 40-15 when Sampras launched a serve that was called out by a

Doubles finalists
Michibata, Connell,
Seguso and Flach line-
up with sponsors and
the tournament director.
(Tom Fey)

linesman. Forget, who saw the ball was in by about a foot, indicated to chair umpire Dana Loconto that the serve was good. He gave up the ace and the set was tied at 2-2. 'It doesn't happen that often,' Forget said. 'I am especially prone to doing it whenever I play someone who is fair like Pete.'

Forget beat the world's No. 1 player, Becker, to reach the final. After his semi-final loss, Becker explained to reporters he hoped to increase his slim lead over second-ranked Edberg by playing at Indianapolis the following week while Edberg remained idle. To that statement came the reply from a reporter that Edberg had just accepted a wild card into New Haven. A surprised Becker said 'Really? That son-of-a....'

Competition for computer rankings effects all players, but most players know the Thriftway ATP is not just a about the action on the court. The tournament has become a player favourite for the variety of non-tennis activities available such as a championship golf course adjacent to the tennis facility and a nearby amusement park. One player took a break from tennis while in Cincinnati in order to experience a childhood dream. Jim Courier got to suit up in a Cincinnati Reds uniform and shag fly balls during batting practice before a game with the Los Angeles Dodgers. Courier, a Florida native, grew up a Reds fan by watching the Major League Baseball team during spring training in Florida. And if it weren't for nerves, mighty

Courier would have stood at the plate. But, the French Open champ later confessed, he 'wimped out.' 'I did make a great backhand catch at the wall. I think I took a dinger (home run) away from someone,' Courier said. 'I had the opportunity to meet some famous people this week, and my head was spinning a little. When you get a chance to do stuff like this, it's great.'

Ken Flach's and Robert Seguso's heads might have been spinning a little as they sliced easily through a star-studded doubles field that included every doubles player ranked in the top 16. The duo beat Grant Connell and Glenn Michibata 6-7, 6-4, 7-5 in the doubles final to collect their second title of the year.

While there was familiarity in the doubles final, the singles final was Edberg-less for the first time since 1986, and Swede-less for the first time since 1982. Edberg, who gained the No. 1 ranking at the 1990 Thriftway ATP with a win over Michael Chang in the quarter-finals, won the title in 1987 and 1990. And for the past eight years, either Edberg, Mats Wilander or Anders Jarryd made up at least one-half of the singles final. If having a Swede in the final is the norm at the Thriftway ATP Championship each year, the tradition is to break attendance records. This year was more of the same as 144,059 attended, the most ever. 'It's like the Kentucky Derby or the Indianapolis 500,' said Paul M Flory, the tournament director at the

Thriftway ATP Championship for the past 17 years. 'When it's August in Cincinnati, it's the place to be.' There's many a good reason why, as the stadium is one of the finest in the tennis world. With seating for 10,300 – and every seat has a back or is a proper chair – the stadium rises from the plains of Southwestern Ohio to envelop both spectator and player into a truly enjoyable venue to view a tennis match. The stadium is a true bowl, with 10 luxury skybox suites lining the upper rim of the facility. Four super-luxurious boxes are in the midst of the north stands, each with private hospitality rooms accessible by private stairways beneath the north stands. A 65-seat airconditioned, enclosed media box overlooks the action on Stadium Court.

More than $1.8 million has been donated to the Children's Hospital Mecical Center since 1974.

But the tournament is not about tennis alone. It's played for the benefit of Cincinnati's Children's Hospital Medical Center, one of the world's leading paediatric medical centres. More than $1.8 million has been donated by the tournament to the charity since 1974, and every year sick children enjoy visits at their bedsides by players. This year Edberg, Jonas Svensson, Kent Kinnear, Ugo Colombini, Pat Galbraith, Brent and Kirk Haygarth, Scott Melville and Chuck Swayne visited the children. Also during the week, players conduct clinics on public courts for children of the various neighbourhoods in Cincinnati and nearby Dayton. Every year, hundreds of children benefit from personal tennis lessons from some of the sport's biggest stars.

Andrei Cherkasov, red racket aloft, produced another consistent display by reaching the quarter-finals. *(Russ Adams)*

Czechoslovak Open Tennis Championships

By Richard Evans

Prague, 5-11 August
Tournament Director: Jan Kodes

From the way the immigration officer casually flipped back one's passport with hardly a glance, to the guitars and songs that echoed the length of the Charles Bridge at night, it was easy to realise that Prague had rediscovered the lightness of being. After

One Czech champion to another – Jan Kodes, new tournament director of the Prague Open, hands the trophy to the bigger, modern version of himself, Karel Novocek.

an absence of five years, a visitor could taste the change in atmosphere as tartly as a slug of slivovitz. One of the world's most beautiful cities, draped under the grey cloak of communism for so long, was wearing a smile again and when tournament director Jan Kodes dropped his ticket prices for the Czechoslovak Open, tennis fans brought those smiles with them to the fine stadium that sits on an island in the middle of the Vitava River.

Even before the new hero Karel Novacek, had stepped on court, crowds were queuing up for tickets in the hot August sunshine. Kodes, who had grown up on these courts before going on to win Wimbledon and the French Open, was gratified to see such positive public response but, being a cautious man, he was not satisfied until Novacek had made it all the way through to the final. 'We need Karel to do well,' Kodes said early in the week. 'After winning so much elsewhere the public will not understand if he fails at home.'

Only insiders knew just how easy it would have been for Novacek to have done just that. He had arrived direct from winning the Head Cup in Kitzbuhel and, with one days's rest, had needed to battle his way past such dangerous opponents as Veli Paloheimo and Renzo Furlan. Novacek, a huge man of 6' 4", plays a massively physical game of

Prague was tasting freedom in many ways in the sunny summer of '91. One way people enjoyed themselves was to take advantage of affordable ticket prices by packing the stadium court.

tennis that puts constant pressure on his reserves of stamina. 'I was really tired after beating Paloheimo,' Novacek admitted. 'But once I had got through the Furlan match, I started to feel OK again.'

Kodes had fretted over the outcome of that second round match and with good reason. Furlan, an Italian of high promise whose game can sometimes be as full of intrigue as the Ludlum novels he loves, pushed Novacek all the way to the third set tie-break and then only succumbed by seven points to five. In the semi-final Thomas Muster, who had beaten defending champion Jordi Arrese in the second round, predictably proved just as tough as Furlan for Novacek who eventually came through 7-5 in the third.

Having made the final, the big Czech found a very familiar face waiting for him. Magnus Gustafsson, whom he had beaten in the Kitzbuhel final, had proved that his levels of guts and

determination matched those of Novacek. Troubled by an arm injury in Austria, the Swede had stopped off in Munich for a medical examination on his way to Prague and played most of the week with pain killers. That, however, did not stop the newcomer to the top ten from sweeping past his first three opponents in straight sets and then outlasting the rugged Guillermo Perez-Roldan 7-5, 6-7, 6-2 in the semis. In the final, Novacek, to the delight of the supportive crowd, defeated Gustafsson 7-6, 6-2 to claim his fourth ATP Tour title of the year – more than any other player at that date.

Unhappily Gustafsson's heroics were the cause of him having to withdraw from the US Open two weks later but for Novacek the victory in front of his own people – winning when he had to win, when it was almost demanded of him – proved his temperament was becoming almost as solid as his power-packed game.

155

GTE/U.S. Men's Hardcourt Championships

By Jessica Harris

Indianapolis, 12-18 August
Tournament Director: Stephen DeVoe

Indianapolis had the complete package,' said tennis great Marty Riessen. 'They had the biggest names, exciting matches, enthusiastic crowds, and wonderful facilities,' he explained. 'The real kicker is that the players love the friendly hospitality and the terrific activities. If the players enjoy themselves off the court, it shows up on the court. Almost every player rates Indy as one of his favourite weeks of the year ... no wonder they've won the IBM/ATP Tournament of the Year award three years in a row.'

The names were storied: Becker, Courier, Sampras, Agassi, Wheaton. The teams were tennis household words: Flach/Seguso, Leach/Pugh, Davis/Pate, Jarryd/Fitzgerald. The matches were riveting. Boris Becker and David Wheaton put the ball in a blur when they collided at full speed in the semis. Minutes later, Jim Courier and Pete Sampras plumbed every line of stadium court as they struck and counterstruck brilliantly.

Pete Sampras. *(Russ Adams)*

The final had the capacity crowd roaring as Becker and Sampras used every shot they owned to search and destroy. The mixture of power and placement was irresistible. First serves whistled and volleys snapped to open court. It brought home to the packed crowds the full power and speed of the men's game – something that is not always evident from a television screen.

The doubles was also dramatic as the world's best were tested to the limit by young, talented newcomers. Jared Palmer and Jonathan Stark, Stanford teammates, fought and scratched their way to the semis before losing to Ken Flach and Robert Seguso. In the other half, hometown favourites Kent Kinnear and Sven Salumaa slashed their way to the finals with upset after upset, capped by a classic three-tie-breaker win over Scott Davis and David Pate. The final was vintage doubles, with both teams attacking, and the ball frequently finding the sharpest angles and the farthest corners of the court.

Todd Witsken, a drummer himself, tries to learn from Chester Thompson of Genesis. *(Peter Bick)*

Off the court, the players were never short of something to do. ATP Tour's Weller Evans, Director of Player Services, put it this way: 'The tournament volunteers at Indy have a knack for making the players feel at home. They're all so friendly and helpful. And they come up with the craziest stuff to do. It's just a great week.'

Some of the 'crazy stuff' included a music room for private lessons with Chester Thompson, lead drummer to Phil Collins and Genesis. The Superstars Competition pitted the players against each other in skills ranging from shooting baskets to video simulated motorcycle racing. The winner, Peter Lundgren, took home a TV entertainment centre. Competitive instincts were further aroused when teams of players went to war against each other with paintball guns in a darkened 'war games' room. Five thousand shots were fired, none in anger.

Boris Becker made several unforced errors when he played his first softball game as more than 40 players took part in three hotly contested games. The European players demanded a replay in soccer.

Wives and 'significant others' went from the elegance of style shows to the exuberance of roller balding. Mark Miles, now CEO of the ATP Tour, and his predecessor Hamilton Jordan, started this tradition of hyper-activity at the Indianapolis tournament. At the end of the week, the players tend to be exhausted. But they always come back for more.

When 3500 young tennis players came for the tournament's Nike Junior Jamboree, Pat McEnroe, Rick Leach, Jim Pugh and Roscoe Tanner, along with 15 other ATP players, conducted clinics and mingled freely for an entire morning. The event's director, Jenny Pearson, said that 'a lot of kids went home all pumped up about tennis.'

Sponsors got some 'court time' too. Roscoe Tanner, Nick Bollettieri, Tim Mayotte, Kelly Evernden and a host of ATP players, set up clinics and match play with sponsor representatives. 'You can't believe Roscoe Tanner's serve until you see it go by you,' one sponsor exclaimed. Kelly Evernden summed it up, 'The pieces came together

better than ever this year. The players and the fans seemed to genuinely enjoy each other. That's all anyone can ask for.'

Tournament director Steve DeVoe and C.O.O. Bill Hoffman both agree, the difference in Indianapolis can be measured by the people who volunteer. They're capable, conscientious, and co-operative. The players and the fans recognise this, and each of them responds to the other to the benefit of all. It's a rare piece of chemistry that Indianapolis is proud of.

Boris Becker tries his hand at soft-ball – one of many off-court distractions for the players in Indianapolis. *(Peter Bick)*

Former Wimbledon finalist Roscoe Tanner, who now works occasionally as a commentator, interviews Patrick McEnroe at courtside. *(Peter Bick)*

Enter a competition in Indianapolis and you can win a motorbike – like Christian Bergstrom. *(Peter Bick)*

Volvo International Tennis Tournament

By Jim Shea

New Haven, 12-18 August
Tournament Director: James Westhall

Granted, a field that includes Jimmy Connors, John McEnroe, Ivan Lendl, Stefan Edberg, Derrick Rostagno and Michael Chang is going to draw a crowd but the big attraction of the 1991 Volvo International was the new facility.

The Connecticut Tennis Center, located next to the Yale Bowl in New Haven is the third largest tennis-only facility in the world behind the sites of the U.S. Open and the French Open. The stadium seats 15,000 and was constructed in less than a year at a cost of $15 million from some 1665 precast concrete pieces. The paint was barely dry when the players and fans arrived for the opening rounds. The reviews were a rave. The players found a large lounge with television and video games, a cafeteria, locker room, trainers' area and laundry. The media worked in a well-equipped area, right next door to an interview room complete with stage and microphones. And each of the fans who attended the tournament found every seat in the stadium offered an unobstructed view of the action.

Attendance reflected both the field and the facility. More than 146,000 fans attended this year's Volvo, a 26,000 increase over 1990. 'It was exciting and encouraging to see such an enthusiastic turnout for our inaugural year in this beautiful new stadium,' said Volvo International tournament director Jim Westhall. 'Not only did we exceed our total expectations, but the 146,000 mark represents the highest nine-day total of any tournament on the ATP Tour in North America and one of the highest worldwide.'

Petr Korda

The $1 million tournament began in 1973 at the Mount Washington Hotel in New Hampshire. From 1975 to 1984 it was played at the Mount Cranmore Tennis Club also in the Granite State, and then moved to Stratton Mountain in Vermont from 1985 to 1989. The Volvo International came to New Haven after the state of Connecticut agreed to provide funding for a new stadium.

The 1990 tournament was played in a temporary stadium, in the same spot where the permanent facility now stands. Westhall was beaming like a proud new father all week long. On more than one occasion he harked back to the early days of the tournament when a handful of fans sat on a grassy hillside to watch the tennis at the Mount Washington Hotel.

The inaugural New Haven Volvo was known for the early exits of the seeded players, and the 1991 tournament proved to be just as tough a venue for crowd favourites. Jimmy Connors, who would dazzle the tennis world with his play at the U.S. Open two weeks later, fell to Malivai Washington in the opening round, as did Andres Gomez, Jimmy Arias and Todd Woodbridge. Entering the quarter-finals, Edberg and Lendl were left behind, soon to be followed by McEnroe and Chang.

The finals between Goran Ivanisevic and Petr Korda was played at high noon on a day soaked with heat and humidity. Korda used the weather to his advantage, running Ivanisevic all over the court until the 108° temperatures on the playing surface finally caught up with him. In 61 minutes, Korda won 6-4, 6-2 to take home the $137,000 title. An hour later, Korda returned to Stadium Court to compete in the doubles finals with partner Wally Masur. The duo defeated defending champions Jeff Brown and Scott Melville 7-5, 6-3, sending Korda on his way with an additional $27,000.

The tournament also featured a legends event that included such past greats as Ilie Nastase, Rod Laver and Fred Stolle. There was also a celebrity doubles affair involving Sports Illustrated model Elle MacPherson, former Pittsburgh Steelers quarterback Terry Bradshaw and Connecticut governor Lowell Weicker. While the focus of the week certainly was tennis, Westhall and his staff also provided players and their families with plenty of other diversions. Some of the off-court activities were softball, windsurfing, roller blading, volleyball, golf and eveen polo. It was also possible to get a manicure or a massage. And then there were parties, lots of parties.

The city of New Haven was also delighted with this year's tournament. Facing tough times during the region's recession, downtown business owners were looking to the Volvo for a boost. And they got it. Merchants tied the Volvo to an eight-day festival downtown, and reported substantial increases in sales. The crowds the festival attracted also helped the city in the public relations department. Shoppers found the downtown area to be anything but a haven for street crime.

The new $15 million Connecticut Tennis Center glows during night-time action at the Volvo International.
(Russ Adams)

Norstar Bank Hamlet Challenge Cup

By Pat Calabria

Long Island, 19-25 August
Tournament Director: Wendy Parr

If you were looking for omens last summer, the Norstar Bank Hamlet Challenge Cup was the place to be. Built into a cosy, compact site in the middle of bustling Long Island, the Hamlet served up one surprise after another, beginning a minor problem with the weather ... it was called a hurricane. On the first afternoon, Hurricane Bob roared through the site, toppling sponsors' tents, muddying parking lots, soaking the DecoTurf courts and postponing play. An omen? Hours later,

the night programme went on as scheduled and Hurricane Ivan – that's Ivan Lendl – roared and raged, too. But after hotly disputing several line calls, Lendl won his match over Carl Uwe-Steeb 6-4, 3-6, 6-3. So that storm passed by quickly, too.

There would be more, of course, topped by the fact that Jimmy Connors, nearing his 39th birthday, staged several brilliant matches to reach the quarter-finals before being ousted by defending

Wendy Parr, Gary Stevens of North Shore University Hospital, Stefan Edberg and Ed Schroeder of IBM participate in another donation from the IBM/ATP Charities Program. *(Michael Baz)*

NORSTAR BANK HAMLET CHALLENGE CUP

champion Stefan Edberg. That turned out to be a prelude to the events which would take place at the U.S. Open, a 45-minute drive down the Long Island Expressway at Flushing Meadow. It was at the Open that Connors made his storybook run into the semi-finals, captivating the crowds, the officials, even the other players.

Connors clearly was the star of the Hamlet, if not the winner. That honour went instead to Lendl, whose surprisingly easy 6-3, 6-2 romp over Edberg in the championship match was the one event that didn't turn out to be a harbinger of anything (Edberg winning the Open, Lendl surviving double match point in his first-round match). Connors racked up a 6-3, 6-4 win over Todd Martin and eliminated Nicklas Kulti by the roller-coaster score of 1-6, 6-4, 6-0, losing only eight points in the third set, to resounding cheers. And how did Connors feel about that syrupy introduction? 'I liked it,' he said, 'Hey, I wrote it.' What he couldn't write was a script that had him dethroning Edberg, the Hamlet's resident pro. But, boy, he tried. Edberg's hard-fought 6-3, 4-6, 6-4 victory in sweltering heat and humidity disappointed the crowd, but heartened Connors. When he said after losing to Jim Courier at the Open, 'I just wanted to get out there and be able to compete again, and I proved I can,' it sounded familiar. Turns out, he'd said that at Long Island, too, after losing to Edberg.

Edberg went on to defeat qualifier Olivier Delaitre in the semi-finals to set up the title match against Lendl, long a favourite of the Long Island crowds. Lendl, some recalled, once showed up late for a Hamlet match after being caught in traffic. Desperate, he drove on the shoulder of the Expressway, showed up 15 minutes late, and won. Later, he explained: 'I had to drive on the grass.' It was, perhaps, his greatest triumph on the surface.

This year required no such theatrics. But Lendl did defeat John McEnroe 6-3, 7-5 in a semi-final battle that, if it didn't quite turn back the clock to more glorious days, at least slowed time down a little. There were flashes of the old days: Lendl's topspin lob that puzzled McEnroe and dropped him to 0-40 en route to breaking his serve in the second

Ivan Lendl was on his toes as he overwhelmed Edberg in the final. *(Michael Baz)*

set; Lendl facing break point in the next game and replying with two service winners and an ace to save the game; McEnroe nailing a service return for deuce, rifling a forehand for the ad and whacking a forehand passing shot to break back at 3-4.

But Lendl's 11th ace concluded the 11th game at 6-5 and then he broke McEnroe to finish the match, and kept the momentum rolling against Edberg to win his record fifth Hamlet championship, seven years after he won the first time, in 1984. Edberg won just five games, extended Lendl to just one hour and 21 minutes on the clock, was broken six times, and at one point in the match surrendered 13 points in a row.

With that commanding performance, Lendl earned the $32,400 first prize, not to mention some relief after a season filled with injuries and disappointment. 'Winning is what keeps me going,' Lendl said. 'I like winning. I really do.' All things considered, the weather wasn't so bad, either.

OTB International Tennis Open

By Annamie Athayde

Schenectady, 19-25 August
Tournament Director: Nitty Singh

Flying frisbees, romantic walks, boating on the lake; for 51 weeks of the year Schenectady's Central Park is just like any other down home playground for the all-American family. Then all of a sudden every summer this ordinary park becomes the scene for an extraordinary tennis tournament; extraordinary because the one thing you won't hear is the rustle of dollar bills, francs changing hands or pounds paying for tickets. This tournament is free to anyone in the mood for world class tennis.

Schenectady is a sleepy town in North New York State. It's horse-racing country – the famous Saratoga race track is nearby. But when OTB decided they wanted to create a new sporting facility to bring the local community together, they chose tennis. The result was not simply another set of tennis courts but a major tournament where, as Tournament Director Nitty Singh says, 'everyone can have fun'. A tournament where you can wander from court to court or take a picnic lunch to one of the park benches and watch the action from monitors set up in the trees. And if the pressure gets too much, take a break and head for the children's playground for a training session on the swings.

It's not just a relaxing time for the fans. The Spanish contingent of Javier and Emilio Sanchez, Francisco Clavet and coach Pato Alvarez spent the week camped out with the Gomez family under a tree at courtside. Complete with magazines and provisions they only occasionally looked up to check whether they were due on court. Michael Stich marked the week by hitting his first ever hole-in-one on the golf course of the Mohawk Country Club just down the road. 'I'm having a lot of fun here,' he remarked, 'and for me, that's great. I've been able to get away from tennis while I'm here and play some golf and now my tennis is starting to get fun again.'

It was an important break for Stich. The new Wimbledon champion was under the sort of pressure that only comes the way of a new big star on the circuit. Pressure made even greater by the presence of the world's press assessing his chances for the coming week's U.S. Open. Some were surprised to see him in Schenectady but he had promised Nitty Singh at the French Open that he would be there and he was 'determined to honour the commitments I made before Wimbledon. Wimbledon is just a tournament like any other.' It was a determination the other players came to regret as he powered his way through the opening rounds.

Todd Woodbridge, who met Stich in the quarter-finals, made it clear that Stich's successes have had an effect not merely on the young German but

Stich cropped Emilio Sanchez in Schenectady – although the haircut came later. *(J.B. Salgado)*

Michael Stich, winner on grass at Wimbledon and clay in Stuttgart now triumps on hardcourt, too. *(Thomas Toohey Brown)*

on the attitude of his opponents too. Even in sleepy Schenectady, the atmosphere in Stadium Court when Stich walked on was electric with tension and anticipation. Every move he made from the first point to the last was greeted with sighs and exclamations from the packed stands. As Woodbridge commented, 'he's getting an aura around him like a Becker or an Edberg or one of those players ... You just have to stick in there and play him'. Unfortunately for Emilio Sanchez, meeting Stich in the final, sticking in there did not quite do the trick.

Stich's powerful serve and delicate touch at the net proved unshakeable. Despite Sanchez's athleticism and determination, which raised applause even from his opponent, he knew when he was beaten and in true laid-back Schenectady style, when Stich effortlessly put away yet another volley, Sanchez handed his racquet to the ballboy. He then had to stand back and see the ballboy not only confidently take the racquet in hand with some spirit but return Stich's serve. The roars of appreciation from the crowd were deafening.

However, the ballboy's luck didn't last any longer than Sanchez's and the match finally went to Stich 6-2, 6-4.

It really wasn't Sanchez's day. Later the same afternoon partnered by Andres Gomez, he went down in a tough doubles final to younger brother Javier, and Todd Woodbridge, 3-6, 7-6, 7-6.

Whilst the players packed away their racquets and Michael prepared to Stich it to someone else at the US Open, the children of Schenectady returned to the swings their grandparents had played on over 100 years ago. And who knows, perhaps in 10 years time it might be one of them collecting the cheque for $18000.

U.S. Open

By Bud Collins

**Flushing Meadow, 26 August-8 September
Tournament Director: Marshall Happer**

All right, so there were 127 guys at Flushing Meadow, including a devastating chap called Edberg. But who knew – or cared? The one and only people's choice was recycled James Scott Connors. He was 'runnin' across the Meadow, pickin' up lots of forget-me-nots...' as goes the old Sinatra lyric from 'You Make Me Feel So Young'. The Meadow was

Kissing the cup Bjorn Borg never got to hold – victory tastes specially sweet for Stefan Edberg. *(Joyner)*

The Duchess of York was one of the more celebrated fans drawn to the U.S. Open by Jimmy Connors' heroic advance. Connors' agent Ray Berton in the background – the royal bodyguards, as ever, to the fore. *(Serge Philippot)*

old Jimbo's young-feeling playground, and he took the 1991 Open with him, if not the trophy (which he's won five times anyway). He turned it into the U.S. (as in Unexpectedly Senescent) Open, and refused to move over for youth until the next-to-last day when a lifelong admirer, 21-year-old Jim Courier caught up with him, emphatically, 6-3, 6-3, 6-2. But by then such strongly touted defenders as the defender himself, Pete Sampras, 1989 champ Boris Becker, Wimbledon champ Michael Stich, Glitz Kid Andre Agassi and old rival John McEnroe were on the street. After Jimmy's deluge: anticlimax.

Stefan Edberg, putting all his desires, experience, poise, punch and champion's presence into an explosive 122-minute package, outwhacked and overwhelmed Courier, 6-2, 6-4, 6-0, to prove that he hadn't caught Borg's Disease after all. Flushing had never been happy camping ground for Edberg. It was ever doldrumsville – until this time he imitated a sharp-edged zephyr for two weeks. Stefan had been zero-for-eight Opens, approaching Bjorn Borg's Swedish record of zero-for-ten. But from the first round failure in 1990, against Alexander Volkov, Stefan took

flight first-class in phoenix fashion to win his first U.S. (a fifth major) on merely the loss of single sets, early on, to Bryan Shelton and Jim Grabb. In the third set he had to serve out three set points, 0-40, 4-5, to stay ahead of Shelton. After that only Michael Chang in the fourth round came remotely close to Stefan, 7-6 (7-2), 7-5, 6-3. Not since Aussie Mal Anderson in 1957 had a guy gone from worst to first in a year's time to capture the U.S. Sweden came in for a piece of the doubles prize, too, as Anders Jarryd accompanied Aussie John Fitzgerald to a 6-3, 3-6, 6-3, 6-3, victory over American's David Pate and Scott Davis.

However, the story was the senescent – yet ageless – Connors, right from the start when the other McEnroe (Patrick) had him wrapped in a shroud at two sets to love and 3-0 in the third. Was this the way James would vanish – without even holding a customary Open birthday party (his 39th)? But, kill the obituary – and stop the presses – Connors began to yearn and burn and signal with that body language of yore that his strokes were coming in from the cold. Somehow he crept from the tomb in a four-hour, 18-minute two-day battle that started Tuesday night and concluded at 1.35 Wednesday morning in a 4-6, 6-7 (4-7), 6-4, 6-2, 6-4 victory. Yet, this was the same Connors who had won his first Open in 1974, a year Carly Simon was warbling 'Haven't got time for the pain...' Jimmy didn't have time either. 'I'm well again, a factor again,' he chortled, reappearing at Flushing after missing 1990 because of a gimpy left wrist, seemingly a career-ending wound. 'I found the right surgeon to put the wrist together, but it took a while to get back to this level.' Connors came into his twenty-first Open through the backdoor, a wild card ranked 174th. (He'd been No. 936 as the season commenced).

From that opening tribute to himself (and 4000 night owls remaining from a full-house gathering), Jimmy just kept piling the unlikely onto the improbable in jitterbugging

167

Reflections of night time play at Flushing Meadow through the sensitive lens of Frenchman Serge Philippot.
(Serge Philippot)

all the way to his fourteenth semi-final, the oldest to get so far since a guy he remembered well: slick little Aussie Ken Rosewall. Rosewall had been a bit older than 39 when he lost both the Wimbledon and U.S. title bouts to a brash basher by the name of, uh, Connors. Most tennis devotees were not pleased then by those results. Connors snickered, 'Wonder if I'll ever be a sentimental favourite?' never imagining he'd be playing at such an unimaginable age. He found out. Affirmatively.

Krickstein, immediately a victimiser by startling eighth seeded Andre Agassi, in a straight-set first-rounder, would soon become another astounding victim of Connors. That was in the fourth round. To get there Jimmy, his forehand firing better than in a very long time, and the familiar backhand bravado in gear, whipped Michiel Schapers and an awed 10th seed Karel Novacek in six sets. Arriving at his birthday, Connors was cushioned by the memory that he had almost always blown out a foe as well as the candles on 2 September. But nothing prior could compare to his good

fortune this natal anniversary, a four-and-a-half-hour climb to one of the most exiting triumphs of his long tennis life: 3-6, 7-6 (10-8), 1-6, 6-3, 7-6 (7-4). Krickstein, who had grasped, and missed, two set points in the second, strode to a lookin'-safe 5-2 lead in the fifth. He didn't fold. Connors bent him, though twice two points within defeat as Aaron served for it at 5-4. Deserting his home-sweet-baseline in the closing, tie-breaking act, Jimmy charged incessantly as his mob cheered him relentlessly to the wire. 'That's why Jimmy's a legend,' sighed Krickstein, as lonely in that raging arena as Dukakis against Bush.

The legend, underpinned by amazing legs, fattened in the quarters, another late night special as Jimmy, two points from trailing rugged Paul Haarhuis by two sets, revved up again. Conqueror of John McEnroe on the same court two years before, Paul – the best little Haarhuis in the Netherlands – was fresh from sending the red-bearded ex-champ, Boris Becker, home red-faced in straight set defeat. Haarhuis was outdoing Connors to 6-4, 5-4, with serve. Whereupon Jimmy, stealing a huge break point with four scrambling lobs and a backhand rip, prolonged the second set and was on his way to the semis in four sets.

Well before, the stunner of the 1990 semis, John McEnroe, had been ejected in a post-midnight five-set screamer by Chang. Left as Connors's companions were Courier, Edberg and three-time champ Ivan Lendl. Lendl, one of the Open's post-World War II greats (eight straight times a finalist until 1989), had willed and skilled his way from two sets down past a would-be first round saboteur, the young dynamite serving Dutchman, Richard Krajicek. Krajicek served for it at 6-5 in the third, had two match points there, plus a 4-2 lead in the subsequent tie-breaker. But Lendl, 31, hung double tough and the 19-year-old Krajicek wilted. Thus invigorated, Lendl outgunned Goran Ivanisevic, and cooled the best looking player up to that moment, Wimbledon ruler Michael Stich, 6-1 in the fifth. Stranded overnight by a third-set downpour, Stich and Lendl resumed on the Thursday with the German still as fluidly aggressive and oppressive as at the Big W. He won the third set, jumped to a 3-0 lead in the fourth set tie-breaker, and appeared home. Abruptly Stich came apart. His serve faltered to let the opportunistically returning Lendl back into it, and Ivan exploited his lanky opponent's discouragement.

That same afternoon, the 361-day reign of Pete Sampras ended in the forehand barrages and razor-edged competitiveness of Courier, 6-2, 7-6 (7-4), 7-6 (7-5). Pete acted relived with the 'monkey' – championships expectations – 'off my back.' But he was publicly chided by Connors: 'That kind of pressure is what this is all about. That's a crock, talking about a monkey.'

Edberg, seeming a gorilla in fine, malevolent tune, played the last two matches about as serve-and-volleyingly handsomely as anyone ever did at the Meadow.

He blasted Lendl, 6-3, 6-3, 6-4, and reacted to Courier's challenge majestically. By beating Edberg, who he stopped in Paris, and adding the U.S. to his French title, Courier would have been regarded as No. 1 for the year, regardless of any computerised sentiment. But Edberg, feeling No. 1-ish himself, permitted Courier to look longingly at only two break points. Both were instantly removed with service winners, and Jim, though he resisted determinedly, was helpless. 'It was a dream, the way I played,' said Edberg, modestly yet accurately.

But what everybody would remember longer was the happy hallucination of James Scott Connors.

'Oh yeah! 39 years old and don't I feel great!' Jimmy Connors in his element at Flushing Meadow. *(Joyner)*

Grand Prix Passing Shot

By Nelson Monfort

Bordeaux, 9-15 September
Tournament Director: Jean-Pierre Derose

Guy Forget, flanked by Bordeaux mayor Chaban Delmas, a former Prime Minister of France (left) and tournament director Jean-Pierre Derose reclaims his Passing Shot title. *(Serge Philippot)*

Everybody was expecting HIM. After Jimmy Connors' amazing feats at the US Open the previous week, posters had been proliferating around Bordeaux with each round that Jimmy won at Flushing Meadow. Hardly anticipating that he would still be in action in New York two days before he

was due in the world's most famous wine-growing country, Connors was in need of a stronger grape than was available in Bordeaux in order to get his 39-year-old legs functioning again in so short a time.

So, as many knowledgeable people had begun to fear, the message arrived at the eleventh hour. Connors, rather than flying to France, was hobbling home to Florida. Tournament Director Jean-Pierre Derose's disappointment was proportional to his expectations, and he could do nothing except hope that Connors would continue to defy the athletic norm by behaving more like Bordeaux's Premier Cru and get better with age. There is always 1992!

Strangely, the decision to change decades of tradition and switch this long-standing event from clay to hard court only enhanced the French players' chances of success. In view of the upcoming Davis Cup semi-final against Yugoslavia at Pau, which was due to be played on a hard surface indoors, captain Yannick Noah had insisted on the switch and was vindicated beyond his wildest dreams.

When the Swedish ace Jonas Svensson seemingly increased Derose's problems by showing a total lack of form in losing to the little-known Olivier Delaitre, the door opened for a flood

The French took over Bordeaux with six Frenchmen reaching the quarter-finals, including Fabrice Santoro (left) and Cedric Pioline. *(Serge Philippot)*

Oliver Delaitre from Metz, reached an ATP Tour final for the first time. *(Serge Philippot)*

of French players to burst through to the quarter-finals. There were six in all who were still alive at that stage and four – Delaitre, Thierry Champion, Cedric Pioline and title-holder Guy Forget – fought their way through to the semis to create a little piece of history. Never before, since Open Tennis came into being in 1968, had four Frenchman reached the semi-finals of an official tournament.

As the dominant player in France, Forget, who had blossomed into a genuine world star in the twelve months that had elapsed since his previous victory at the 'Passing Shot' was not going to let that kind of opportunity go by. After beating the promising Pioline, Forget easily defeated Delaitre in a final that didn't exceed an hour 6-1, 6-3 to join Karel Novacek as the only player, by mid-September, to have won four titles on the ATP Tour in 1991.

Just to emphasise the extraordinary home-grown dominance of this event, Forget teamed with Arnaud Boetsch to win the doubles title as well, defeating the German pair of Patrick Kuhnen and Alexander Mronz 6-2, 6-2.

Aberto da Republica

By Ricardo Acioly

Brasilia, 9-15 September
Tournament Director: Ricardo Bernd

The plane makes an eye-catching descent into the capital of Brazil. With no other towns for hundreds of miles, the lights of the city really stand out – a gleaming reminder that Brasilia was built out of nothing just 35 years ago in the heart of this vast land, specifically as a political centre for the nation. It now holds over 1.5 million people who converged from all over Brazil, including myself and my family. The layout of the city is very simple.
It was mapped out just like an aeroplane, with wings pointing north and south and the fuselage heading east and west. The wings are mainly residential areas while the long line of buildings forming an avenue wider than the Champs-Elysee house all the government agencies.

It was in the centre of this avenue, at the cockpit end of the 'plane' that six Supreme courts were laid for the Alberto da Republica, including a 7000-seat stadium. Being surrounded by the National

In downtown Brasilia, there is space for just about anything, including a Centre Court and its satellites. *(Nilton Lazzarini)*

Andres Gomez on top of a podium for the first time since the 1990 French Open. *(Nilton Lazzarini)*

Congress on one side and ministry buildings on the other was not a common sight for players used to more conventional venues. But this is Brazil and last year, remember, we played the Rio de Janeiro tournament on a beach. It really felt good for me to be back home playing a tournament and staying with my parents for a change. The Saturday before the tournament started I invited some players, ATP Tour staff and local friends to a bar called Chopp Expresso. A band performs every Saturday and as I like to play guitar and the band's leading guitarist is a particular friend of mine, I ended up on the stage, performing a few songs. By the end of the evening I was really psyched!

Most players were having a tough time adapting to the changing conditions. During the day the sun shining down on the rubberised courts made them very slow while at night, as the air cooled, they became pretty fast. It was like playing two different tournaments and upsets were bound to happen. Two of the biggest came on Wednesday when Sandon Stolle and Marcelo Saliola defeated the two top seeds, Karel Novocek and Emilio Sanchez respectively. Neither Karel nor Emilio enjoyed the funny bounces and, by then I was not feeling too funny myself, having lost to

Pablo Arraya after a satisfying first round success against Pedro Robolledo. However, I was making good progress in the doubles with my partner Mauro Menezes, a fellow Brazilian from Sao Paulo, and, after a tight-fought straight win over Bryan Shelton and Duke Odizor, we found ourselves in the final against Kent Kinnear and Roger Smith.

The doubles final was scheduled for Saturday night and I was really excited that evening. There we were in the cockpit of the 'plane' in front of a packed stadium court, including my parents and friends. Mauro and I had been playing well all week and needed just one more positive performance to keep the title in Brazil. Unhappily Kent and Roger did not care too much about our hopes and aspirations! With Kinnear returning like a mad man and Smith coming up with a serve every time we had a break point, we found it impossible to prevent them from snatching a deserved straight set victory. Our disappointment was not allowed to last long. Within minutes the whole centre of the city was treated to an enormous firework display – twenty minutes of colour and noise that ended with a grand finale that saw special effect fireworks cascading down the side of the government buildings like waterfalls. The whole thing went off with a Brazilian bang and I was delighted to have put up a good performance in my home town.

Meanwhile Andres Gomez had been enjoying his best week since winning the French Open 18 months before. After a classic South American battle against Argentina's Martin Jaite, the big man from Ecuador came through to beat the last Brazilian survivor in the singles, Danilo Marcelino, in Saturday's semi-finals while in the other half of the draw, Emilio's younger brother, Javier Sanchez fought back from a set down to defeat Bryan Shelton. Some people had doubted whether Gomez would ever win another ATP Tour title when his form slumped after winning Roland Garros but Andres is a fighter and, even though Sanchez played well enough to grab the second set, Gomez proved you can still be a champion at 31.

Barclay Open

By Patricia Jolly

Geneva, 9-15 September
Tournament Director: Daniel Auberson

At the 1991 Barclay Open, and for the second time in a couple of months, Thomas Muster 'outgrunted' enemy-brother and countryman Horst Skoff in the singles final. The two Austrians, both famous for their loud way on the court, had already been featured in the 1991 Florence championship round that had also turned to Muster's advantage.

Muster defeated defending champion Skoff 6-2, 6-4, but he wasn't keeping close track of the score. He did not bother to raise his arms in a sign of victory until the chair umpire pointed out that it was all over. 'I thought it was 5-2 for me,' he later laughed.

Commenting about his victory, Muster confessed a soft spot for the Parc des Eaux Vives where the Barclay Open is held. There, he reconnected with the Tour in 1989, after being sidelined for six months by his severe Key Biscayne knee injury. 'I started to practice again here with Marc Rosset who, at the time, had just broken through,' he recalled. 'I only competed in the doubles, but it was a great feeling to be around people who believe in you.'

Each year, the Barclay Open offers a young talent the chance of battling on the main field.

If Austrians are widely recognised as major assets for world-class tennis, the Parc des Eaux Vives was the theatre of thrilling performances by new faces. Because his tennis was almost pure perfection, the Geneva crowd almost forgave Soviet wild card recipient Andrei Medvedev for brutally ousting local hero Marc Rosset 6-2, 6-1 in the first round. The Barclay Open makes a point of offering a promising young talent the opportunity of battling on the main field each year. For the 1991 edition, Tournament Director Daniel Auberson had picked the 1991 French Open Junior Champion, 17-year-old Andrei Medvedev. 'What can I say,' commented a bitterly disappointed Rosset. 'I practised like crazy and he still beats me bad; I don't know what to think any more.'

Medvedev who started on the men's Tour only in May, aroused great interest. In four IBM/ATP Tour events played, he had made it only once through the first round upon his opponent's retirement. In Geneva, he thoroughly prepared each match by long talks with his coach who, as a retired Soviet Tour pro, had once played against some of his opponents.

Some of the qualifiers also posted stunning wins. 'I probably won because I feel absolutely no pressure,' said Salvadorian Miguel Merz, a 24-year-old jewellry designer, after defeating Patrick Baur. German Carsten Arriens unexpectedly defeated number eight seed Omar Camporese 6-3, 6-4 in the first round. And Argentinian Christian Miniussi defeated Renzo Furlan and Goran Prpic before losing in the quarter-finals to Medvedev.

Although out of the singles main draw, Marc Rosset paired up for the first time with last year's singles runner-up Sergi Bruguera to win the doubles 3-6, 6-3, 6-2 against Swedish duo Per Henricsson and Ola Jonsson. He helped raise money for the charity programme 'Médicins sans frontiers' by auctioning his racket during the official dinner.

The agony and the agony of winning. For Thomas Muster, the ecstasy comes later on if exhaustion does not set in first. *(Team Reporters)*

Swiss Indoors

By Rene Stauffer

Basel, 23-29 September
Tournament Director: Roger Brennwald

Roger Brennwald was all smiles when he reflected on his tournament, talking about the 'best Swiss Indoors of all times'. The attendance of 61,900 spectators marked a new tournament record, and none of them regretted coming. Swiss hero Jakob Hlasek, who with a ranking of 18 was only the 6th seeded player at the start of the tournament, managed to overcome stiff challenges, beating Jan Gunnarson, Carl-Uwe Steeb, Kevin Curren, Alexander Volkov and John McEnroe on the way to his fifth overall title, his first of the year and his first in his adopted home country. 'When I came to Switzerland with my family in 1968, the people here were very friendly to us,' Hlasek said after what he described as his biggest success so far. 'I consider this victory as a sign of gratitude to the Swiss public, which supported me during my matches like I have never been supported before.' Since Hlasek also won the doubles with his first-time partner Patrick McEnroe, he left Basle with his highest pay-check of $118,250.

When the biggest Swiss tournament started, nobody – except tournament director Brennwald – really considered Hlasek as a title challenger. The attention focused on Wimbledon champion Michael Stich, defending champion John McEnroe and Jimmy Connors, who was playing in Basle for the fourth time in a row and who made

his first appearance in the ATP Tour after his glorious progress to the semi-finals of the U.S. Open. Top-seeded Stich, tired after an exhausting weekend in Kansas City, where he and his team had lost in the semi-finals of the Davis Cup against the United States, went out in the first round, losing 6-3, 6-3 against the Swede Christian Bergstrom. But that was the only disappointment for the public, with the exception of the first-round loss of Swiss Marc Rosset, who missed two matchpoints against Kevin Curren. Jimmy Connors did much better, beating qualifier Laurent Prades, No. 4 seeded Petr Korda and Amos Mansdorf in straight sets, on his way to the semi-finals. To the delight of almost everybody, John McEnroe was in similarly great shape, reaching the final four with wins over Laurent Prades, his brother Patrick as well as Bergstrom.

The match everybody had been waiting for since the draw became a reality: John McEnroe against Jimmy Connors. The two living American legends had played against each other officially 32 times, McEnroe leading 19-13. But their meetings had become less and less frequent: they had played only twice over the last five years, Connors winning at the Canadian Open in 1987, as well as in Toulouse in 1989. McEnroe showed no signs of respect during this semi-final, managing to produce what he later called his 'best match of the

Ball boys and ball girls receive the traditional gold-wrapped chocolates from Swiss No. 1 Jakob Hlasek - a popular winner in Basel. *(Bernard Rohner)*

year'. The New Yorker went on to win 6-1, 6-3, but had a lot of praise for his older opponent. 'If Jimmy continues like that, he will soon be back in the top twenty.' Although on the losing side, Jimmy Connors also enjoyed the encounter, acknowledging: 'He served well, volleyed well and moved well. He was sharp all the way round.'

The drama and emotion anticipated in the match between Connors and McEnroe charged the first of the two semi-finals. But the semi-final between Alexander Volkov and Jakob Hlasek was equally dramatic: it developed into a nail-biting thriller spread over two and a half hours and culminating in three tie-breaks. Both players held their serves throughout the first two sets, Hlasek winning the first tie-break 7-3 and losing the second 5-7. Volkov then moved ahead 3-0, but a controversial line call helped Hlasek back into the match. After saving one match point at 4-5, he forced another tie-break, coming back from 1-4 to win it 7-5. It was a win which filled the St Jakobshalle with joy and excitement.

When the final began, the Stadium was sold out for the fourth day in a row, with most of the 9,000 spectators cheering for Hlasek. McEnroe led the series 4-2 but had lost two of the previous three encounters with his former doubles partner. McEnroe achieved an early service-break, but Hlasek fought back with the help of the crowd. He served and volleyed brilliantly, leaving McEnroe perplexed when he won the tie-break with a perfectly placed cross-court-volley which won the first set tie-break 7-4.

Hlasek gained confidence after the first set and I got a little bit flat at the wrong moment', McEnroe said after the match. 'He really outplayed me, playing great tennis.' Hlasek never let the former world number one back into the match, breaking his service another four times with superb returns and passing shots and ending up a 7-6, 6-0, 6-3 winner. 'This win I will never forget. Maybe I will even tell my grandchildren about it,' Hlasek said. He had become the first Swiss winner of the Swiss Indoors.

39th International Championship of Sicily

By Nick Kennerley

Palermo, 23-29 September
Tournament Director: Cino Marchese

It's the best kept secret of the ATP Tour ', said umpire Gerry Armstrong as he adjusted the head-rest on his sun-lounger. Picture the scene: a swimming pool under a Saracan tower on a promontory surrounded by a beautiful blue sea. Under a cloudless sky the English umpire was discussing the finer points of tennis officialdom with tournament supervisor Mark Darby. Occasionally they abandoned their sun-loungers in favour of a cooling dip off the rocks. Swimming like a fish nearby was Communications Manager, Meg Donovan, who was also enjoying this rare opportunity to unwind. Breakfast had been a cappucino and a couple of pastries in a nearby restaurant, the sort of place that is ideal for people-watching. Nearly all the players participating in the 39th International Championship of Sicily were staying in the picture-postcard little fishing port of Mordello.

Another world away, but in fact only 12 kilometres by road, in the bustling town of Palermo, the tennis tournament was playing out a series of dramas with the Monte Pellegrino providing a magnificent backdrop to the theatre.

The charismatic Cino Marchese immediately saw the value of Yannick Noah to the tournament.

Enter Emilio Sanchez stage-left. The 26-year-old Spaniard was determined to break the Palermo jinx that had prevented him getting past the first round in three previous appearances. With 'eye of newt and toe of frog' the three witches gave him more than Banquo's ghost to trouble him, with tough matches against Martin Jaite and Thomas Muster en route to the final. His easiest match was his semi-final against Marian Vajde, the victor of a night-time encounter against Italian Diego Nargiso. This had been an exciting three-setter more reminiscent of an AC Milan/Inter Milan clash than a tennis match, with the crowd chanting and shouting for one man or the other and jumping up and down on the wooden platform that made up the stands.

The other half of the draw had seen the return of the charismatic Yannick Noah, who had recently been denied a wildcard entry to the U.S. Open. The tournament director here, Cino Marchese, a charismatic figure with his hair shining like a beacon, immediately saw the value of Noah to the tournament. The seats were full every time he played and even when he was drawn against the Italian, Claudio Pistolesi, he was the darling of the tournament. Above all he had come to play tennis and not the fool. There were moments of sheer brilliance and incredible athleticism, though a lack of match practice and of overall physical fitness eventually let him down. He fell in a three-set thriller to Jordi Arrese, who in turn met the French fresher Frederik Fontang in the semi-final.

Enter the French fresher stage-right. Fontang shot to a three-love lead in the first set and took it 6-3. Arrese replied with a three-love lead in the second and took that 6-2. At 4-4 in the third, Fontang broke Arrese's serve and served for the match. He too was broken. 5-5. Arrese served again but lost a close fought game. At 6-5 Fontang once again served for the match, only to squander two match

points and the game. In the tie-break Arrese saved two more match points before succumbing to Fontang in a highly disputed final point. Arrese argued that the chair umpire had missed a not-up call, but later television replays vindicated the umpire. Egged on by a vibrant Sicilian crowd, pure theatre had become melodrama.

As if to say he didn't believe in jinxes, let alone witches, Sanchez polished off the first set of the final, 6-1, in just half an hour. Fontang realised that he had to start putting some pressure on the Spaniard to have any chance at all and attacked his backhand. In the second set Fontang won a hard-fought first game, the turning point of the match. He broke the Sanchez serve in the next game and took the set 6-3. In the decider Fontang raced to a 4-0 lead, but this in turn spurred on the Spaniard to display incredible touch and timing with his drop shots, the hallmark of a world class clay courter. At 3-5 down Sanchez was serving to save the match when the Frenchman suffered an agonising cramp attack. He almost defaulted but somehow staggered on to the end of the game, miraculously breaking Sanchez's serve and winning the title. A kiss from girlfriend Valerie gave him just enough strength to stand up for the trophy presentation. The play had now changed from *Macbeth* to *Romeo and Juliet*. The producer, in his day job as tournament director, (Cino Marchese), single handedly held back the effusive Italian crowd.

It was a frustrating day for Emilio Sanchez because he then went on to lose the doubles final playing with his brother Javier. They were defeated in three sets by the Dutchmen, Jacco Eltingh and Tom Kempers, and by the Palermo jinx.

Frederik Fontang, a shock winner in Palermo, with girlfriend Valerie. *(A. Tonelli)*

One of the sponsors, Peugeot, capitalised on the theatrical nature of the tournament laying on a poolside dinner with syncronised swimmers, a light show and the launch of their new baby 106. Meanwhile back by the hotel pool in Mondello, umpire Gerry Armstrong towelled down after another refreshing dip in the deep blue sea and quietly repeated 'Palermo's the best kept secret on the ATP Tour. Let's keep it to ourselves – don't tell anyone.' Oops, sorry Gerry!

Queensland Open

By Tim Prentice

Brisbane, 23-29 September
Tournament Director: Graham Lovett

Milton Tennis Centre, nestled comfortably in the heart of sports-mad Brisbane, proved a drought-breaker in more ways than one during the $250,000 Queensland Open Championships. Australia's sunshine capital was experiencing an unusually dry spell for early spring and with temperatures hovering up around the 31°C mark, the locals were lamenting the lack of rain for more than two months.

On the ATP Tour, 'touch' players were also in the grip of a worrying title shortage. Power players, those with the cannonball serves and Howitzer groundstrokes to match, were pocketing one title after another. Enter Italian left-hander Gianluca Pozzi, aged 26 and with a world ranking of 136 – and Brisbane rain-clouds!

On the tournament's third day, the skies opened, dousing Brisbane and its outdoor (plexipave) court surface with its first rain for 65 days. By this time, Pozzi had already served notice that he was going to be a menace as the event unfolded. In the early rounds he fought long and hard to subdue Australian youngsters Sandon Stolle and Todd Woodbridge – each in three sets – to manufacture a quarter-final meeting with American Jim Grabb. With his racket strung at a lowly 44 lbs, the lanky Italian continually mixed up his shots, confusing and

Gianluca Pozzi became the first Italian ever to win a title in Australia. *(Sun Newspapers, Brisbane)*

Jason Stoltenberg holds
all the aces against the
mixed doubles team of
Samantha Thomson and
Andrew Kratzman. *(Sun
Newspapers, Brisbane)*

frustrating all challengers with deft placement and uncanny court coverage. At times, observers thought they were watching extracts from some John McEnroe-Ramesh Krishnan handbook. Pozzi's feathery touch and all-round steadiness prevailed 6-3, 6-1 over Aussie Jason Stoltenberg in the semi-final.

At the other end of the draw, American Aaron Krickstein was making shorter work of the opposition. After straight-setting Aussie pair John Fitzgerald and Mark Woodforde in the early rounds, the 1990 Brisbane finalist outmanoeuvred South African Wayne Ferreira 6-4, 6-3 in the quarters. Krickstein then out-slugged the hard-hitting Russian star Andrei Chesnokov 7-5, 6-4 in a tense semi-final.

The local fans expected anything but a Pozzi-Krickstein final but coming from the part of Australia that produced such all-time greats as Rod Laver and Roy Emerson, they turned up in good number (and voice) for the title decider.

Bamboozled by the Italian's precision placement and lack of pace, Krickstein dropped serve three times in the 102-minute match, won by Pozzi 6-3, 7-6 (7-4). It was an excited Pozzi who accepted the winner's cheque for $32,400 and his maiden ATP Tour singles title. Krickstein earned $19,090 and just failed to pass the magical $2 million mark in career earnings.

I had nothing to lose and just tried to play as relaxed as possible,' said Pozzi after becoming the first Italian ever to win a singles title in Australia. 'I played solid tennis throughout the week and made few mistakes. I knew I could do it.' Krickstein acknowledged that Pozzi was clearly the better player on the day. 'I was never able to get good rhythm on my returns and my serve nor did I feel comfortable hitting the ball,' he said. According to IBM Matchfacts, the American finished the week with 13 aces, just one fewer than Australia's Stoltenberg who sprang the biggest upset by ousting top seed and titleholder Brad Gilbert in the quarter-finals.

The Queensland Open doubles final featured the virgin combination of John Fitzgerald and Canada's Glenn Michibata. With a minimum of fuss, the top seeded duo powered to the final where they were confronted by the Aussie tandem of Todd Woodbridge and Mark Woodforde. Urged on by the enthusiastic gallery, the 'Woodys' rallied back from a service break down in the first set to clinch the final after a tightly fought tie-break – their fourth doubles triumph of the year.

The Queensland Open again served as a strong lead-up event for the rich Australian Indoor Championships in Sydney and will be recorded in tennis history books as a 'Drought Breaker' for a couple of special reasons.

Australian Indoor Tennis Championships

By Bruce Matthews

Sydney, 30 September-6 October
Tournament Director: Graham Lovett

He didn't win the tournament. He wasn't even around on finals day. Yet Goran Ivanisevic's legacy to the Australian indoor championships was immeasurable. His quarter-final and semi-final shoot-outs are as enshrined in the memories of those fortunate to be there as Stefan Edberg's name is similarly indelibly etched on the winner's trophy. Simply, gallant Goran was acclaimed the hero while satisfied Stefan ran off with his first Australian indoor singles title.

It's in no way disrespectful to Edberg to dwell on the power of Ivanisevic. Not merely to light up the IBM radar gun, but the smile on Graham Lovett at the sight of ticket box queues to Sydney's 12,000-seat Entertainment Centre. Even the flag-waving fervour of the noisy groups of Croat supporters, drawn by Ivanisevic's outspoken defence of his homeland's independence fight, was dampened as they temporarily forgot the political stance to ride the left-hander's awesome serve in a bold bid to reach another final.

For a while it seemed Edberg would stagger under the sustained bombardment of heavy first serves and Ivanisevic spotted the door slightly ajar at 4-3 with two serves to follow in the deciding set tie-break. But the world No. 1 emphatically kicked it shut, grabbing four of the next five points for the

4-6, 7-6, 7-6 semi-final victory suitably acknowledged by a standing ovation from the 10,000 truly fortunate spectators.

For the second successive night Ivanisevic had packed the cheap seats with young compatriots who would normally dispense their hard-earned dollars on Friday and Saturday nights at the harbour city's cinema strip less than a kilometre from the tournament site. Word spread fast of his ace-inspired 7-5, 7-6 quarter-final triumph over Andre Agassi. Croatia's self-appointed sporting ambassador fired a staggering 27 aces which the American later admitted was 'the most successful anyone has ever served against me'. Rather than be distracted by the often untimely support for his opponent, Agassi fed off the energy generated by the raucous 9000 fans. It was more the atmosphere generally reserved for local boxing world champ Jeff Fenech's bouts at the same venue. This time the humbled lost on points but no friends from one of the most sustained slugging matches ever witnessed in an Australian tennis tournament.

The fourth seeded American twice stood one point from squaring the match when Ivanisevic trailed 5-6 in the second set. Yet the 20-year-old from Split saved both in characteristic style – with thunderous aces. Gallant Agassi held eight break

The 12,000-seat Entertainment Centre packed out for the most successful Uncle Toby's event Graham Lovett had ever promoted. (Craig Gabriel)

points in that critical second set, only to watch helplessly as Ivanisevic saved seven with aces. 'I just wanted a look at one second serve on a break point,' Agassi lamented. 'I really can't look at myself and say I screwed it up. I was far from outmuscled and the only thing he did better than me was his first serve. Twenty-seven aces, incredible.' Agassi was still so hyped an hour later that he ordered two pizzas and settled down to watch a late night doubles match.

Lovett was moved to describe the quarter-final as 'the best atmosphere and tension in the 19 years of this tournament'. Appropriately, Ivanisevic thanked the loyal supporters he had mustered to courtside following an emotional pledge earlier in the week that he would be prepared to lay down his racket and pick up a rifle to defend his homeland in the civil war raging across Yugoslavia at the time. 'Aside from Davis Cup, that's the best crowd I've played in front of. They were great and I played great. I always play good in Australia,' Ivanisevic said.

Edberg hasn't got a bad Down Under record either, adding the Uncle Tobys sponsored indoor to his two Australian Open crowns. It often follows that finals day can be anti-climactic when compared to outstanding semi-final duels. And so it was as Edberg publicly dissected Brad Gilbert with the clinical precision of a skilled surgeon. So commanding was the Swede's 6-2, 6-2, 6-2 Sunday afternoon romp that the defenceless American, normally renowned for service returns, held just one break point. Gilbert was almost

apologetic to the crowd for such a lopsided 97-minute final, particularly considering the quality of the semi-finals.

Really, Gilbert's only chance was to reproduce the guile that somehow manufactured the amazing counter-attack which overran Pete Sampras 1-6, 7-5, 6-3 in their semi-final. He trailed 1-6, 2-4 before summoning his deft touch and vast experience to defuse the Sampras power and turn the match around with staggering speed. But against Edberg there was no escape from a tardy start. Gilbert's run to the final at least compensated for his early exit the previous week in Brisbane where he was defending Queensland Open titleholder. The wily tour veteran dragged young South African Wayne Ferreira back to reality with a 6-1, 6-4 whipping in the quarter-finals before conjuring the great escape against Sampras. Ferreira looked back on Sydney with satisfaction too after ousting three-times champ Ivan Lendl 6-4, 2-6, 7-5 in the third round.

But in the end it was Edberg who tightened his grip on the world No. 1 ranking. The new titleholder illustrated his more relaxed manner nowadays by opening a champagne magnum motor-racing style and spraying photographers from the victory dais on court. He then permitted himself a quick swig from the huge bottle to delight the fans. It was brief indulgence for the 25-year-old multi-millionaire who as runner-up had watched Boris Becker perform a similar spontaneous act the previous year. Funny, Stefan doesn't copy anyone these days. He leads by example.

Grand Prix de Toulouse

By Bruno Cuaz

Toulouse, 30 September-6 October
Tournament Director: Christian Bimes

Foie gras, pate en croute and ice cream: the menu was not your ideal diet. However, Guy Forget had made a point to attend the official dinner, held in the prestigious Salle des Colonnes of the Hotel-Dieu, on the eve of the Grand Prix de Toulouse singles final. Amos Mansdorf, his opponent, sat at a different table and tried the typical south-west French food more cautiously. In honour of the French Tennis Committee gathered in Toulouse, and of his guests, tournament director Christian Bimes offered a Mozart concert performed by a band selected among the National Orchestra of Toulouse.

The next day though, the atmosphere was back to sports with the final of the tenth Grand Prix de Toulouse and a rather easy 6-2, 7-6 victory for Guy Forget over Mansdorf, in the very city where the current top French player captured his first career title in 1986. Forget's father and grandfather had also once won this tournament. This time, Forget's mother and brother supported him as he won his fifth 1991 title after Sydney, Brussels, Cincinnati and Bordeaux. This success firmly settled him in his No 6 spot in the IBM/ATP Tour rankings, and secured his qualification for the ATP Tour World Championships. Never since the creation of the event in 1970 had a Frenchman won five tournaments in the same year, not even Yannick Noah.

Forget was, however, almost reluctant to play the tournament as he was suffering from influenza which was being treated by antibiotics, as well as having chronic tendonitis in his right knee that caused him to play with an impressive knee brace that reminded one of Yugoslav Goran Prpic's. But, 'Don't worry,' Forget explained, 'the pain is not proportional to the size of the knee brace.'

En route to the victory, Forget was mainly worried by two big servers. First Marc Rosset, who led 6-3, 3-2 in the quarters before bowing out to Forget's mental toughness, which enabled him to exploit his opponent's weaknesses and reverse the course of the match. The next day, in the semis Forget was up against 19-year-old Richard Krajicek. The young Dutchman, 6'4" tall, had masterfully ousted John McEnroe 6-2, 6-2 in the quarter-final round, and the once No 1 had praised his talent: 'I can see him among the top five very soon.' Krajicek's serve seemed unstoppable, and only in the last game Forget made the break. In that game, Krajicek passed only two first serves out of six. The Dutchman later explained that a hamstring injury had ruined the end of his match. Unfortunately, this great hope has now faced several minor injuries that might make him fall into the category of physically weak players.

The other revelation of the event was the Swedish junior player, Thomas Enqvist, winner of the 1991 Australian Open Junior and of the U.S. Open Junior. Enqvist got through the qualification rounds before putting up a superb fight against Marc Rosset in the second round of the singles main draw. Like his rival, Junior Soviet Andrei Medvedev, Enqvist firmly established himself on the men's tour. Toulouse presented new faces, but it was also the scene of Amos Mansdorf's return. His fantastic backhand delighted the crowds throughout the week. Israel's Number 1 had an extremely rough time at the start of the 1991 season, with the anguish of the Gulf War, followed by a more pleasant event, his wedding, which also shook and moved his private life. Toulouse was his first 1991 final, and he proved to be back to his best. However, in the final Forget was better and a French victory was undoubtedly the most appropriate way to celebrate the tenth anniversary of the Grand Prix de Toulouse.

Someone said he was as tall as Wilt Chamberlain. 'No, he isn't' said John McEnroe who knows about these things. The gregarious Mr. Hene, a French-based American artist, was happy to pose with John, his agent Sergio Palmieri (left) and tournament director Christian Bimes. *(Richard Evans)*

Athens International

By Lauren Goldenberg

Athens, 30 September-6 October
Tournament Director: Dionyssis Gangas

The 1991 Athens International proudly unveiled its new home for the final leg of the clay court season of the IBM/ATP Tour. Located on spacious land at the outskirts of the town, the courts at the recently completed Olympic Tennis Center are situated amongst a world-class sporting complex that includes an 80,000-seat stadium, velodrome and natatorium.

In fitting Olympic style, Barcelona's Sergi Bruguera, who stepped onto the clay courts in Estoril in April and captured his first career singles title, walked off the court in Athens with his third tournament victory and an impressive 38-9 clay court match record for 1991. In the one-hour and 28-minute final Bruguera battled with compatriot Jordi Arrese for a 7-5, 6-3 triumph.

In the third all-Spain final of 1991, Bruguera at last came out the winner following two consecutive losses to Emilio Sanchez in Barcelona and Gstaad. Bruguera successfully relied on his improved serve and attack game to secure the match in a hard-fought battle from the baseline. 'Arrese is one of the best clay court specialists,' explained Bruguera who converted on his sixth match point opportunity with an ace to win the match. 'He fights the whole match and doesn't give any presents. He is difficult to beat.'

Bruguera, who only the week prior played on the indoor courts of Basel, managed to readjust his game to the clay surface he prefers.

But the weather in Athens wreaked havoc on the new courts as play began under torrid, late summer skies forcing continuous water breaks to keep the choking dust at bay. Then without notice, winter rolled in from the north over the surrounding mountains dropping temperatures dramatically and producing incessant rain. Several matches were delayed including an exciting two-day come-from-behind win for Bruguera in the semi-finals against Austrian Thomas Muster. Muster took the first set easily and appeared to be on his way to his second final of the year, but Bruguera fought back to take the second set before the rain stopped the match early in the third with Bruguera up a service break. After a six-hour delay, the young Spaniard needed only nine minutes to finish off the Austrian for a 1-6, 6-2, 6-0 win and a berth in the final. Just four hours later, he returned to the court against Arrese and won the title.

Following the singles in a midnight doubles match, the Dutch duo of Jacco Eltingh and Mark Koevermans dropped the first set, but rallied back to defeat Menno Oosting and Olli Rahnasto 5-7, 7-6 (3), 7-5 for their first title as a team.

Sergi Bruguera finishing the year as he began it, having spanned Europe, winning trophies in Estoril, Monte Carlo and now Athens. *(Studio Kominis 3)*

Seiko Super Tennis

By Leo Schlink

Tokyo, 7-13 October
Tournament Director: Jun Kamiwazumi

Cherry blossom, sake, wondrous hospitality and fabulous Seiko Super Tennis form the vaunted Japanese fare on the IBM/ATP Tour each October. This year, the cavernous Metropolitan Gymnasium had something more to contend with – two typhoons!

Outside the imposing edifice of brilliant architectural precision, Japan's 21st typhoon of the season expelled a venomous barrage of rain and wind causing landslides throughout their nation... Within the stadium's vast boundaries, Swedish stylist Stefan Edberg unleashed similar acts of dynamism and, in the end, the understated serve-volley maestro was able to dispatch five opponents at the comfortable cost of just two sets dropped for his sixth win on the tour this season.

Ultimately the challenge of contending with the Edberg tempest, which had begun with victory at Flushing Meadow, and continued to gather momentum with another triumph at Sydney, fell to Californian Derrick Rostagno, who underlined a giant-killing reputation with successive wins over Boris Becker (quarter-finals) and Ivan Lendl (semi-finals). In the end, however, Rostagno's brave bid was of little avail. Edberg, with facile economy and an irresistible will to succeed, eventually triumphed 6-3, 1-6, 6-2 after overcoming a second-set scare. The result was doubly rewarding for Edberg

who earned $122,700 – and a gold racket valued at $64,000. Little wonder the Swede was last seen clasping his briefcase with more animation than ever. The outcome was equally deserved for tournament director Jun Kamiwazumi and an invariably industrious committee, for whom the largest problem was easily and rapidly solved. Capacity crowds, doubtless grateful to find as safe and as pleasurable a haven as the Metropolitan Gymnasium (which cost the not inconsiderable figure of $8000 an hour to keep open each day after 9pm) merely underlined the success of the 14th Seiko tournament.

By virtue of byes into the second round, and imposing form thereafter, Edberg, Andre Agassi, Ivan Lendl and Boris Becker – the four big guns as they were known locally – advanced to the quarter-finals where they were joined by Michael Chang, Goran Ivanisevic, David Wheaton and Derrick Rostagno. Classic confrontations by any measure. Appropriately, Edberg posted the swiftest transition into the semi-final round after a clinical 6-2, 6-2 dismissal of the ever-popular Michael Chang who, in his anxiety to become more offensive, may have facilitated Edberg's passage.

Ivanisevic, who somehow managed to put aside the difficulties of competing internationally while his native Croatia struggled

188

for self-rule, was spectacularly impressive in ousting a disconsolate Agassi for the second week in succession with a 6-3, 6-4 margin.

Lendl, the defending champion, avenged his Wimbledon defeat to the Minnesotan, Wheaton – but not before a titanic confrontation had left the Czechoslovakian to consider the closeness of the 7-6, 7-5 result.

On a drama-filled day, Rostagno seized the opportunity he had craved since a net-cord averted victory over Becker in the 1989 U.S. Open when, clutching a match point, Rostagno was denied by Becker's shot which caught the tape and bounced into undefended territory. History shows, of course, that Becker went on to win the U.S. Open. This time, however, the tennis gods looked upon Rostagno more favourably enabling him to win 7-6, 4-6, 6-3. The American, who became tennis' 98th millionaire in the course of a memorable week, was not done with yet. A 7-6, 6-2 success over Lendl underscored the crafty Californian's continued emergence.

In the top half, Edberg and Ivanisevic provided an intriguing joust to match their 4-6, 7-6, 7-6 encounter the previous week in Sydney. Again Edberg would prevail. This time the score was 4-6, 7-6, 7-5. Little wonder, then, both players felt a touch of deja vu. So to the final. Split sets ensured the decider would go to the wire. A brace of volleying errors from Rostagno's racket proved critical and allowed Edberg to express a greater insistence on victory. 'I'm just feeling good,' said Edberg, after registering his 17th consecutive win. 'The U.S. Open did a lot for my confidence and helped me believe in myself more. I'm on a winning streak, which happens once in a while.'

American duo Jim Grabb and Richey Reneberg knew exactly how Edberg felt. Eight days after teaming up for their first title of the season at Sydney, Grabb and Reneberg eclipsed top seeds Scott Davis and David Pate, 7-5, 2-6, 7-6 (7-5). Their Asian odessy came too late, however, for Grabb and Reneberg to qualify for the ATP World Doubles Championship in Johannesburg.

Boris Becker tries his hand at the traditional Seiko ceremony while Stefan Edberg and Shuzo Matsuoka look on. (Akio Matsumoto)

Holsten International

By Richard Evans

Berlin, 7-13 October
Tournament Director: Jochen Grosse

Arnaud Boetsch learning how to handle a press conference in Berlin. *(Richard Evans)*

With methodical precision and inexhaustible energy the polar bear was doing his laps in the water surrounding his rocky home at the Berlin zoo. Players wandering by from their nearby hotels could admire the huge creature's stoic stamina as well as the remarkable agility he showed, backflipping Olympic style off the wall underneath the gaping tourists.

Come October ATP Tour pros have stamina on their minds. Some find sufficient reserves of energy to make the final push, others would rather be in a pool somewhere, even if somewhat warmer than that enjoyed by our friend, the polar bear.

Petr Korda was for the push rather than the pool. Ever since an ankle injury at Key Biscayne back in March had impeded his progress, this cheerful Czech had seemed hell bent on making up for lost time, winning New Haven and reaching the final at Washington DC and Montreal in an impressive North American campaign. Now, at a tournament keen to start afresh in new surroundings, having moved to the spacious Deutschlandhalle from more cramped quarters the previous year, Korda was instrumental in wiping the slate clean. In the very first round, he removed the reigning champion, Ronald Agenor, 6-3 in the third and then, in the quarters, beat the 1990 finalist, Alexander Volkov, 6-3, 5-7, 6-1.

By that time sparse crowds had witnessed some strange happenings. Top seed Michael Stich, searching for inspiration in front of too many empty seats during an afternoon session, never discovered it against the ever-determined Anders Jarryd in the quarters and left many of his fans wondering why they had only bought tickets for the weekend.

Karel Novacek, whose performances over the year proved he had stamina to match any bear, was also caught by a veteran campaigner on one of those days when nothing works and went out in the first round to Kevin Curren.

Patrick Kuhnen, surprisingly finding himself the last German survivor, made the most of the No. 2 seed's early departure by beating Cedric Pioline on his way to the semi-final. But defeating a second Frenchman proved too much for Kuhnen who lost in straight sets to Arnaud Boetsch, a talented young man who thus made his first appearance in an ATP Tour final. Despite losing

6-3, 6-4 to Korda, Boetsch – who had played brilliantly to defeat Jonas Svensson 6-2, 6-1 in the second round – had taken a significant step forward in a career that promises to take off in 1992.

For Korda the week was a triumph. Not only did his versatile left-handed game enable him to quell Jarryd's challenge in the semis before outsmarting Boetsch but he also found the time – and the stamina – to help Novacek earn his first ever doubles title with a hard fought 3-6, 7-5, 7-5 win over Jan Siemerink and Daniel Vacek in the final.

There is someone else crucially connected with this tournament who has stamina – Jochen Grosse. Transferring his event from Frankfurt has not been an easy task but now, with the assistance of IMG's marketing talents and the benefit of a better venue, there is no reason why the tennis fans of Berlin should not come out and support a tournament that matches this year's young finalists for potential.

Riklis Israel Tennis Center Classic

By Lauren Goldenberg

Tel Aviv, 7-13 October
Tournament Director: Ian Froman

For the past fifteen years, the Israel Tennis Center has provided the children of Israel with a special quality of life through the sport of tennis. Over 150,000 children, in 11 centers around the country, have benefited from this unique programme that successfully uses tennis as a vehicle for enrichment, education and sportsmanship. For the week of October 7, the children of the Ramat Hasharon center put aside their rackets and lend their courts to the professionals of the IBM/ATP Tour for the 13th annual Riklis Israel Tennis Center Classic.

At this year's tournament a more optimistic atmosphere prevailed after a difficult inauguration onto the IBM/ATP Tour in 1990 due to the Gulf crisis. A record number of players descended upon the Holy Land to compete for the $150,000 purse.

An unlikely candidate claimed the $18,000 first prize. Qualifier Leonardo Lavalle, who came into the tournament ranked 218, became the 15th first-time singles title winner this year with a 6-2, 3-6, 6-3 win over South African Christo van Rensburg in a nearly two-hour Saturday final. The lanky left-hander from Mexico City is the third qualifier to capture a title in 1991. 'It's been a dream week for me. I was just hoping to get through qualifying,' the 24-year-old Lavalle said. 'I was just planning to get some practice. This is spectacular.' Lavalle ends an eight-year singles title dry spell for Mexico. Paul Ramirez last won in Caracas in 1983.

On the way to the final, Lavalle disposed of the top seed Russian Andrei Cherkasov in the quarter-finals, but the Mexican's success in Tel

Leo Lavalle – a surprise Mexican winner in Tel Aviv.
(Tennis Sport Israel)

Why is this man smiling? Gilad Bloom at the player's party. *(Tennis Sport Israel)*

Aviv was not limited to singles. With partner Javier Frana of Argentina, the top-seeded pair reached the doubles final falling to the first-time pair and second-seeded duo of David Rikl of Czechoslovakia and Michiel Schapers of the Netherlands 6-2, 6-7 (7), 6-3.

Van Rensburg also experienced success and renewed confidence with his result in Tel Aviv. Plagued with a difficult year, van Rensburg fell out of the top 100 for the first time since 1986. The likeable South African, who has played in Israel several times and captured the Challenger title in Jerusalem the week before Tel Aviv,

apologized to the crowds for defeating the two local favourites, Israelis Amos Mansdorf and Gilad Bloom, on the way to his first singles final since Orlando last year.

Special guests at the Riklis tournament included a group of 450 overseas founders, major contributors to the Israel Tennis Centers who came to Israel to celebrate the 'Bar Mitzvah' year of the tournament, a religious observance marking adulthood. With its special brand of Israeli hospitality, the Riklis Israel Tennis Center Classic has matured into one of the most enjoyable and popular weeks on the IBM/ATP Tour.

Grand Prix de Tennis de Lyon

By Richard Evans

Lyon, 14-20 October
Tournament Director: Gilles Moretton

A year before, troubled and hurting, Pete Sampras had been forced to withdraw from Gilles Moretton's fine tournament with shin splints. The Californian teenager was just beginning to discover that being the youngest ever U.S. Open champion was not as much fun as he might have thought. It was a much wiser and much happier Sampras who finally honoured his commitment to this popular event in France's second city and the state of his mind was refelected in the state of his play. *Formidable!*

Far from dropping a set, Sampras lost only eighteen games all week on the medium fast indoor carpet. The stinging penetration of his first serve and the smooth fluency of an overall game that hides no weaknesses proved far too much for opposition that would, under normal circumstances, have been considered highly dangerous. Wimbledon quarter-finalist Thierry Champion was swept aside 6-1, 6-3, in the second round and two-time French Open semi-finalist Jonas Svensson was also allowed only four games. In the semi-final, Brad Gilbert

Brad Gilbert chats to tournament director Gilles Moretton (left) and Patrice Dominquez, the former French No1 who is now head of sport at La Cinq TV.
(Richard Evans)

Plenty for Pete Sampras to smile about as he hoists the Korloff trophy. But it was a different story when he returned for the Davis Cup Final. (Serge Philippot)

was hoping for a repeat of his victory over Pete at the Sydney Indoors just two weeks before. The hope was stillborn. Sampras obliterated one of the Tour's most experienced and solid campaigners 6-1, 6-2.

The top half of the draw had been full of interest. The talented, two handed French teenager Fabrice Santoro ended Marc Rosset's reign as defending champion in the first round but then found himself confronted by a player he might only just have heard of – Johan Kriek. After being off the Tour for more than a year, Kriek was benefitting from the new ATP Tour ruling that allows players a certain number of direct entries at their old ranking once they have recovered from injury.

Blazing away in that style reminiscent of old, Kriek startled Santoro 6-4, 6-4 but was then surprised himself by the power and accuracy of Olivier Delaitre whose weekend wedding to Emmanuelle had only seemed to heighten his determination to prove that he, too, was a force in French tennis.

In the first round Delaitre had repaid Moretton's offer of a wild card with one of those presents tournament directors receive with reluctance – the elimination of their top seed. An impressive

title winner in Toulouse just two weeks before, Guy Forget now found himself bundled out of the first round 1-6, 6-4, 6-3 by a stocky, pugnacious competitor who looked just as well built for the job of scrum half in France's World Cup rugby team as he did for the Davis Cup squad he would soon be joining. Even after puncturing Kriek's return, Delaitre was not finished. No 3 seed Sergi Bruguera was his next victim in the semi-finals and by now the enthusiastic crowds who had been packing the circular seating in the pleasingly designed Palais de Sports day and night all week were fully behind their new found hero.

But the Lyonais fans know their tennis and they quickly realised the only thing to do on finals day was to sit back and admire tennis of supreme quality from the young man who had earmarked the gold, silver and bronze Korloff trophy for himself from day one. Pete Sampras was an emphatic winner 6-1, 6-1 and an exceptional champion.

In the doubles the increasingly effective partnership of Tom Nijssen and Cyril Suk continued their late charge for Johannesburg and the ATP Tour World Doubles Finals by securing the title with a 7-6, 6-3 win over Steve Devries and David MacPherson.

CA Tennis Trophy

By Hermann Fuchs

Vienna, 14-20 October
Tournament Director: Leo-Gunther Huemer

In Vienna you usually have a house-warming party when you move into a new apartment or a new house; a custom that tournament director Leo-Gunther Huemer adopted for the CA-Trophy. On the evening after the qualification round all players as well as sponsors and people helping in the organisation met for a social gathering in the players' lounge of the Vienna Stadthalle. Apart from the almost proverbially delicious Viennese food and low piano music, two magicians guaranteed the success of the party. Their tricks with cards and ribbons and their ability to make things disappear and reappear inspired admiration and almost neverending applause.

The morning after the organisers probably would have given a bundle for the ability to make something appear. At a presentation of his racket company that also featured top alpine and nordic skiers ('Fischer' only entered tennis after having produced skis for decades) the main attraction was missing. Michael Stich, seeded number one at the CA-Trophy, excused himself because he had to see a doctor in Germany. A dislocated vertebra that had to be put in place would delay his arrival for several hours. This made suspicious people immediately see the message as an excuse for an early loss or even a no-show altogether.

Mark Kratzmann and Jason Stoltenberg need to lean and stretch at the opulent Plaza Hotel after flying in from Tokyo. *(Richard Evans)*

The sceptics were proved wrong. Impressively. Not only did the Wimbledon champion show up in time for the already scheduled TV-talkshow at the City Hall, he also showed clearly why he is ranked in the top five on the IBM/ATP computer. After 'mandatory' wins over Leonardo Lavalle and Patrick McEnroe on his 23rd birthday, he almost destroyed old nemesis Anders Jarryd who had not only beaten him in Vienna last year, but also only a few days before in Berlin.

I feel great,' Michael stressed several times, 'I really enjoy playing here.' Maybe a night at the Andrew Lloyd-Webber musical *Phantom of the Opera*, that was on his agenda on a free evening, also played some small part in that...

So it was no big wonder that Stich was playing a leading role in THE match of the tournament. Of the many top games that the fans saw in the course of the week (Andrei Cherkasov versus Amos Mansdorf for instance, which the Russian won after three tie-breaks, a first ever for Vienna; or Richard Krajicek's win against the young Austrian Thomas Buchmayr; or Jan Siemerink's surprise victory over second-seeded Jakob Hlasek – to name only a few), the semi-final of the number one seed against 23-year-old Czechoslovakian Petr Korda just beat everything. Some absolutely fantastic rallies made the 8000 fans cheer for minutes. And again the German surprised everybody: even when his opponent hit the most unbelievable shots, Stich was all smiles. What a positive contrast to the robotesque way a lot of players behave on the court.

The final could not quite meet the high expectations that the semi-final had created. Jan Siemerink (who after Hlasek had also beaten the number one local hero, last year's finalist Horst Skoff, and German Charlie Steeb) was way too nervous to really challenge Michael Stich.

My game is all serve-volley,' the teenager from the Netherlands explained, 'but my serve just did not work today.' A statement that was underlined by three double faults in the very first game. So it took Stich only 105 minutes to win all three sets 6-4 – and by doing so to become the only player to win at least one tournament of the IBM/ATP Tour on each of the four surfaces this year. Grass at Wimbledon, clay in Stuttgart, hard courts in Schenectady and now Supreme in Vienna.

For the 1990 winner Anders Jarryd, this time eliminated by Stich in the quarter-finals, the doubles was a little bit of a consolation. Together with South African Gary Muller he won a dramatic final against number one seeds Hlasek and Patrick McEnroe.

Gary Muller looking relaxed and colourful in front of a photographic mural of the Vienna Woods. *(Richard Evans)*

Stockholm Open

By Georges Honsi

Stockholm, 21-27 October
Tournament Director: Johan Flink

In a way, it was a repetition of what happened at the Australian Open last January. The bottom line is that Boris Becker won the tournament after a long and thrilling final. And on both occasions, the German champion was lucky to reach the final as, earlier in the tournament, he came awfully close to losing to the same man: Omar Camporese. In Melbourne, Becker ended up winning 14-12 in the last set. At the Globe Arena in Stockholm if the final result 4-6, 7-5, 6-3 doesn't look as impressive, the danger for him was at least as big. Hitting huge serves one after the other, and controlling the baseline rallies with his usual touch, Camporese went up to lead by one set and 3-1 in the second. He even held a point for 4-1 and his serve to come. An hour later, Becker left the court victorious. 'Every time I meet Camporese, he plays some incredible tennis, and I know that sooner or later he's going to beat me,' Becker admitted afterwards. From that moment, Becker started playing better and better after every match. In the quarters, he avenged his loss to Pete Sampras last summer in Indianapolis, by defeating 'Petie' 7-5, 7-5, and went on to dominate the world number 3 player, Jim Courier in three sets.

Stockholm doubles champions John Fitzgerald and Anders Jarryd watch Niklas Jarryd struggle to get into the yoghurt.
(Richard Evans)

Still talking – Stefan Edberg and Boris Becker after their thrilling five set final. *(Gianni Ciaccia)*

As astonishing as it may sound, the finals which opposed Becker to Stefan Edberg, the crowd's favourite, was the first meeting between the top two players in the world in 1991. They hadn't played each other since the Paris Indoor final last year when Becker was forced to retire after just a few games. But for Becker, the challenge was particularly interesting. He was trying to capture his first tournament since his success in Australia at the start of the year. A victory would also end the streak of 21 straight matches won by Edberg, since his loss to Lendl in the Long Island final. And by retaining his title in Stockholm Becker would remain at least for another week, the number 2 player on the IBM/ATP Tour computer. Still, Edberg was the clear favourite, having really impressed in the semi-finals against Aaron Krickstein who could only win four games. 'I could hardly play any better,' Edberg admitted after defeating Krickstein. 'I'm not afraid of him,' Becker claimed firmly to the Swedish press trying to make him say the contrary.

In the final, although he didn't look the victor all the way, Becker finally proved able to get his second tournament win of the year. For that, he needed three hours and 17 minutes to defeat Edberg, and get crowned for the third time in Stockholm. After Edberg won the first set 6-3 breaking serve twice, he played a careless service game allowing Becker to benefit from an early break. 'That was the turning point,' Becker admitted later. 'Suddenly, I was back in the match. And once I won the second set, I felt like I had a chance to win the match.'

But he didn't expect at this stage what was going to happen in the third set where the Swede went for everything, hardly missing a shot. 'There wasn't much I could do at this stage, but I thought he couldn't go on playing that well for very long. I thought he was going to calm down sometime hopefully.' Suddenly, in the fourth set, Edberg started missing more first serves allowing his rival to attack him. At the same time, Boris picked up

Gianni Ciaccia's view of the spectacular Globe Arena. *(Gianni Ciaccia)*

the level of his own serve. That made the difference. 'I just lost the rhythm of my serve. I felt pain on my right elbow for one game but then it went away,' Edberg explained, refusing to give any excuse for winning four games in the last two sets.

The 13,000 people who filled the Globe Arena's Stadium was a little disappointed to see the champion refuse to make a speech before receiving the trophy. 'After three and a half hours, it is difficult to find the right words. In general, I'm not a big speaker. I just want to leave the stadium and be by myself,' Becker explained later. No one can blame him for that. But he admitted this week was very special to him. 'To tell the truth, every victory over Edberg is important. Every time we meet, I try very hard to win. But it certainly does feel good to win a whole tournament again, especially when you beat the number 6, 3 and 1 in a row.'

Runner up in Stockholm for the second year running, Edberg was sure disappointed not to win at home. 'It would have been nice also to win by 22nd straight match as I would have beaten my own record set last year. But at least, this year, it was a good final.' But Edberg wasn't the only Swede to do well that week. The surprise came from David Engel, a member of the famous Tim Klein team. Coming from he qualifying rounds, Engel upset Nicklas Kulti in the first round and then realised the best win of his career so far by defeating David Wheaton. It didn't look very good for Engel on court number 1 when Wheaton capture the first set and went on to a 4-1 lead in the second. 'At this stage, he lost a little bit of intensity, and I played very well,' explained Engel who finally won 7-6 in the third set. And although he lost to Pete Sampras in the following round, he has nothing to blush about as he threatened 'Petie' all the way only bowing out 6-4 in the third. This remarkable week was still not enough for Engel to be chosen by the Swedish tennis journalists' association 'Gurs och Gräs' as the satisfaction of the year. Under the presidency of Björn Hellberg, the association had its biannual meeting during the Stockholm Open and elected Thomas Enqvist for his remarkable performances in the junior Grand Slam events this year.

There were many impressive recoveries during the week similar to Engel's against Wheaton. Jakob Hlasek facing Jan Siemerink in the second round saved three match points - two in the second and one in the third set - to come out as the winner after he trailed 2-5 in the final set. One should also mention Aaron Krickstein's fine week where he upset the Wimbledon champion Michael Stich in the second round finishing with a love set in the third. 'I'm hitting the ball better than ever now that I've changed racket,' said Krickstein who went on the semi-finals.

Although ranked third in the world, it was somewhat surprising to find Jim Courier in the semi-finals where he lost to Becker. This was his first tournament since playing the U.S. Open final six weeks earlier. 'I had to withdraw from Sydney and Tokyo because of a shoulder tendinitis. I had played so much that my whole body was broken,' Courier said. Most evidently he was back in perfect shape.

The Stockholm Open attracts international TV coverage. Here Italy's Ubaldo Scanagatta interviews Jim Courier. (Richard Evans)

Bliss Cup

By Lauren Goldenberg

Guaruja, 21-27 October
Tournament Director: Ricardo Bernd

Paradise revisited. The IBM/ATP Tour returned to Guaruja, Brazil for the second event of 1991 for the start of a three-week tennis adventure in the Southern Hemisphere. The inaugural Bliss Cup, hosted by the Casa Grande Hotel, officially opened the summer season of this seaside retreat. The stadium, built around the hotel courts, afforded two splendid views: on one side the beach with its inviting blue water and pristine white sand and on the other side, the lush, green mountains which separate Guaruja from the industrial city of Santos and the bustling metropolis of Sao Paulo beyond.

The action on the beach was matched only by the action on the courts and the enthusiastic crowds witnessed a series of tennis firsts. In the

Finalist Markus Zoecke seems to be listening to winner Javier Frana despite attendant distractions. *(Nilton Lazzarini)*

The beach is never very far away when tennis is played in Guaruja. *(Nilton Lazzarini)*

final, the left-handed Argentinian Javier Frana, captured his first career singles title with a 2-6, 7-6 (1), 6-3 victory over the giant serving German and first-time finalist Markus Zoecke. In an impressive effort of sheer guts and determination, Frana battled his way through the draw coming from behind after losing the first set in three of his five matches to become the 16th first-time singles winner this year on the IBM/ATP Tour.

The slow hardcourt surface of the Casa Grande courts was the perfect equaliser for the 32-draw with its eclectic mix of claycourt specialists and proven hardcourt players. Among the claycourters were several 1991 title winners including the top seed Thomas Muster of Austria, looking for his first win on hardcourts since September 1990 at the U.S. Open, Guillermo Perez-Roldan of Argentina, and Spaniard Jordi Arrese. Local hero Luiz Mattar and Dutchman Paul Haarhuis headed the opposition in battle for the $150,000 in prize money. In the end, the two serve and volleyers, Frana and Zoecke, managed to outplay the rest under a blazing Brazilian sun. 'This is the best day of my life,' Frana said after the match. When asked about the secret to his win over the powerful German,

he said, 'I concentrated really well due to my past experience with top players and in Davis Cup. I think this was the difference.' Frana, who started out the year at No. 183, came into Guaruja ranked 79 following several impressive results throughout the season including a final finish at Newport. His title run broke his previous career high ranking of 70 (in April 1988) to a new mark of 62. Zoecke also claimed a new personal best from 91 to 67.

The 'Double Dutch' theme continued to prevail on the IBM/ATP Tour with the latest duo of Paul Haarhuis and Jacco Eltingh claiming the doubles title at Guaruja with a 6-3, 7-5 defeat of the first-time tandem of Bret Garnett and Todd Nelson of the United States.

The action in Guaruja was not limited to the tennis courts. The competition moved daily to the beach for intense soccer clashes while others preferred body surfing in the unpredictable waves of the Atlantic. In the cool, refreshing evenings, the heavily anticipated Miss Nivea beauty contest and an inspiring show by popular Brazilian singer Jane Duboo entertained an appreciative group of players and sponsors.

Open de la Ville de Paris

By Philippe Bouin

Paris, 28 October-3 November
Tournament Director: Patrice Clerc

At last! The Paris Open tournament, the highest prize money Series Championship with $2 million, has taken six years to get to 'its' final. At long last! Six years were needed for this rich heir to the former French Indoor International Championship to enjoy a French winner.

After a three-hour 46-minute tight final, punctuated by 53 aces, Guy Forget went up to the net to shake the hand of his defeated opponent, Pete Sampras. At the same time, the entire stadium with its 14,660 spectators gave him a standing ovation. Guy Forget had just killed two birds with

Guy Forget – a rare trophy for a victory of rare importance for French tennis.
(David Vincent)

A quarter past three and a long afternoon ahead for Pete Sampras who went down in a five-set thriller. (Gianni Ciaccia)

The 1991 tournament gave Paris satisfaction. Nothing was missing, neither the stars, nor the surprises, nor the emotion, nor a great final. A cocktail able to satisfy the most demanding crowd: the Paris Open public being the most demanding crowd in the world. And the most enthusiastic.

Though the 'clay planet' of the French Open is mainly reserved for the affiliated members of the French Tennis Federation, the Paris Open tickets are put on sale to the public. In that way, Bercy's public is probably the youngest and the most popular in the world, at least during the first three days. Going through Paris, from clay to Taraflex, tennis gains not only speed but also power. Cruelty as well. By the end of the tournament, when ticket prices rise, the population in the stadium is back to the age and behaviour which suit the higher class visitors to the sponsors' village. This village is a superb copy of the wine and spirit stores which were formerly found in the district of Bercy, entirely devoted to the spirits trade.

As the Flushing Meadow public, the Bercy public like to see blood run. The first was that of the young French player, Fabrice Santoro. A stroke of luck played a nasty trick on this young 18-year-old hope, twice chosen in the French Davis Cup team this year. In fact, the draw produced his own captain, Yannick Noah, as his opponent for the first round. Just out of his singing retirement (his first record was in the top of the charts in France last summer), Noah decided to test himself in Bercy having in mind a possible return for the Davis Cup final - France versus the United States - a month and a half later in Lyon. On good form, serving as in his best days, supported by the public, the captain gobbled up his young lieutenant, 7-5, 6-3. Stimulated by the approaching Davis Cup, other French players came through, such as qualifier Rodolphe Gilbert who beat Anders Jarryd in the first round 2-6, 7-5, 7-5; and Arnaud Boetsch. Beating Andrei Chesnokov in the first round, Arnaud took the opportunity of Michael Stich's withdrawal (because of a tennis elbow injury) to reach the second round. Another Russian player, Alexander Volkov, was to stop him in the quarter-final, 7-5, 6-2.

one ball: his win and the way he managed it, gave both the tournament and its winner national prestige which up to now was missing for both of them.

Since Yannick Noah's win at the French Open in 1983, Paris was longing for such a triumph. Of course, Boris Becker's win in 1986 and 1988 and Stefan Edberg's in 1990 added great names to the list of tournament winners; of course, the five sets final won by Tim Mayotte against Brad Gilbert in 1987 was an epic one. However, Paris never fascinated the crowd. Indeed, the previous year, the tournament was included in the ATP Tour and nine of the top ten players were in the draw. Because of these two factors, 97,000 spectators had come to the Palais Omnisport de Paris Bercy, a record for an indoor tournament with only one session a day. But, 1990 had a miscarried final: due to his thigh injury, Boris Becker had to give up after only six games. And Paris was left unsatisfied.

Aided by a little good fortune, Jonas Svensson's Parisian love affair continued at Bercy. *(Gianni Ciaccia)*

In the meantime, a lot of blood had run. First of all, blood of old celebrities. The same day, on Wednesday, Yannick Noah, John McEnroe and Jimmy Connors disappeared. Easily defeated by Derrick Rostagno, 6-3, 6-3, Noah could verify that two weeks of jogging were not enough to sweep the toxins of a year's retirement away. After a tight first round against defeated Agenor (5-7, 6-4, 6-2), Jimmy Connors, as at the U.S. Open, was under Jim Courier's thumb 6-2, 6-3, to the great displeasure of his adoring public. As far as John McEnroe was concerned, he had to deal with one of the most dangerous players of the moment,

Goran Ivanisevic. It was a sparkling fight. McEnroe was given one penalty point. Ivanisevic served 16 aces. Strength was on the side of youth.

After the old players, it was the stars' turn to be thunderstruck. On Thursday, the first three top players vanished. First of all, Becker gave up, knocked flat not by Jonas Svensson but rather by a 'flu virus which kept him in bed. As a result, he had to inevitably give up his No. 2 ranking to Jim Courier at the end of the week. This new responsibility did not make the French Open winner particularly happy: hardly a few hours after Becker had scratched,

Courier fell as well, knocked out by Omar Camporese's subtle punch; the Italian player had already beaten Jakob Hlasek in the previous round.

Another French Open champion, Michael Chang, happened to be the hero of the day. And, as in the 1989 French Open final, his victim was Stefan Edberg. Though Edberg had started well by winning the first set 6-2, he was playing his 93rd singles of the year. In the end, tiredness caught up with him when Chang, thanks to unquestionable progress, started an attacking game. An hour and a half later, Edberg left the tournament downcast.

In the quarter-finals, Chang and Svensson got the better of Korda and Novacek, the two Czechoslovakian players who, at the end of the week, were going to join Lendl among the top ten. For his part, Pete Sampras dictated his game to Alexander Volkov (6-2, 6-3). Sampras had done the hardest work in the previous round; he had beaten Ivanisevic in spite of the 26 aces served by a boy who had explained the day before that he didn't want to be referred to as a Yugoslavian.

Easy victor over Patrick McEnroe in the first round (6-3, 6-2), Guy Forget had more problems beating Rostagno, 4-6, 6-3, 6-1, and later Omar Camporese, 6-1, 3-6, 6-3. Once he was in the semis, he was more efficient against Svensson (7-5, 6-4) than Sampras, who lost one set against Chang, 2-6, 6-4, 6-3.

In the final, for quite a while the American gave the impression that he was going to be the winner. Though he lost the first set at the tie-breaker, Sampras was more aggressive and led two sets to one and 3-1 in the fourth. Forget then showed the progress which had already enabled him to win five tournaments this year. He leapt at Sampras's throat, and thanks to a series of winners, snatched the fourth set. Being back two sets all, and cheered by an enthusiastic crowd, Forget was not going to release his prey. After a three-hour 46-minute match, he could brandish the trophy (the work of Italian sculptor Lucio Fanti), a bronze genealogical tree inscribed with the names of all the players.

In the doubles, Anders Jarryd and John Fitzgerald were delighted to add the Paris Open title to their list for the year, which included the French Open, Wimbledon and the U.S. Open. But the most watched match proved to be the quarter-final won by Ken Flach and Robert Seguso against Yannick Noah and Henri Leconte, with the Davis Cup final waiting on the horizon.

The mock columns and statues in the players dining room are appreciated almost as much as the food. Anders Jarryd, John Fitzgerad (forefront) Laurie Warder and Wally Masur tuck in. (Richard Evans)

Kolynos Cup

By Jonathan Marks

Buzios, 28 October-3 November
Tournament Director: Paulo Ferreira

If you think that you've seen all there is to see on the tennis tour you haven't until you've been to one of the ATP Tour's Brazilian events. For here you must expect the unexpected and marvel at crowds who wander in from the beach to take in a match and end up making the competitors look positively over-dressed.

Extravagant corporate hospitality characterises tournaments in Brazil and the Kolynos Cup was to be no exception. Guests of Kolynos were treated to more than a mere marquee and a couple of canapes. Lodged on their very own island, Nas Rochas, they were entertained throughout the week with parties that sambaed well into the early morning. The traditional tournament cars were replaced by 'courtesy cruises' that ferried the guests to a tournament that rarely got under way before the early afternoon. Nor was the players' chosen mode of transport particularly conventional. In what is, after all, Senna country the pros hired beach buggies for the week and when not sighted tearing down the town's main drag they were to be found racing each other on one of Buzios' beautiful local beaches.

Emilio Sanchez and Thomas Muster, seeded first and second, held pole positions in one of the strongest draws seen in Brazil. The Spaniard,

Spain's Jordi Arrese, triumphant after winning his first hardcourt title. (J.B. Salgado)

The new Brazilian No. 1
Jaime Oncins looks
suitably pleased.
(J.B. Salgado)

however, was to be the victim of a poor start, despatched by the in-form German Marcus Zoecke in the first round. Muster survived until the quarter-finals but was put out by Francisco Roig in a tight three-set battle. Local attention was focused on Jaime Oncins whose progress as far as the last eight had ensured a sufficient injection of computer points to lift him above Luis Mattar and into the position of Brazilian number one. As Oncins progressed to the semis and local excitement and expectations reached fever pitch it seemed possible that the weekend's tennis on the mainland might equal the party atmosphere at Nas Rochas. But just as the crowd were undressing and gearing up for a good Saturday afternoon of tennis the unexpected happened – it rained.

At a tournament where nothing was being done by halves it would have been foolish to count on a light drizzle or a passing shower. It poured for the whole weekend, and when play was finally abandoned late on Sunday afternoon both the semi-finals remained unresolved. It seemed for a while

as if the only competitor that would leave Buzios with a winners cheque would be the young lady who had been crowned 'Miss Kolynos' at Saturday night's rather damp proceedings at Nas Rochas.

But on Monday the rain abated and Oncins and Arrese progressed to the final. Oncins had strong hometown support behind him but Arrese, who had dealt with the media circus surrounding his match with Borg in the spring, had too much experience, too cool a head and, in the end, too many shots for his younger opponent to combat. A Spanish clean sweep was completed when a revitalised Casal and Sanchez saw off Frana and Lavalle in the doubles final.

As the players and tour officials breathed a collective sigh of relief and hurried off to the next event in Sao Paolo, there was time for them to reflect that Buzios had come close to surprising even these veterans of Brazilian events. Who could have predicted just how close we had come to settling a Brazilian tournament indoors?

Diet Pepsi Indoor Challenge

By Chris Martin

Birmingham, 4-10 November
Tournament Director: Josh Ripple

Michael Chang carved himself another piece of tennis history – albeit a small one – when he won the Diet Pepsi Indoor Challenge in November. The 19-year-old from Placentia, California, became the first tennis player to win a tournament at what was at the time a brand new site, the 6,500 seater National Indoor Arena in Birmingham. The $500,000 tournament was only the second event of any kind to be staged there. It was of course nothing to match his previous entry into the history books as the youngest French Open winner in 1990 but it was nevertheless the perfect way for Chang to end a title drought that had lasted more than a year. 'It always feels good to win no matter what time of year it is,' said Chang after beating Guillaume Raoux 6-3, 6-2 in the 66-minute final.

Producing his best in the final week of the regular season is becoming something of a habit for Chang. It was his third successive trip to the final of this event which from 1976 until the 1990 tournament was played at the Wembley Arena in London.

But Chang will not be the only player to have fond memories of his first visit to Birmingham. Raoux will also have a warm glow in his heart when he looks back. Although he did not meet a seed until the semi-finals where he beat fellow

countryman Thierry Champion 6-3, 6-4, he certainly had to work extremely hard for his first appearance in a tour final in four years of trying. Along the way he played two exhausting three-set matches back to back and in the end that proved too much for the bespectacled Frenchman. 'I didn't play my first match until Wednesday and I didn't get a break so it was very tiring for me'.

John McEnroe and Pat Cash, two more regulars from the tournament's London days joined Chang as the star attractions – although not for too long. Unfortunately for the tournament a somewhat lacklustre McEnroe ran into an in-form Alexander Mronz of Germany, a player who has often threatened to shoot down a big name but never quite managed it., This time he stuck to his guns defeating the former world number one 6-3, 4-6, 6-3 in the first round on the Wednesday night. On Thursday McEnroe was on his way back to New York via Concorde. These days McEnroe's game is engulfed in frustration, not at the officials, although they do still test his wrath, but at his racket. For some reason it just won't do what it is told.

But Cash playing his first tournament since Wimbledon at least lasted one round longer than McEnroe before falling to the unpredictable Ronald Agenor of Haiti. For a change Cash's

Despite the switch from London to Birmingham, there was still no stopping Michael Chang who won his second indoor title in Britain. (Bob Thomas Photography)

absence from the circuit was not through injury as it had so often been in the past. 'I was just really tired and missed my wife and kids, so I took a long break to be with them.' As a result future appearances on the tour by the 1987 Wimbledon champion could be few and far between. 'I have worked very hard over the years and now I don't really want to commit myself to play as much as I used to. But having played at Birmingham I must say I still enjoy doing battle,' said Cash. The 26-year-old Australian then added, 'As far as the tournament is concerned I think it was very well run and has a good future.'

Despite an apparent lack of enthusiasm from the Birmingham public the joint organisers Pro-Serve and the Lawn Tennis Association are determined to mould the event into something the locals will be proud of. In a bid to increase the profile of the tournament and attract more star names the prize money will be increased for 1992 to $600,000. Certainly the LTA are standing firmly behind the event. Their chief executive Ian Peacock said in his organisation's financial report for 1991, 'Although we made a loss on the event this year I am confident that in the magnificence of the National Indoor Arena the tournament can be turned around and become a popular feature of the British tennis calendar.' And he added: 'It is important to keep the event in Britain in order to avoid compounding the British perception that tennis is only played four weeks of the year in June and July.' The LTA has another two years of their contract with the NIA to run. However, judging by those words and with a little help from the public who were noticeable mainly for their absence, the arena could be hosting a major tennis event for several years to come.

Bayer Kremlin Cup

By Eugene L. Scott

Moscow, 4-10 November
Tournament Director: Eugene L. Scott

Pushkin lives. The greatest storyteller in Russian history would have a field day plucking plots from events in his country over the past twelve months. Indeed these political plots have had dramatic beginnings, uncertain mid-sections and few conclusions – a fertile playground for a poet's imagination.

A Russian (Andrei Cherkasov) defeating an American (Tim Mayotte) in last year's final of the first major tennis championships on the largest landmass on earth, was at least a pilot in the name of perestroika, glasnost and failed coup. What possibly could be a convincing encore? Try this unlikely theme. The finalist (Jakob Hlasek) trails 0-5 in his first round final set against Branislav Stankovic. He survives, progresses to the championship round against the same Cherkasov and himself holds a handful of match points only to fall in a third-set tie-breaker. Thus a Russian defends his initial career triumph in an unlikely homeland for such fairy-tale endings.

A postscript would make a first-year history student blush at its sweaty irony. The winners of the doubles title were Germans Jelen and Steeb over Russians Cherkasov and Volkov some fifty years after Herr Ribbentrop signed his villainous non-aggression pact with comrade Molotov.

Happy on court, Andrei Cherkasov found the litter from the failed coup a more sombre sight. (Art Seitz)

The marvel of sports is its uncompromising emphasis on the present. 'Whom did you beat today?' is the sole relevant question (and quest). One's socio-political colouring (past or present) has no bearing on the outcome of the morning's match. It has always been so. The doubles pairings at the Kremlin cup scoffed at history. Mansdorf and Medvedev. An Israeli and a Ukrainian. Bahrami and Riglewski. An Iranian and a German. Oosting and Poliakov. A Dutchman and a Russian. A get-togehter of the same men not so long ago would have been treasonous. Yet today these international tandems rely on each other for their daily bread.

There were times in 1991 when the Krenlin Cup itself seemed un unlikely happening. If the Gulf crisis wasn't enough to make all sporting morally irrelevant then the aborted August coup in Russia imperilled the site's city existence. The power of sport, however, is so compelling that in the minds of experts, the Kremlin Cup would have continued even if the dreaded coupsters had triumphed. You see, they would have needed any conceivable optimistic sign to the west that the situation in the Soviet Union was normal. And what is more normal than sport?

Nearly 100,000 fans attended the week's matches which is more than the glory years of the Masters at Madison Square Garden, although to be fair to both events, New York has a veritable cornucopia of cultural competition to contend with while the Kremlin Cup, on the other hand, is the year's most important sporting affair in the USSR.

If I am not mistaken, the 18,447 fans at the final was the largest crowd of the indoor season. And perhaps of any indoor season. So much for the good news. Even the bad news (that the preponderance of tickets sold for roubles) has turned out to be not very bad news at all. Surprisingly, ticket revenues – just like in Schenectady where admission is free – are not looked to for significant income. More astonishing is that of the tournaments eighty assorted Western and Soviet sponsors, not one invested in the tournament

Eighteen thousand packed the arena but outside the Kremlin, there was just Andrei Chesnokov. (Art Seitz)

because of a besotted passion for tennis. For each it was a sound corporate decision to clear the way to do business in a country which has no word for either private or profit.

The Kremlin Cup is a shameless showcase for the effusive internationalism tennis projects. Imagine an Iranian carpet impresario uniting a German aspirin company, a Moscow editor, a U.S. publisher, a Swiss chef and the prime minister of Russia, which a few weeks before the tournament began became the prime minister of what remained of the USSR). Such a partnership, had it occurred ten yers ago (the year Bjorn Borg retired) would have landed the protagonists (and some antagonists as well) head first in a boggy gulag 10,000 miles from the centre strap in the Olympic Stadium. Pushkin move over. More likely, roll over.

213

Banespa Open

By Lauren Goldenberg

Sao Paulo, 4-10 November
Tournament Director: Ricardo Bernd

The final victory of the 1991 IBM/ATP Tour prior to the season-ending championships belonged to lucky Christian Miniussi of Argentina. The 24-year-old and eight-year tour veteran became one of the luckiest losers in tennis history when he captured his first career singles title at the Banespa Open in Sao Paulo, Brazil with a come from behind 2-6, 6-3, 6-4 defeat over the hometown favourite and new Brazilian number one, Jaime Oncins. The luxurious and grand Hotel Transamerica in the Santo Amaro section of the sprawling metropolis of Sao Paulo was the setting for this culminating event and the exciting one-hour and 51-minute final.

After eight years on the Tour, Christian Miniussi moved stylishly towards his first singles title. *(Joveci de Freitas)*

Miniussi, the first and only lucky loser to win a title this year on the IBM/ATP Tour, netted a main draw spot following the withdrawal with a back injury of fifth seed Thomas Muster. In the first round, Miniussi successfully defeated recently crowned Guaruja champion and fellow compatriot Javier Frana in straight sets. His second-round opponent, German Lopez of Spain, was then forced to withdraw with a foot injury sustained when jumping from the stands. That put Miniussi into the quarter-finals where he surprised another fellow countryman and rising star, Gabriel Markus. In the semi-finals, Miniussi then soundly defeated the tournament's sportsmanship award winner and crowd pleaser, Andres Gomez, to earn a berth in his first career singles final. His luck even extended into the doubles competition where Miniussi and partner Gustavo Luza, also from Argentina, were awarded a walkover in the first round after Emilio Sanchez withdrew with a hip problem.

The holder of four career doubles titles with four fellow Argentinians, Miniussi retained his composure during the singles final after dropping the first set to become the 18th first-time winner this year on the IBM/ATP Tour. 'This is the luckiest week in my life,' explained the blond-haired, blue-eyed Latin following the match. 'After I won the first match against Frana I knew I was lucky. I even won at cards that night! There was no pressure on me. My goal here was just to get through qualifying.' The win propelled the claycourt specialist from No. 116 to No. 83 in the rankings; the first time he had been in the top 100 since May 1988. Miniussi's success this year included a quarter-final finish at Geneva and a round of 16 appearance at the French Open, both as a qualifier.

Oncins, affectionately known as 'Jaiminho' or 'Little Jaime' despite his nearly 6'5" frame, was playing in his second final in as many weeks after a career best showing at Buzios. Again with a one set lead, Oncins was unable to capitalise despite the enthusiastic support from the crowd, which included several family members and friends. In Buzios, Oncins had earned enough

Andres Gomez helped Jaime Oncins to the doubles title in between some careful putting practice. *(Joveci de Freitas)*

points to become Brazil's new No. 1 following 28-year-old Luiz Mattar's five-year reign. 'I can't believe it,' Oncins declared when asked about the double loss. 'I really thought I had a good chance, but I made the same mistake as last week. I didn't attack, I didn't have enough courage. Miniussi used these same tactics to beat me.'

Oncins found some consolation in the doubles competition, capturing his first career title with the veteran Andres Gomez with a 7-5, 6-4 win over doubles specialist Jorge Lozano of Mexico and Brazilian tennis hero Cassio Motta.

ATP Tour World Championship

By Ron Atkin

Frankfurt, 11-17 November
Tournament Director: Zeljko Franulovic

It was Pete Sampras, closing out the year in a blaze of brilliance, who held aloft the huge blue crystal crown as winner of the 1991 IBM/ATP Tour World Championships in Frankfurt's Festhalle. Sampras, 20, defeated his good friend, sometime doubles partner and golf companion Jim Courier 3-6, 7-6, 7-3, 6-4 in the first all-American final since John McEnroe beat Arthur Ashe in 1979. It was a victory worth $1,020,000 and more than doubled Sampras's earnings for the year.

The only blemish on his week was defeat by Boris Becker in the final round robin match in the John Newcombe Group. As he first defeated Michael Stich and Andre Agassi in group matches, Ivan Lendl in the semis and Courier on the culminating night Sampras pushed his game to ever-higher levels of skill. Courier eventually acknowledged the inevitable in the final and afterwards paid Sampras full tribute: 'He has the ability to hit shots the rest of us can't hit and don't even think about hitting.' Sampras concurred: 'When I am playing well I go for outrageous shots. That's what makes me great and sometimes not so great. It's the risk I take.'

From August until the climax of the Frankfurt tournament Sampras won 37 of his 43 singles matches. But in none of those contests did the Californian play better than in the semi-final

Clench-fisted triumph for Jim Courier takes him to the Frankfurt final. *(Russ Adams)*

Power and style – Pete Sampras on his way to the ATP Tour title. *(Gianni Ciaccia)*

against Lendl. The 31-year-old Lendl, a five-time winner of the event, qualifying for his 12th straight year and appearing in his 50th match, had sailed through the groups as the only contestant with a 3-0 record. He delivered 28 aces in those three matches and never dropped serve.

Yet Lendl was thrashed 6-2, 6-3, his worst loss of 1991 and biggest defeat in those 12 years of play in this prestigious season's-end tournament. 'That was the best two sets I have ever played,' said Sampras. 'From the first point I felt great. I was serving well and returning unbelievably. Everything I hit turned to gold.'

Some of the Sampras serves were clocked at 120 mph, his returns - struck breathtakingly early - drew gasps of disbelief from the crowd of 8500 and in seven games, from 4-2 in the first set until 5-0 in the second, Lendl collected only 13 points, four of them with aces. It was all over in 67 minutes.

If the Lendl match and, to a lesser extent, the contest against Courier, were the peaks of Sampras's week, the crux of it all was a marvellous battle with Becker on the final night of the groups. Sampras had to face a German folk hero inspired by the adulation of the sell-out audience. Sampras needed to emerge from that set with at least one set in order to guarantee himself a spot in the semi-finals and for a long time he looked unlikely to get it.

Becker swept the first set 6-4 and had three points to break for a 5-4 lead and serve out for the match. Sampras survived to take the set into the tie-break, which he won 7-3. Becker, who never had a break point against him in the match, failed to hold serve at all in that tie-break and it cost him a place in the semi-final. At Frankfurt last year Becker fled the Festhalle immediately after his semi-final loss to Agassi. This time he hung around, wearing a big smile because, he said, he knew he had played well. So well, in fact, that Sampras praised him as the best in the world. 'He has it all,' said Sampras. 'The speed, the mobility, a huge serve, incredible guts.'

Becker also has a special place in the hearts of the German nation but in Frankfurt this year what he did not have was a place in the semi-finals, which many members of the public found difficult to understand and hard to bear.

At least Becker went out with every gun blazing gloriously. For Germany's other qualifier, Michael Stich, the Wimbledon champion, it was a miserable occasion. He failed to win any of his three matches in the John Newcombe Group and after being beaten by Becker lamented that it was rough for a German to play on home territory and find everybody in the crowd against him.

Karel Novacek, a late replacement when the top seed Stefan Edberg pulled out because of renewed problems with his long-term knee injury,

Once again the Festhalle was a visual treat when decked out for the second IBM/ATP World Championship.
(Gianni Ciaccia)

Much effort but no title this time for Agassi.
(Russ Adams)

Agassi's semi-final pitted him against Courier, his conqueror in the final of the French Open. And Courier, despite a stated preference for outdoor tennis, repeated on the Greenset carpet what he had done to Agassi on the clay of Paris. The score this time was 6-3, 7-5 rather than five sets, but the margin of superiority was emphatic.

In the final it seemed early on that Courier might still be on enough of a high to repel the power of Sampras. The white-capped redhead from Florida looked capable of ending a memorable year on a fantastic note as he pocketed the first set. But as Sampras hotted up the pace Courier found more and more trouble holding serve. He fought off five break points, dropped serve in the 11th game of the second set, only to break right back, but lost the tie-break 7-5. That was, in effect, the end for Courier. In the last two sets, despite serving no more than nine aces, Sampras dropped a mere nine points on serve and it remained only for Edberg to join the finalists on court for the presentation ceremony and to accept a diamond and gold tennis ball as the year's top player on the ATP Tour.

It had been another highly successful occasion for the beautifully decorated Festhalle, for the supportive city of Frankfurt and for the IBM/ATP Tour.

was the only other player to fail to win a match, in his case in the Ilie Nastase Group. The new number one seed, Jim Courier, set the high level of competition which was maintained throughout a week of excellent matches by defeating Novacek 6-7, 7-5, 6-4 in the opening contest, battling back from 3-1 down in the second set.

On the same opening night, long after midnight, Agassi had silenced the home fans by defeating Becker 6-3, 7-5. It was his fifth straight win over the German and an indication that the hard-hitter from Las Vegas, winner of the ATP title in Frankfurt in 1990, was again a force to be reckoned with, despite having squeezed into the 1991 event in eighth and last place.

Beaten in three sets by Sampras, Agassi bounced back to defeat Stich 7-5, 6-3 in his last group match, ensuring his own place in the semi-finals and denying Becker any hope of getting through.

A sponsor's logo, a new and much-acclaimed Greenset court and a hot but thoughtful Pete Sampras. *(Gianni Ciaccia)*

ATP Tour World Doubles Championships

By Dave Beattie

Johannesburg, 18-24 November
Tournament Director: Keith Brebnor

The ATP Tour decision to bring their showpiece of the year – the World Doubles Finals – to South Africa met with success that surpassed all expectations. Not surprisingly there were problems, technical, organisational and, particularly, political. But they were all swept away in five days of glorious tennis that left no doubt that the ATP decision was the right one; and that Johannesburg, if not the entire country, was 'sold' on the doubles game. The organisational hitches were understandable. No decisions on South Africa as a venue for World Doubles Finals

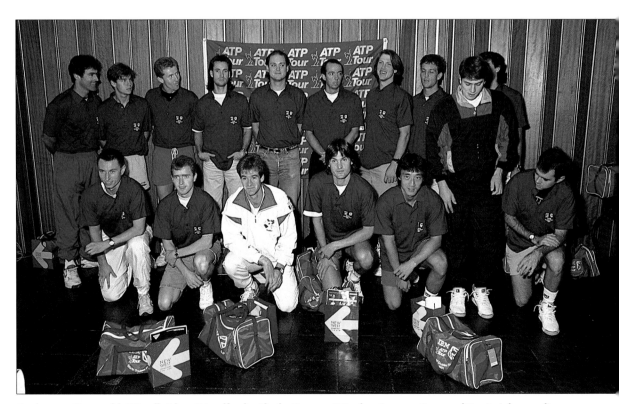

Back row: Fitzgerald, Woodbridge, Woodforde, Flach, Seguso, Warder, Jensen, Pate and Davis (obscured). Front: Suk, Nijssen, Jarryd, Connell, Michibata, Witsken, Galbraith. *(Gordon Simmonds)*

Glenn Michibata helps to integrate South African tennis at the ATP Tour clinic. *(Gordon Simmonds)*

or any other international event could be made before the local administration achieved unity, and before the sports moratorium on international contact was relaxed.

The first objective was considered achieved when two of the three local 'controlling' bodies united to form Tennis SA. The third body, the Tennis Association of SA (TASA), refused to join. They considered the lifting of the moratorium to be premature, and maintained that without their presence in Tennis SA, there was no unity. But with the blessing of the majority of people of all races, Tennis SA, under Chris Ngcobo, prevailed, and shortly afterwards, the moratorium was lifted. While the news was greeted with great joy, it left the organisers hard pressed for time. That they put

on an event of such magnitude, in such a professional manner at such short notice was a tribute to the ATP Tour and to tournament promoter Keith Brebnor and the staff of Tennis SA.

But it was the players, almost to a man, who really 'sold' the event, on and off the court. They took time out to give a clinic at a township, Kwa Thema, where the ATP Tour Charirties Programme made a donation that would help build a tennis centre in the impoverished area. The players also entertained almost 300 children of all races at Ellis Park.

The Johannesburg tennis public is notorious for its apathy when it comes to tennis. They will watch it on television – it ranks as one of the most popular viewing sports in the country – but they

221

won't go 'live' unless there is a McEnroe, Connors or Agassi in the offing. Perhaps, after missing out on top quality tennis for a couple of years, they were simply hungry. If they were, the eight doubles teams must have left them sated.

The venue itself was perfect. The focal point was the 5000-seater Standard Bank Area, standing like a jewel in the old tennis complex at Ellis Park, only a few blocks east of the centre of the Golden City. In the complex are a number of hardcourts, occupied this time by gaily covered marquees, small fast-food outlets, sponsors' shops. And the old centre court, scene of so many historic matches, including South Africa's only win in the Federation Cup, became the ATP control and media centre.

Day One of the tournament almost brought disaster. A group of TASA supporters, backed by more radical black quasi-political groups, carried out their threat to disrupt the tournament. Some slipped into the arena, and with the first match – between Grant Connell and Glenn Michibata and Pat Galbraith and Todd Witsken – only 90 minutes old, the demonstrators struck. Plastic bags containing seeds and sand exploded on the court. The demonstrators were removed from the arena, and after continuing outside, were escorted away by police.

It was an hour before the match was resumed, and although Connell reflected the views of many when he said afterwards: 'I never at any time felt physically threatened' there was grave concern among ATP and Tennis SA officials. But Tennis SA president Ngcobo said: 'The show must go on.' It did, and there were no more unpleasant incidents. In fact, the tournament grew in stature. After a first night attendance of about 50 per cent, the demand for tickets swelled to gold rush proportions. The last three nights were sold out.

The disruption apart, the first day's play was scintillating, the only flaw among the gem-like performances being the abject display from Scott Davis in particular, and his partner David Pate. They never did find their touch and failed to win a single match in the round robin phase of play.

In the same section, the Forbes/Segal Group, ambidextrous Luke Jensen and Laurie Warder were entertaining and the 'Woodies' – Mark Woodforde and Todd Woodbridge – became the crowd favourites. But it was Robert Seguso and Ken Flach, reaching again for the greatness of the 80's, who swept their way unbeaten to the semi-finals, where they took out Connell and Michibata in two tie-break sets. Meanwhile the world's No. 1

pair John Fitzgerald and Anders Jarryd rolled through the Hewitt/McMillan Group unbeaten. But they had to call on all their skill and experience in the semi-finals, coming from 2-5, and 0-2, to win 7-5, 6-2 against the 'Woodies'.

Perhaps after such a splendid week of tennis, expectations were too high for the final. Whatever the reason, it failed to provide the icing on the cake. Flach, in particular, and Seguso, looked lacklustre, Fitzgerald and Jarryd were called on to produce no more than the consistency that had been a hallmark of their play all week, in order to pick up the winners' cheque for $100,000. The match lasted 131 minutes, and the score was 6-4, 6-4, 2-6, 6-4. But set against the background of a week of captivating, riveting tennis, the downbeat final will soon be forgotten

After three Grand Slam triumphs at Roland Garros, Wimbledon and Flushing Meadow, Anders Jarryd and John Fitzgerald add the final touch to a great year in Johannesburg. *(Gordon Simmonds)*

The 1991 Challenger Circuit

By Russell Barlow

Frederic Fontang – Challenger success propelled him towards the top 200. (A. Tonelli)

The Challenger Circuit is aptly named. The challenge facing an aspiring Stefan Edberg or Boris Becker today is huge. With so many talented professionals jealously guarding their positions amongst the upper echelons of the ATP computer ranking, breaking into the top 200 in the world can be a daunting task.

But, with the continued growth of the Challenger Circuit, orchestrated out of the ATP Monte Carlo office, the path is open and the task, though difficult, far from impossible.

The Challengers, offering prize-money ranging from $25,000 to $100,000, often with hospitality, are spread around the globe so as to minimise the amount of travel required for young hopefuls with limited funds.

Owing to the importance of maintaining a substantial circuit of events for young professionals, the ATP has been dedicated to the improvement in both number and quality of Challengers, as well as bringing professional tennis to those parts of the world where there are no ATP Tour events. Part of this dedication to the Challenger Circuit is the ATP Tour Pro Classic, held at

the ATP Tour headquarters in Ponte Vedra Beach, Florida, which was won this year by young professional Johnathan Stark from the United States. This event, under the direction of ATP Tour Director of Tennis, Brian Gottfried, also featured an exhibition by some of the Senior Tour players for 1992, with Fred Stolle, Ken Rosewall, and others participating in doubles exhibitions.

The success and popularity of the 1991 Challenger Circuit is shown by the comparison with that of the previous year. The total number of events rose from the 1990 total of 70 to 95 in 1991; with a similar increase in prize money from $3.95 million to $5.425 million.

Covering 35 countries throughout the world Challengers are now played in exotic locations like Guadeloupe in the French West Indies, on the beach of Brazil in Fortaleza, and in Singapore, Asia's bustling tourist location. Also 1991 saw in-roads into Eastern Europe, with new events played in Warsaw, Bucharest and Prague, as well as a very successful event in Istanbul, Turkey organised by the inimitable Bekir Emre.

In spite of what may seem a delightful travel schedule, the competition at the Challengers is fierce, with the stars of tomorrow fighting for vital IBM/ATP Tour ranking points which will allow them to rise to the level of being accepted into the main draws of the ATP Tour events.

1991 saw many of these competitors rising through the ranks, some literally bursting onto the scene. One such example in the autumn, was Massimo Valeri, ranked 519 in August, who due to a quarter-finals showing in Merano and winning Messina, rose to 195 within one month on the IBM/ATP Tour computer rankings. French player Frederic Fontang showed the way this year when he began ranked 215, and by reaching the semi-finals in Zaragoza, was accepted into the main draw of the San Marino ATP Tour event where he reached the final. He followed this performance by reaching the final of the Cervia Challenger and winning Merano attaining the position of 104 by early September. He then went on to seize his first ATP Tour title by scoring an upset victory in the final of Palermo. After that triumph, his ranking had soared to 61.

Zimbabwe's Byron Black is another young professional who broke through this year. Black began the year ranked 453 and won titles in Winnetka and Madeira, was runner-up in Cherbourg and Istanbul and semi-finalist in the Azores. As of November, Black had reached the 116th position on the IBM/ATP Tour world rankings.

One of Italy's most promising younger players earned his place on the ATP Tour this year by virtue of his performances on the Challenger Circuit. Stefano Pescosolido began 1991 ranked 140 and reached number 66, earning half of his total points in Challengers by winning Porto and Parioli, and reaching the finals in Guadeloupe and Siracusa. Similarly, Spain's Carols Costa rose from 114 to 58, earning half of his total points in Challenger with wins in Siracusa and Venice, and a finalist position in Merano, among other performances.

Not only do the Challengers provide opportunities for the younger players, they also serve as a means for regular ATP Tour players to return to the circuit after injury or lack of performances at the higher level. Argentine Alberto Mancini, who had a difficult year in 1990, returned to the tennis scene in early 1991 by playing Challengers in South America on his favourite clay court surface. By virtue of a semi-final performance in Sao Paulo and winning the Santiago Challenger, Mancini was back on the winning road, and finished 1991 back amongst the top 25 players in the world.

Just as 1991 saw a further increase in spectator attendance at the ATP Tour events, the Challenger Circuit mirrored the increase in the popularity of professional tennis by the public attendance figures at most tournaments. While the traditional events such as Brest, France had more than 20,000 visitors during the week, new events in Bielefeld, Germany and Graz, Austria, actually had sell-out crowds for the last few days of their tournaments.

In all, the 1991 Challenger Circuit enjoyed success as never before experienced, by providing the vital stepping stone to the IBM/ATP Tour for the stars of the future, and delivering professional tennis to the ever-growing numbers of tennis fans throughout the world.

Byron Black, in action here at Grand Champions, was another 1991 Challenger star. *(Cynthia Lum)*

Facts and Figures

Results

31 DECEMBER-6 JANUARY: BP NATIONAL CHAMPIONSHIPS, WELLINGTON $175,000 Winner: RICHARD FROMBERG
Rd 32: Christian Bergstrom d Andrei Cherkasov 76 76; Patrick McEnroe d Bryan Shelton 63 61; Bruce Derlin d Dimitri Poliakov 62 46 64; Javier Sanchez d Sergio Casal 63 36 63; Richard Fromberg d Luis Herrera 75 62; Marian Vajda d Francisco Clavet 64 62; Ramesh Krishnan d Brett Steven 62 26 75; Luiz Mattar d Kelly Evernden 64 64; Omar Camporese d Brian Garrow 61 61; Markus Zoecke d Daniel Vacek 63 63; Robbie Weiss d Renzo Furlan 67 62 64; Thomas Hogstedt d Karel Novacek 64 16 64; Alex Antonitsch d Joao Cunha-Silva 62 64; Andrew Sznajder d Tarik Benhabiles 64 63; Jaime Oncins d Malivai Washington 61 16 76; Lars Jonsson d Alexander Volkov 64 62. **Rd 16:** Bergstrom d McEnroe 63 62; Poliakov d Sanchez 62 64; Fromberg d Vajda 62 62; Krishnan d Mattar 61 75; Camporese d Zoecke 62 60; Hogstedt d Weiss 63 63; Sznajder d Antonitsch 64 62; Jonsson d Oncins 62 62. **QF:** Bergstrom d Poliakov 62 76; Fromberg d Krishnan 57 64 75; Camporese d Hogstedt 63 76; Jonsson d Sznajder 62 62. **SF:** Fromberg d Bergstrom 63 57 76; Jonsson d Camporese 57 63 76. **F:** Fromberg d Jonsson 61 64 64.
DOUBLES: Luiz Mattar/Nicolas Pereira d John Letts/Jaime Oncins 46 76 62.

31 DECEMBER-6 JANUARY: AUSTRALIAN MEN'S HARDCOURT CHAMPIONSHIPS, ADELAIDE $175,000 Winner: NICKLAS KULTI
Rd 32: Magnus Larsson d Boris Becker 64 36 76; Slobodan Zivojinovic d Mark Kratzmann 63 36 76; Patrik Kuhnen d Veli Paloheimo 60 64; Todd Woodbridge d Guillaume Raoux 76 61; Udo Riglewski d Sergi Bruguera 75 63; Fabrice Santoro d Thierry Champion 62 63; Nicklas Kulti d Aki Rahunen 64 60; Magnus Gustafsson d John Fitzgerald 62 63; Michael Stich d Jean-Philippe Fleurian 64 64; Gilad Bloom d Sandon Stolle 67 76 64; Jason Stoltenberg d Jacco Eltingh 63 64; Jimmy Arias d Horst Skoff 76 30 Ret.; Mark Woodforde d Eric Koevermans 62 76; Martin Sinner d Eric Jelen 63 76; Paul Haarhuis d Brad Pearce 61 36 62; Jim Courier d Alexander Mronz 36 62 61. **Rd 16:** Larsson d Zivojinovic 76 76; Kuhnen d Woodbridge 75 62; Santoro d Riglewski 76 75; Kulti d Gustafsson 46 61 61; Stich d Bloom 75 61; Arias d Stoltenberg 62 64; Sinner d Woodforde 46 63 64; Courier d Haarhuis 64 64. **QF:** Larsson d Kuhnen 76 36 63; Kulti d Santoro 63 60; Stich d Arias 36 63 63; Courier d Sinner 76 63. **SF:** Kulti d Larsson 75 63; Stich d Courier 64 76. **F:** Kulti d Stich 63 16 61.
DOUBLES: Wayne Ferreira/Stefan Kruger d Paul Haarhuis/Mark Koevermans 64 46 64.

7-13 JANUARY: HOLDEN N.S.W. OPEN TOURNAMENT OF CHAMPIONS, SYDNEY $250,000 Winner: GUY FORGET
Rd 32: Wally Masur d Ivan Lendl 26 76 Ret.; Derrick Rostagno d Horst Skoff 62 64; Martin Jaite d Guillaume Raoux 62 64; Andrei Cherkasov d David Wheaton 62 60; Guy Forget d Scott Davis 63 63; Todd Woodbridge d Magnus Larsson 62 75; Fabrice Santoro d Carl-Uwe Steeb 75 62; Aaron Krickstein d Jason Stoltenberg 67 61 61; Johan Anderson d Jay Berger 63 64; Jimmy Arias d Petr Korda 57 62 62; Michael Stich d Alexander Volkov 64 63; Jakob Hlasek d Nicklas Kulti 76 62; Richard Krajicek d Mark Rosset 63 62; Darren Cahill d Sergi Bruguera 64 16 64; Amos Mansdorf d Mark Koevermans 63 36 61; Magnus Gustafsson d Jonas Svensson 36 64 64. **Rd 16:** Rostagno d Masur 64 76; Jaite d Cherkasov 61 61; Forget d Woodbridge 61 60; Santoro d Krickstein 75 16 63; Anderson d Arias 64 63; Stich d Hlasek 36 76 64; Cahill d Krajicek 64 64; Gustafsson d Mansdorf 76 63. **QF:** Rostagno d Jaite 61 63; Forget d Santoro 61 62; Stich d Anderson 63 60; Gustafsson d Cahill 75 64. **SF:** Forget d Rostagno 60 62; Stich d Gustafsson 76 64. **F:** Forget d Stich 63 64.
DOUBLES: Scott Davis/David Pate d Darren Cahill/Mark Kratzmann 36 63 62.

7-13 JANUARY: BENSON AND HEDGES NEW ZEALAND OPEN, AUCKLAND $175,000 Winner: KAREL NOVACEK
Rd 32: Emilio Sanchez d Renzo Furlan 64 61; Malivai Washington d Steve Guy 63 62; Jean-Phillipe Fleurian d Brett Steven 26 61 62; Eric Jelen d Gilad Bloom 63 16 64; Chuck Adams d Richard Fromberg 63 64; Christian Bergstrom d Javier Sanchez 62 61; Jaime Yzaga d Kelly Evernden 62 76; Luiz Mattar d David Engel 06 76 64; Omar Camporese d Francisco Clavet 62 63; Lars Jonsson d Martin Sinner 36 62 63; Grant Connell d Veli Paloheimo 75 16 64; Karel Novacek d Alexander Mronz 36 75 63; Alex Antonitsch d Udo Riglewski 63 60; Patrik Kuhnen d Ramesh Krishnan 62 64; Marian Vajda d Robbie Weiss 61 63; Andrei Chesnokov d Aki Rahunen 64 61. **Rd 16:** E Sanchez d Washington 46 36 76; Fleurian d Jelen 63 61; Bergstrom d Adams 63 46 76; Mattar d Yzaga 62 62; Jonsson d Camporese

75 36 75; Novacek d Connell 64 64; Kuhnen d Antonitsch 46 64 75; Vajda d Chesnokov 61 57 75. **QF:** Fleurian d Sanchez 62 76; Mattar d Bergstrom W/O; Novacek d Jonsson W/O; Vajda d Kuhnen 46 63 64. **SF:** Fleurian d Mattar 36 64 63; Novacek d Vajda 64 46 60. **F:** Novacek d Fleurian 76 76.
DOUBLES: Sergio Casal/Emilio Sanchez d Grant Connell/Glenn Michibata 46 63 64.

14-27 JANUARY: AUSTRALIAN OPEN, MELBOURNE $2,057,306 Winner: BORIS BECKER
Rd 128: Stefan Edberg d Dimitri Poliakov 61 76 62; Eduardo Masso d Brad Pearce 67 61 67 63 86; Pat Cash d Karel Novacek 62 64 61; Christo van Rensburg d Mark Kratzmann 63 61 75; Nuno Marques d Joao Cunha-Silva 46 64 16 63 64; Jaime Oncins d John Arbanas 63 63 75; Gilad Bloom d Diego Perez 75 62 63; Jim Courier d Jan Gunnarsson 63 64 62; Jimmy Arias d Andrei Chesnokov 60 63 46 26 64; Bart Wuyts d Lars Jonsson 57 57 64 76 97; Jaime Yzaga d Daniel Vacek 64 64 62; Michiel Schapers d Martin Sinner 63 62 26 62; Christian Saceanu d Jeff Tarango 26 63 62 36 75; Mats Wilander d Heath Denman 76 63 64; Richard Fromberg d Peter Doohan 64 76 75; Brad Gilbert d David Wheaton 64 46 63 76; Ivan Lendl d Tarik Benhabiles 61 61 63; Scott Davis d Alex Antonitsch 36 62 64 63; Magnus Gustafsson d Jamie Morgan 61 60 63; Wally Masur d Sandon Stolle 61 62 63; Patrik Kuhnen d Guillaume Raoux 75 64 76; Ctislav Dosedel d Javier Frana 75 26 63 63; Amos Mansdorf d Andrew Sznajder 60 63 63; Aaron Krickstein d Simon Youl 64 64 64; Jason Stoltenberg d Jakob Hlasek 06 64 75 64; Mark Koevermans d David Pate 64 62 36 26 60; Jan Siemerink d Jose Francisco Altur 63 63 63; Carl-Uwe Steeb d Claudio Pistolesi 62 62 63; Goran Prpic d Jim Pugh 63 62 36 62; Luiz Mattar d Nicklas Kulti 64 75 67 63; Ramesh Krishnan d Eric Jelen 76 Ret.; Goran Ivanisevic d Sergi Bruguera 64 06 61 64; Mark Woodforde d Emilio Sanchez 06 75 76 62; Bryan Shelton d Paolo Cane 76 46 63 64; Anders Jarryd d Gary Muller 64 63 61; Grant Connell d Niclas Kroon 61 64 62; Patrick McEnroe d Thomas Hogstedt 46 46 63 61 63; Johan Anderson d Aki Rahunen 62 64 63; Todd Witsken d Kelly Jones 60 61 60; Jay Berger d Magnus Larsson 63 64 60; Andrei Cherkasov d Derrick Rostagno 36 64 61 46 108; Darren Cahill d Jonathan Canter 61 64 63; Petr Korda d Alexander Volkov 61 16 16 64 75; Richard Krajicek d Fabrice Santoro 26 61 62 63; Cristiano Caratti d Broderick Dyke 62 36 64 63; David Engel d Kelly Evernden 63 26 61 60; Glenn Layendecker d Udo Riglewski 63 63 46 67 62; Peter Lundgren d Leonardo Lavalle 76 36 76 61; Jonas Svensson d Thierry Champion 63 64 61; Francisco Clavet d Andrew Castle 67 62 61 62; Todd Woodbridge d Mark Kaplan 16 63 63 61; Christian Bergstrom d Cedric Pioline 64 62 16 76; Martin Jaite d Luis Herrera 63 61 36 67 64; Michael Stich d Malivai Washington 46 57 76 61 64; Alexander Mronz d John Fitzgerald 64 64 64; Guy Forget d Horst Skoff 76 62 64; Lars Wahlgren d Marc Rosset 46 26 76 63 97; Wayne Ferreira d Fernando Luna 61 63 62; Jacco Eltingh d Robbie Weiss 36 62 63 75; Jean-Philippe Fleurian d Renzo Furlan 61 60 60; Omar Camporese d Markus Zoecke 36 62 76 64; Paul Haarhuis d Javier Sanchez 26 61 62 76; Marian Vajda d Brian Garrow 26 64 75 63; Becker d Vajda 64 61 63. **Rd 64:** Edberg d Masso 61 62 63; Cash d van Rensburg 76 64 64; Oncins d Marques 63 60 62; Courier d Bloom 62 63 62; Arias d Wuyts 63 61 62; Yzaga d Schapers 76 64 62; Wilander d Saceanu 76 63 36 46 64; Gilbert d Fromberg 46 64 46 60; Lendl d Davis 76 63 62; Gustafsson d Masur 75 36 76 60; Kuhnen d Dosedel 62 64 64; Krickstein d Mansdorf 75 36 76 62; Koevermans d Stoltenberg 63 63 63; Siemerink d Steeb 62 57 46 64 62; Prpic d Mattar 63 61 61; Ivanisevic d Krishnan 64 36 61 61; Woodforde d Shelton 76 63 63; Connell d Jarryd 61 75 62; McEnroe d Anderson 63 63 57 61; Berger d Witsken 61 63 60; Cahill d Cherkasov 46 26 63 75 75; Krajicek d Korda 46 76 63 64; Caratti d Engel 36 62 63 64; Layendecker d Lundgren 36 16 75 63 64; Svensson d Clavet 62 75 36 61; Woodbridge d Bergstrom 61 06 62 76; Stich d Jaite 63 76 76; Forget d Mronz 67 64 64 62; Ferreira d Wahlgren 62 64 76; Eltingh d Fleurian 61 36 76 36 61; Camporese d Haarhuis 75 75 36 63; Becker d Vajda 64 61 63. **Rd 32:** Edberg d Cash 76 75 62; Courier d Oncins 63 61 61; Yzaga d Arias 36 76 61 63; Wilander d Gilbert 76 61 64; Lendl d Gustafsson 46 62 63 62; Krickstein d Kuhnen 64 64 61; Siemerink d Koevermans 46 62 64 36 61; Prpic d Ivanisevic 63 64 63; Woodforde d Connell 64 36 75 63; McEnroe d Berger 61 75 75; Krajicek d Cahill 67 63 63 76; Caratti d Layendecker 64 64 57 46 75; Woodbridge d Svensson 75 62 61; Forget d Stich 76 76 46 63; Ferreira d Eltingh 62 64 62; Becker d Camporese 76 76 06 46 1412. **Rd 16:** Edberg d Courier 46 60 64 57 62; Yzaga d Wilander 75 26 61 36 61; Lendl d Krickstein 62 62 61; Prpic d Siemerink 76 67 60 76; McEnroe d Woodforde 62 64 61; Caratti d Krajicek 63 64 67 36 64; Forget d Woodbridge 64 36 63 64; Becker d Ferreira 64 76 64. **QF:** Edberg d Yzaga 62 63 62; Lendl d Prpic 60 76 62; McEnroe d Caratti 76 63 46 46 62; Becker d Forget 62 76 63. **SF:** Lendl d Edberg 64 57 36 76; Becker d McEnroe 67 64 61 64. **F:** Becker d Lendl 16 64 64 64.

DOUBLES: Scott Davis/David Pate d Patrick McEnroe/David Wheaton 67 76 63 75.

4-10 FEBRUARY: MURATTI TIME INDOOR CHAMPIONSHIPS, MILAN $600,000 Winner: ALEXANDER VOLKOV
Rd 32: Ivan Lendl d Magnus Larsson 75 46 75; Cristiano Caratti d Peter Lundgren 76 62; Diego Nargiso d Omar Camporese 75 64; Nicklas Kulti d Marc Rosset 63 64; Carl-Uwe Steeb d Michael Chang 61 75; Karel Novacek d Ronald Agenor 64 62; Thierry Champion d Mark Koevermans 64 76; Aaron Krickstein d Amos Mansdorf 60 61; Jakob Hlasek d Todd Witsken 76 62; Anders Jarryd d Roberto Raffa 60 61; Jan Gunnarsson d Claudio Mezzadri 63 63; Andrei Chesnokov d Sebastian Sorebini 63 63; Alexander Volkov d Cedric Pioline 64 67 64; Eric Jelen d Christo van Rensburg 64 62; Pat Cash d Andrei Cherkasov 75 46 76; Goran Prpic d Goran Ivanisevic 63 36 64. **Rd 16:** Caratti d Lendl 64 16 76; Kulti d Nargiso 76 61; Steeb d Novacek 46 76 64; Krickstein d Champion 40 Ret.; Hlasek d Jarryd 63 06 64; Gunnarsson d Chesnokov 64 63; Volkov d Jelen 63 36 76; Cash d Prpic 75 63. **QF:** Caratti d Kulti 63 61; Steeb d Krickstein 63 76; Hlasek d Gunnarsson 60 76; Volkov d Cash 64 63. **SF:** Caratti d Steeb 76 67 63; Volkov d Hlasek 64 63. **F:** Volkov d Caratti 61 75.
DOUBLES: Omar Camporese/Goran Ivanisevic d Tom Nijssen/Cyril Suk 64 76.

4-10 FEBRUARY: VOLVO TENNIS, SAN FRANCISCO $250,000 Winner: DARREN CAHILL
Rd 32: Andre Agassi d Jeff Tarango 76 63; Udo Riglewski d Marcos Ondruska 61 63; Kevin Curren d Scott Davis 75 63; Luis Herrera d Gary Muller 64 76; Brad Gilbert d Patrik Kuhnen 63 36 62; Alexander Mronz d Rick Leach 63 62; Dan Goldie d Jim Grabb 64 57 63; Tim Mayotte d Tomas Carbonell 64 76; Darren Cahill d Thomas Hogstedt 62 63; Guillaume Raoux d Brian Garrow 61 61; Mark Kratzmann d Veli Paloheimo 63 76; John McEnroe d Andrew Sznajder 63 60; Wally Masur d Brad Pearce 61 64; Ramesh Krishnan d Aki Rahunen 76 76; David Pate d Paul Chamberlin 63 75; Andres Gomez d Brian Devening 46 64 64. **Rd 16:** Agassi d Riglewski 36 64 63; Curren d Herrera 46 76 62; Gilbert d Mronz 63 63; Goldie d Mayotte 26 76 75; Cahill d Raoux 57 64 63; McEnroe d Kratzmann 64 76; Masur d Krishnan 63 63; Pate d Gomez 16 64 62. **QF:** Agassi d Curren 62 64; Gilbert d Goldie 61 57 64; Cahill d McEnroe 76 36 63; Masur d Pate 61 46 76. **SF:** Gilbert d Agassi 61 62; Cahill d Masur 46 64 75. **F:** Cahill d Gilbert 62 36 64.
DOUBLES: Wally Masur/Jason Stoltenburg d Ronnie Bathman/Rikard Bergh 46 76 64.

4-10 FEBRUARY: CHEVROLET CLASSIC, GUARUJA, BRAZIL $150,000 Winner: PATRICK BAUR
Rd 32: Rodolphe Gilbert d Luiz Mattar 63 62; Pablo Arraya d Pedro Rebolledo 63 62; Shuzo Matsuoka d Jose Francisco Altur 26 63 64; Jacco Eltingh d Jimmy Brown 64 61; Gabriel Markus d Renzo Furlan 63 64; Patrick Baur d Olivier Delaitre 63 46 62; Diego Perez d Thierry Tulasne 62 63; Fernando Meligeni d Cassio Motta 62 64; Jaime Oncins d Mauro Menezes 60 32 Ret.; Henrik Holm d Gianluca Pozzi 62 67 75; Martin Wostenholme d Lawson Duncan 76 61; Pablo Albano d Horacio de la Pena 06 64 76; Tarik Benhabiles d Marcelo Saliola 64 61; Chris Garner d Christer Allgardh 67 76 64; Fernando Roese d Johan Carlsson 64 76; Danilo Marcelino d Marcelo Filippini 63 64. **Rd 16:** Gilbert d Arraya 63 36 64; Matsuoka d Eltingh 64 63; Baur d Markus 46 76 62; Perez d Meligeni 60 63; Holm d Oncins 46 62 63; Wostenholme d Albano 64 62; Garner d Benhabiles 62 76; Roese d Marcelino 62 76. **QF:** Matsuoka d Gilbert 64 62; Baur d Perez 63 76; Wostenholme d Holm 26 63 75; Roese d Garner 63 10 Ret. **SF:** Baur d Matsuoka 57 63 76; Roese d Wostenholme 63 64. **F:** Baur d Roese 62 63.
DOUBLES: Olivier Delaitre/Rodolphe Gilbert d Shelby Cannon/Greg van Emburgh 62 64.

11-17 FEBRUARY: US PRO INDOOR TENNIS CHAMPIONSHIPS, PHILADELPHIA $1,000,000 Winner: IVAN LENDL
Rd 64: Ivan Lendl bye; Guillaume Raoux d Dan Goldie 64 76; Renzo Furlan d Veli Paloheimo 46 75 64; Gary Muller bye; Derrick Rostagno bye; Chuck Adams d Grant Stafford 62 62; Cristiano Caratti d Jeff Tarango 75 64; Michael Stich bye; Brad Gilbert bye; Tomas Carbonell d Gilad Bloom 61 61; Udo Riglewski d Glenn Layendecker 63 67 60; Paul Haarhuis bye; Darren Cahill bye; Thomas Hogstedt d Ramesh Krishnan 63 61; Kevin Curren d Mark Kratzmann 63 67 64; Jay Berger bye; Jim Courier bye; Jim Grabb d Patrik Kuhnen 64 64; Aki Rahunen d Grant Connell 76 75; Mark Koevermans bye; Wally Masur d Christo van Rensburg d Brad Pearce 62 61; Alexander Mronz d Horacio de la Pena 62 62; John McEnroe bye; Tim Mayotte bye; Wayne Ferreira d Jean-Philippe Fleurian 75 64; Jaime Yzaga d Anders Jarryd 63 63; Petr Korda bye; Patrick McEnroe bye; Malivai Washington d Alex Antonitsch 74 46 60; Milan Srejber d Scott Davis 64 67 63; Pete Sampras bye. **Rd 32:** Lendl d Raoux 61 75; Muller d Furlan 67 63 64; Adams d Rostagno 75 63; Stich d Caratti 62 64; Gilbert d Carbonell 63 63; Haarhuis d Riglewski 61 63; Cahill d Hogstedt 64 62; Curren d Berger 61 62; Grabb d Courier 62 64; Rahunen d Koevermans 61 62; Masur d van Rensburg 46 76 63; J McEnroe d Mronz 61 62; Ferreira d Mayotte 64 62; Korda d Yzaga 64 63; Washington d P McEnroe 60 63; Sampras d Srejber 62 75. **Rd 16:** Lendl d Muller 76 63; Stich d Adams 64 64; Gilbert d Haarhuis 76 61; Curren d Cahill 67 63 76; Rahunen d Grabb 67 61 63; J McEnroe d Masur 76 63; Korda d Ferreira 75 76; Sampras d Washington 63 76. **QF:** Lendl d Stich 62 76; Gilbert d Curren 46 63 60; J

McEnroe d Rahunen 75 63; Sampras d Korda 64 60. **SF:** Lendl d Gilbert 64 36 64; Sampras d J McEnroe 62 64. **F:** Lendl d Sampras 57 64 64 36 63.
DOUBLES: Rick Leach/Jim Pugh d Udo Riglewski/Michael Stich 64 64.

11-17 FEBRUARY: DONNAY INDOOR CHAMPIONSHIP, BRUSSELS $600,000 Winner: GUY FORGET
Rd 32: Boris Becker d Alexander Volkov 64 36 63; Eric Jelen d Ctislav Dosedel 76 63; Arnaud Boetsch d Horst Skoff 64 26 63; Michael Chang d Todd Woodbridge 64 63; Christian Saceanu d Andre Agassi 63 76; Andrei Cherkasov d Juan Aguilera 62 62; Goran Prpic d Henri Leconte 67 64 62; Andrei Chesnokov d Christian Bergstrom 36 64 64; Marc Rosset d Jonas Svensson 60 64; Ronald Agenor d Carl-Uwe Steeb 62 75; Eduardo Masso d Richard Fromberg 63 67 63; Guy Forget d Amos Mansdorf 46 63 63; Jakob Hlasek d Magnus Larsson 63 63; Mats Wilander d Omar Camporese 64 76; Pat Cash d Karel Novacek 26 76 63; Stefan Edberg d Magnus Gustafsson 60 64. **Rd 16:** Becker d Jelen 76 76; Chang d Boetsch 63 62; Cherkasov d Saceanu 64 62; Chesnokov d Prpic 64 76; Rosset d Agenor 64 63; Forget d Masso 61 62; Hlasek d Wilander 61 75; Edberg d Cash 36 61 64. **QF:** Becker d Chang 75 61; Cherkasov d Chesnokov 75 61; Forget d Rosset 62 75; Edberg d Hlasek 61 62. **SF:** Cherkasov d Becker 26 63 22 Ret.; Forget d Edberg 36 60 63. **F:** Forget d Cherkasov 63 75 36 76.
DOUBLES: Todd Woodbridge/Mark Woodforde d Libor Pimek/Michiel Schapers 63 60.

18-24 FEBRUARY: EUROCARD CLASSICS, STUTTGART $1,000,000 Winner: STEFAN EDBERG
Rd 32: Christian Bergstrom d Jan Gunnarsson 64 36 63; Karel Novacek d Jordi Arrese 76 64; Patrick Baur d Nicklas Kulti 63 75; Jonas Svensson d Richard Fromberg 67 61 60; Goran Ivanisevic d Alexander Volkov 61 62; Eric Jelen d Carl-Uwe Steeb 63 64; Jakob Hlasek d Slobodan Zivojinovic 63 36 76; Guy Forget d Juan Aguilera 62 63; Emilio Sanchez d Amos Mansdorf 76 63; Andrei Cherkasov d Patrik Kuhnen 57 62 76; Jan Siemerink d Horst Skoff 61 60; Sergi Bruguera d Thomas Muster 62 63; Andrei Chesnokov d Magnus Larsson 64 64; Magnus Gustafsson d Marc Rosset 64 61; Omar Camporese d Ronald Agenor 64 62; Stefan Edberg d Markus Zoecke 64 76. **Rd 16:** Novacek d Bergstrom 61 63; Svensson d Baur 64 62; Ivanisevic d Jelen 64 64; Forget d Hlasek 63 64; Cherkasov d Sanchez 64 64; Siemerink d Bruguera 62 63; Gustafsson d Chesnokov 46 63 76; Edberg d Camporese 63 76. **QF:** Svensson d Novacek 76 62; Forget d Ivanisevic 75 76; Siemerink d Cherkasov 75 75; Edberg d Gustafsson 62 63. **SF:** Svensson d Forget 26 76 62; Edberg d Siemerink 64 62; **F:** Edberg d Svensson 26 36 75 62.
DOUBLES: Sergio Casal/Emilio Sanchez d Jeremy Bates/Nick Brown 63 75.

18-24 FEBRUARY: VOLVO TENNIS INDOOR, MEMPHIS $750,000 Winner: IVAN LENDL
Rd 64: Ivan Lendl bye; Wayne Ferreira d Luis Herrera 67 76 63; Gary Muller d Jimmy Arias 67 76 64; Paul Haarhuis bye; Petr Korda bye; Patrick McEnroe d Horacio de la Pena 62 62; Brian Garrow d Ramesh Krishnan 76 36 76; Darren Cahill bye; Andres Gomez bye; Tim Mayotte d Peter Lundgren 63 64; Guillaume Raoux d Renzo Furlan 76 16 63; Cristiano Caratti bye; Derrick Rostagno bye; Mark Kratzmann d Marcelo Filippini 76 16 64; Kevin Curren d Veli Paloheimo 64 61; Jim Courier bye; Michael Chang bye; Jean-Philippe Fleurian d Jim Grabb 64 75; Grant Connell d Scott Davis 62 76; Luiz Mattar bye; Wally Masur bye; Dan Goldie d Jaime Yzaga 63 46 76; Aki Rahunen d Richard Schmidt 64 26 64; Jeff Tarango bye; Michael Stich bye; Alex Antonitsch d Tomas Carbonell 36 76 76; Mats Wilander d Marcos Ondruska 76 57 62; David Wheaton bye; Mark Koevermans bye; Gilad Bloom d Christo van Rensburg 36 63 63; Chris Garner d Brad Pearce 76 62; Pete Sampras bye. **Rd 32:** Lendl d Ferreira 63 36 75; Haarhuis d Muller 63 61; McEnroe d Korda 26 61 75; Cahill d Garrow 64 62; Mayotte d Gomez 64 62; Caratti d Raoux 75 76; Rostagno d Kratzmann 76 76; Courier d Curren 63 64; Chang d Fleurian 64 36 62; Connell d Mattar 63 60; Masur d Goldie 67 75 62; Tarango d Rahunen 63 16 62; Stich d Antonitsch 62 63; Wilander d Wheaton 64 63; Koevermans d Bloom 63 64; Sampras d Garner 76 63. **Rd 16:** Lendl d Haarhuis 62 61; Cahill d McEnroe 63 64; Caratti d Mayotte 36 76 62; Rostagno d Courier 61 64; Chang d Connell 76 67 64; Tarango d Masur 76 64; Stich d Wilander 63 63; Koevermans d Sampras 26 11 4040 Ret. **QF:** Lendl d Cahill 76 63; Rostagno d Caratti 67 62 60; Chang d Tarango 63 75; Stich d Koevermans 64 62. **SF:** Lendl d Rostagno 63 62; Stich d Chang 62 62. **F:** Lendl d Stich 75 63.
DOUBLES: Udo Reglewski/Michael Stich d John Fitzgerald/Laurie Warder 75 63.

25 FEBRUARY-3 MARCH: ABN/AMRO WERELD TENNIS TOURNAMENT, ROTTERDAM $500,000 Winner: OMAR CAMPORESE
Rd 32: Ivan Lendl d Tom Nijssen 63 61; Nicklas Kulti d Christian Saceanu 62 64; Ctislav Dosedel d Henri Leconte 75 57 76; Jakob Hlasek d Pat Cash 62 64; Emilio Sanchez d Libor Pimek 63 63; Anders Jarryd d Amos Mansdorf 64 62; Jan Siemerink d Mark Koevermans 36 64 62; Andrei Chesnokov d Richard Krajicek 64 63; Paul Haarhuis d Jonas Svensson 75 06 63; Magnus Gustafsson d Jordi Arrese 61 30 Ret.; Magnus Larsson d Michiel Schapers 64 46 64; Christian Bergstrom d Goran Ivanisevic 76 76; Karel Novacek d Ronald Agenor 63 61; Javier Sanchez d Todd Woodbridge 61 64; Omar Camporese d Eric Jelen 62 26 62; Alex Antonitsch d Thomas Muster 26 75 62. **Rd 16:** Lendl d Kulti 64 60; Hlasek d Dosedel 63 64; Jarryd d E Sanchez 62 62; Siemerink d Chesnokov 46 63 62; Haarhuis d Gustafsson 63 36 61; Bergstrom d Larsson 62 75; Novacek

d J Sanchez 67 63 63; Camporese d Antonitsch 63 64. **QF:** Lendl d Hlasek 36 63 75; Jarryd d Siemerink 76 62; Haarhuis d Bergstrom 75 63; Camporese d Novacek 64 75. **SF:** Lendl d Jarryd 75 64; Camporese d Haarhuis 67 62 76. **F:** Camporese d Lendl 36 76 76.
DOUBLES: Patrick Galbraith/Anders Jarryd d Steve Devries/David Macpherson 76 62.

25 FEBRUARY-3 MARCH: VOLVO TENNIS, CHICAGO $250,000
Winner: JOHN MCENROE
Rd 32: John McEnroe d Gilad Bloom 62 61; Ramesh Krishnan d Aki Rahunen 61 64; Alexander Mronz d Michael Robertson 62 61; Gary Muller d Jean-Philippe Fleurian 64 64; Petr Korda d Peter Lundgren 76 63; Malivai Washington d Marian Vajda 61 61; Udo Riglewski d Scott Davis 63 76; Veli Paloheimo d Marcelo Filippini 63 26 62; Kevin Curren d Tomas Carbonell 63 67 62; Jaime Yzaga d Jimmy Connors 63 60; Grant Connell d Jim Grabb 61 64; Luiz Mattar d Grant Stafford 63 63; Patrick McEnroe d Brad Pearce 61 67 76; Nicolas Pereira d Ken Flach 67 75 64; David Pate d Luiz Herrera 63 62; Richey Reneberg d Todd Martin 26 76 63. **Rd 16:** J McEnroe d Krishnan 75 63; Mronz d Muller 76 63; Washington d Korda 64 76; Riglewski d Paloheimo 76 63; Yzaga d Curren 61 36 64; Connell d Mattar 61 67 63; P McEnroe d Pereira 64 76; Reneberg d Pate 63 76. **QF:** J McEnroe W/O; Washington d Riglewski 46 63 60; Connell d Yzaga 64 64; P McEnroe d Reneberg 61 76. **SF:** J McEnroe d Washington 76 67 64; P McEnroe d Connell 46 64 64. **F:** J McEnroe d P McEnroe 36 62 64.
DOUBLES: Scott Davis/David Pate d Grant Connell/Glenn Michibata 64 57 76.

4-10 MARCH: NEWSWEEK CHAMPIONS CUP, INDIAN WELLS $1,000,000 Winner: JIM COURIER
Rd 64: Stefan Edberg bye; Martin Jaite d David Wheaton 75 57 64; Darren Cahill d Veli Paloheimo 63 64; Steve Bryan d Juan Aguilera 63 61; Michael Chang d Marcelo Filippini 61 61; Jimmy Arias d Henri Leconte 76 63; Wayne Ferreira d Jean-Philippe Fleurian 64 64; Andres Gomez bye; Guy Forget bye; Tomas Carbonell d Gary Muller 64 61; Derrick Rostagno d Dan Goldie 64 75; Marc Rosset d Peter Lundgren 76 64; John McEnroe d Wally Masur 76 26 75; Jim Grabb d Gilad Bloom 76 26 61; Scott Davis d Javier Sanchez 76 75; Thomas Muster d Goran Ivanisevic bye; Fabrice Santoro d Aki Rahunen 61 64; Glenn Layendecker d Kelly Jones 46 63 63; Michael Stich d Tim Mayotte 63 61; Alexander Volkov d Thierry Champion 67 63 64; Richey Reneberg d Kevin Curren 67 76 76; Renzo Furlan d Cristiano Caratti 57 77 61; Francisco Clavet bye; Emilio Sanchez bye; Sergi Bruguera d Todd Witsken 75 75; Luiz Mattar d Brad Pearce 64 62; Andrei Cherkasov d Petr Korda 75 61; Jim Courier d Guillaume Raoux 64 36 62; Byron Black d Marian Vajda 61 36 63; Goran Prpic d Maurice Ruah 63 61; Andre Agassi bye. **Rd 32:** Edberg d Jaite 63 63; Cahill d Bryan 76 62; Chang d Arias 44 46 61; Ferreira d Gomez 64 76; Forget d Carbonell 61 63; Rostagno d Rosset 75 61; Grabb d McEnroe 76 75; Davis d Muster 63 62; Santoro d Ivanisevic 60 62; Stich d Layendecker 63 76; Reneberg d Volkov 67 62 64; Clavet d Furlan 60 67 62; Sanchez d Bruguera 64 64; Cherkasov d Mattar 75 67 64; Courier d Black 61 76; Agassi d Prpic 63 64. **Rd 16:** Edberg d Cahill 36 75 62; Chang d Ferreira 63 36 64; Forget d Rostagno 63 63; Davis d Grabb 64 64; Stich d Santoro 46 63 64; Reneberg d Clavet 26 63 60; Sanchez d Cherkasov 63 76; Courier d Agassi 26 63 64. **QF:** Edberg d Chang 16 62 75; Forget d Davis 75 61; Stich d Reneberg 60 26 64; Courier d Sanchez 62 63. **SF:** Forget d Edberg 64 64; Courier d Stich 63 62. **F:** Courier d Forget 46 63 46 63 76.
DOUBLES: Jim Courier/Javier Sanchez d Guy Forget/Henri Leconte 76 36 63.

4-10 MARCH: COPENHAGEN OPEN 1991 $150,000 Winner: JONAS SVENSSON
Rd 32: Jonas Svensson d Martin Strelba 76 62; Frederik Fetterlein d Eduardo Masso 36 63 62; Carl-Uwe Steeb d Henrik Holm 36 63 75; Christian Bergstrom d Jacco Eltingh 63 75; Jakob Hlasek d Markus Zoecke 26 64 63; Lars Jonsson d Luiz Herrera 61 60; Christian Saceanu d Michael Tauson 64 75; Ronald Agenor d Alex Antonitsch 46 63 64; Todd Woodbridge d Per Henricsson 62 75; Thomas Hogstedt d Stefano Pescosolido 64 75; Jose Francisco Altur d Andrei Olhovskiy 76 26 64; Karel Novacek d Thomas Enqvist 62 36 64; Anders Jarryd d Barts Wuyts 63 62; Jan Gunnarsson d Patrik Kuhnen 63 62; Mark Woodforde d Jens Woehrmann 26 61 64; Andrei Chesnokov d Patrik Baur 46 62 64. **Rd 16:** Svensson d Fetterlein 63 26 62; Bergstrom d Steeb 36 63 63; Hlasek d Jonsson 63 64; Saceanu d Agenor 63 76; Woodbridge d Hogstedt 63 60; Novacek d Altur 63 62; Jarryd d Gunnarsson 63 62; Woodforde d Chesnokov 62 26 76. **QF:** Svensson d Bergstrom 64 75; Hlasek d Saceanu 36 64 62; Woodbridge d Novacek 76 46 61; Jarryd d Woodforde 61 63. **SF:** Svensson d Hlasek 62 16 63; Jarryd d Woodbridge 60 64. **F:** Svensson d Jarryd 67 62 62.
DOUBLES: Todd Woodbridge/Mark Woodforde d Charles Beckman/David Macpherson 63 61.

15-24 MARCH: LIPTON INTERNATIONAL PLAYERS CHAMPIONSHIPS, KEY BISCAYNE $1,500,000 Winner: JIM COURIER
Rd 128: Stefan Edberg bye; Bruce Derlin d Harold Solomon 62 63; Gary Muller d Scott Davis 76 64; Goran Prpic bye; Juan Aguilera bye; Jaime Oncins d Alexis Hombrecher 63 63; David Witt d Cassio Motta 61 76; Michael Stich bye; Michael Chang bye; Jaime Yzaga d Brian Garrow 64 36 61; Francisco Clavet d Stefano Pescosolido 46 64 61; Henri Leconte bye; Darren Cahill bye; Veli Paloheimo d Renzo Furlan 62 64; Jeff Tarango d Johan Carlsson 75 63; Emilio Sanchez bye; Andrew Agassi bye; Fabrice

Santoro d Guillaume Raoux 26 62 76; Todd Witsken d Alexander Mronz 64 16 63; Magnus Gustafsson d Aaron Krickstein bye; Kevin Curren d Marian Vajda 63 61; David Wheaton d Jim Grabb 63 36 61; Guillermo Perez-Roldan bye; Jakob Hlasek bye; Nuno Marques d Carl-Uwe Steeb 62 62; Arnaud Boetsch d Gilad Bloom 36 63 76; Sergi Bruguera bye; Cristiano Caratti bye; Jimmy Connors d Udo Riglewski 64 64; Rodolphe Gilbert d Thierry Champion 76 61; Pete Sampras bye; Francisco Roig bye; Javier Sanchez d Marcelo Filippini 63 26 60; Wayne Ferreira d Horacio de la Pena 63 Ret.; Franco Davin bye; Derrick Rostagno bye; Ramesh Krishnan d Peter Lundgren 64 64; Tim Mayotte d Malivai Washington 75 62; Andrei Cherkasov bye; Jim Courier bye; Luis Herrera d Brad Pearce 63 60; Paul Haarhuis d Mark Kratzmann 63 62; Karel Novacek bye; Martin Jaite bye; Jimmy Arias d Jean-Philippe Fleurian 16 64 63; Dan Goldie d Andrew Sznajder 75 67 63; Guy Forget bye; Andres Gomez bye; Tomas Carbonell d Thomas Hogstedt 62 60; Jan Gunnarsson d Chris Garner 62 62; Horst Skoff bye; Richey Reneberg bye; Petr Korda d Richard Krajicek 16 63 62; Jan Siemerink d Jason Stoltenberg 76 36 76; Brad Gilbert bye; Alexander Volkov bye; Shuzo Matsuoka d Kelly Evernden 36 61 62; Patrick Baur d Luiz Mattar 76 63; Mark Rosset bye; Patrick McEnroe bye; Kelly Jones d Grant Connell 64 64; Steve Devries d Aki Rahunen 63 62; Boris Becker bye. **Rd 64:** Edberg d Derlin 62 63; Prpic d Muller 64 60; Aguilera d Oncins 63 75; Stich d Witt 62 16 62; Chang d Yzaga 63 62; Leconte d Clavet 62 46 64; Cahill d Paloheimo 60 36 61; E Sanchez d Tarango 67 76 63; Agassi d Santoro 76 46 75; Gustafsson d Witsken 63 26 61; Curren d Krickstein 62 60; Wheaton d Perez-Roldan 44 Ret.; Hlasek d Marques 76 63; Bruguera d Boetsch 64 76; Caratti d Connors 64 63; Gilbert d Sampras 64 62; J Sanchez d Roig 76 62; Ferreira d Davin 76 10 Ret.; Rostagno d Krishnan 67 64 63; Mayotte d Cherkasov 64 61; Courier d Herrera 76 36 63; Haarhuis d Novacek 64 63; Arias d Jaite 76 63; Forget d Goldie 61 63; Carbonell d Gomez 64 26 64; Skoff d Gunnarsson 62 60; Reneberg d Korda 67 76 63; Siemerink d Gilbert 67 64 63; Matsuoka d Volkov 63 75; Rosset d Baur 64 64; McEnroe d Jones 75 60; Becker d Devries 57 63 76. **Rd 32:** Edberg d Prpic 64 62; Stich d Aguilera 64 63; Chang d Leconte 46 63 63; E Sanchez d Cahill 76 61; Agassi d Gustafsson 67 62 75; Wheaton d Curren 06 76 75; Bruguera d Hlasek 61 62; Caratti d Gilbert 64 46 63; Ferreira d J Sanchez 61 63; Rostagno d Mayotte 67 64 63; Courier d Haarhuis 75 36 63; Forget d Arias 61 61; Carbonell d Skoff 06 61 62; Reneberg d Siemerink 76 64; Rosset d Matsuoka 64 64; McEnroe d Becker 61 64. **Rd 16:** Edberg d Stich 64 26 64; E Sanchez d Chang 57 63 64; Wheaton d Agassi 60 75; Caratti d Bruguera 67 36 76; Rostagno d Ferreira 63 16 64; Courier d Forget 76 63; Reneberg d Carbonell 76 76; Rosset d McEnroe 76 61. **QF:** Edberg d E Sanchez 62 76; Wheaton d Caratti 67 62 60; Courier d Rostagno 60 63; Reneberg d Rosset 76 36 63. **SF:** Wheaton d Edberg 63 64; Courier d Reneberg 64 63. **F:** Courier d Wheaton 46 63 64.
DOUBLES: Wayne Ferreira/Piet Norval d Ken Flach/Robert Seguso 57 76 62.

1-7 APRIL: ESTORIL OPEN, $375,000 Winner: SERGI BRUGUERA
Rd 32: Ronald Agenor d Andres Gomez 64 63; Javier Sanchez d Christer Allgardh 46 75 62; Goran Prpic d Aki Rahunen 61 63; Karel Novacek d Omar Camporese 61 63; Francisco Clavet d Andrei Cherkasov 62 46 75; Tomas Carbonell d Cassio Motta 75 63; Nuno Marques d Emanuel Couto 62 36 61; Marian Vajda d Juan Aguilera 75 36 62; Horst Skoff d Marc Rosset 61 16 63; Richard Fromberg d Joao Cunha-Silva 64 46 21 Ret.; Claudio Mezzadri d Jordi Arrese 63 62; Andrei Chesnokov d Horacio de la Pena 64 62; Sergi Bruguera d Mark Koevermans 63 63; Eduardo Bengoechea d Veli Paloheimo 75 46 62; Renzo Furlan d Thierry Champion 26 76 61; Paul Haarhuis d Emilio Sanchez 60 62. **Rd 16:** J Sanchez d Agenor 52 Ret.; Novacek d Prpic 62 75; Clavet d Carbonell 62 76; Vajda d Marques 46 75 63; Skoff d Fromberg 64 62; Chesnokov d Mezzadri 57 75 61; Bruguera d Bengoechea 63 67 63; Furlan d Haarhuis 75 63. **QF:** Novacek d J Sanchez 75 63; Vajda d Clavet 62 06 63; Chesnokov d Skoff 63 61; Bruguera d Furlan 61 63. **SF:** Novacek d Vajda 75 62; Bruguera d Chesnokov 64 26 63. **F:** Bruguera d Novacek 76 61.
DOUBLES: Paul Haarhuis/Mark Koevermans d Tom Nijssen/Cyril Suk 63 63.

1-7 APRIL: SALEM OPEN, HONG KONG $260,000 Winner: RICHARD KRAJICEK
Rd 32: Michael Chang d Kelly Jones 62 63; Christo van Rensburg d Ramesh Krishnan 62 57 75; Gary Muller d Jaime Yzaga 63 64; Tommy Ho d Todd Woodbridge 64 62; Eduardo Masso d Michael Stich 75 64; Richard Krajicek d Neil Borwick 64 67 63; Patrik Kuhnen d John Stimpson 64 64; Anders Jarryd d Udo Riglewski 62 61; Kevin Curren d Aaron Krickstein 76 61; Felix Barrientos d Nick Brown 61 64; Glenn Michibata d Mark Kratzmann 16 76 62; Wally Masur d Jakob Hlasek 64 76; Amos Mansdorf d Gianluca Pozzi 63 67 64; Alexander Mronz d Michael Walker 63 63; Alex Antonitsch d Guillaume Raoux 64 46 75; Todd Witsken d John McEnroe 63 57 76. **Rd 16:** Chang d van Rensburg 75 67 64; Muller d Ho 61 16 63; Krajicek d Masso 61 64; Kuhnen d Jarryd 76 10 Ret.; Barrientos d Curren 16 61 75; Masur d Michibata 63 64; Mronz d Mansdorf 67 64 62; Antonitsch d Witsken 61 76. **QF:** Muller d Chang 57 63 76; Krajicek d Kuhnen 76 26 61; Masur d Barrientos 60 61; Antonitsch d Mronz 36 63 64. **SF:** Krajicek d Muller 62 64; Masur d Antonitsch 46 76 63. **F:** Krajicek d Masur 62 36 63.
DOUBLES: Patrick Galbraith/Todd Witsken d Glenn Michibata and Robert Van't Hof 62 64.

1-7 APRIL: PRUDENTIAL SECURITIES TENNIS CLASSIC, ORLANDO $250,000 Winner: ANDRE AGASSI
Rd 32: Andre Agassi d Brian Garrow 62 64; David Engel d Danilo Marcelino 63 36 76; Bryan Shelton d T J Middleton 63 63; Chuck Adams d

Grant Connell 63 46 63; Brad Gilbert d Pedro Rebolledo 26 61 61; Patrick Baur d Bart Wuyts 64 62; Malivai Washington d Luis Herrera 46 75 64; Nicolas Pereira d Scott Davis 75 61; Jimmy Arias d David Macpherson 76 26 64; David Witt d Tim Mayotte 76 62; Thomas Hogstedt d Johan Anderson 36 63 62; Derrick Rostagno d Jimmy Connors 61 64; David Pate d Chris Garner 63 76; Jeff Tarango d Ken Flach 76 64; Diego Nargiso d Richard Matuszewski 63 76; Pete Sampras d Brad Pearce 62 62. **Rd 16:** Agassi d Engel 64 64; Adams d Shelton 36 76 76; Gilbert d Baur 63 76; Washington d Pereira 61 63; Arias d Witt 67 76 61; Rostagno d Hogstedt 46 62 62; Pate d Tarango 62 67 61; Sampras d Nargiso 63 76. **QF:** Agassi d Adams 64 76; Washington d Gilbert 62 67 62; Rostagno d Arias 61 64; Sampras d Pate 63 63. **SF:** Agassi d Washington 64 76; Rostagno d Sampras 75 64. **F:** Agassi d Rostagno 62 16 63.
DOUBLES: Luke Jensen and Scott Melville d Nicolas Pereira and Pete Sampras 67 76 63.

8-14 APRIL: SUNTORY JAPAN OPEN TENNIS CHAMPIONSHIP, TOKYO $1,000,000 Winner: STEFAN EDBERG
Rd 64: Stefan Edberg bye; Kelly Evernden d Guillaume Raoux 63 63; Jimmy Connors d Jim Pugh 16 64 60; Wally Masur d Eduardo Masso 64 63; Anders Jarryd d Jason Stoltenberg 60 63; Luis Herrera d Jacco Eltingh 62 62; Tim Mayotte d Gary Muller 76 46 63; Michael Stich bye; Brad Gilbert bye; Grant Connell d Jan Apell 76 36 76; Andrew Sznajder d Alex Antonitsch 62 63; Pat Cash d Toshihisa Tsuchihashi 62 75; David Pate d Todd Woodbridge 16 63 63; Patrick Baur d Gianluca Pozzi 64 64; John Fitzgerald d Richard Krajicek 61 64; Michael Chang d John McEnroe bye; Slobodan Zivojinovic d Brian Garrow 60 76; Todd Witsken d Eduardo Furusho 61 63; Amos Mansdorf d Gilad Bloom 62 61; Dan Goldie d Jan Siemerink 64 36 76; John Stimpson d Kentaro Masuda 61 61; Jim Grabb d Jeff Tarango 46 63 76; Jim Courier bye; Jakob Hlasek bye; Udo Riglewski d Mark Kratzmann 64 62; Alexander Mronz d Yasufumi Yahamoto 61 62; Patrik Kuhnen d Aaron Krickstein 62 75; Shuzo Matsuoka d Kevin Curren 76 62; Jaime Yzaga d Christo van Rensburg 61 76; Ramesh Krishnan d Thomas Hogstedt 61 65; Ivan Lendl bye. **Rd 32:** Edberg d Evernden 62 76; Connors d Masur 36 76 75; Jarryd d Herrera 61 60; Stich d Mayotte 75 64; Gilbert d Connell 61 76; Cash d Sznajder 62 64; Pate d Baur 61 64; Chang d Fitzgerald 60 60; McEnroe d Zivojinovic 61 64; Witsken d Mansdorf 62 16 63; Goldie d Stimpson 36 76; Courier d Grabb 67 62 63; Hlasek d Riglewski 76 64; Mronz d Kuhnen 64 64; Yzaga d Matsuoka 61 76; Lendl d Krishnan 63 62. **Rd 16:** Edberg d Connors 64 67 61; Stich d Jarryd 76 62; Cash d Gilbert 46 16 63; Chang d Pate 76 64; McEnroe d Witsken 36 76 64; Courier d Goldie 63 64; Hlasek d Mronz 67 75; Lendl d Yzaga 75 63. **QF:** Edberg d Stich 76 63; Chang d Cash 64 61; Courier d McEnroe 62 62; Lendl d Hlasek 61 64. **SF:** Edberg d Chang 75 62; Lendl d Courier 64 61. **F:** Edberg d Lendl 61 75 60.
DOUBLES: Stefan Edberg/Todd Woodbridge d John Fitzgerald/Anders Jarryd 64 57 64.

8-14 APRIL: TROFEO CONDE DE GODO, BARCELONA $650,000 Winner: EMILIO SANCHEZ
Rd 64: Boris Becker bye; Jean-Philippe Fleurian d Franco Davin 46 76 75; Carl-Uwe Steeb d Eric Jelen 76 62; Sergi Bruguera d Mark Woodforde 60 60; Marc Rosset d Claudio Mezzandri 67 61 64; Javier Sanchez d Jose Francisco Altur 62 75; Roberto Azar d Jose Aparisi 76 36 64; Andrei Chesnokov bye; Andre Agassi bye; Goran Prpic d Tomas Carbonell 63 61; Aki Rahunen d Joao Cunha-Silva 64 64; Karel Novacek d Carlos Costa 63 16 64; Guillermo Perez-Roldan d Lars Jonsson 63 64; German Lopez d Diego Nargiso 63 67 63; Marcelo Filippini d Horst Skoff 76 63; Andres Gomez bye; Jonas Svensson bye; Martin Jaite d Paul Haarhuis 63 62; Renzo Furlan d Henri Leconte 63 63; Magnus Gustafsson d Juan Aguilera 64 60; Alexander Volkov d Fernando Luna 76 67 64; Francisco Clavet d Mats Wilander 63 62; Veli Paloheimo d Alberto Mancini 64 26 64; Goran Ivanisevic bye; Emilio Sanchez bye; Diego Perez d Mark Koevermans 76 61; Francisco Roig d Vincente Dolves 36 62 75; Andrei Cherkasov d Tarik Benhabiles 26 62 61; Omar Camporese d Thierry Champion 61 36 61; Horacio de la Pena d Richard Fromberg 64 64; Jordi Arrese d Marian Vajda 67 75 64; Guy Forget bye. **Rd 32:** Becker d Fleurian 75 61; Bruguera d Steeb 64 61; J Sanchez d Rosset 36 63 34 Ret.; Chesnokov d Azar 76 61; Agassi d Prpic 67 64 75; Rahunen d Novacek 06 62 62; Perez-Roldan d Lopez 75 16 64; Filippini d Gomez 57 64 63; Jaite d Svensson 75 46 62; Gustafsson d Furlan 63 61; Clavet d Volkov 60 61; Paloheimo d Ivanisevic 63 64; E Sanchez d Perez 61 61; Cherkasov d Roig 62 75; Camporese d de la Pena 36 61 62; Arrese d Forget 26 63 75. **Rd 16:** Bruguera d Becker 62 64; Chesnokov d J Sanchez 57 75 64; Agassi d Rahunen 62 63; Perez-Roldan d Filippini 61 60; Jaite d Gustafsson 63 06 75; Paloheimo d Clavet 63 64; E Sanchez d Cherkasov 57 75 63; Camporese d Arrese 63 75. **QF:** Bruguera d Chesnokov 62 75; Perez-Roldan d Agassi 60 67 76; Jaite d Paloheimo 61 46 63; E Sanchez d Camporese 76 46 75. **SF:** Bruguera d Perez-Roldan 64 64; E Sanchez d Jaite 75 62. **F:** E Sanchez d Bruguera 64 76 62.
DOUBLES: Horacio de la Pena/Diego Nargiso d Boris Becker/Eric Jelen 36 76 64.

15-21 APRIL: PHILIPS OPEN, NICE $250,000 Winner: MARTIN JAITE
Rd 32: Martin Jaite d Guy Forget 62 62; Jimmy Arias d Rodolphe Gilbert 76 76; Jordi Arrese d Richard Fromberg 62 64; Renzo Furlan d Juan Aguilera 76 76; Andres Gomez d Nicklas Kulti 60 76; Alberto Mancini d Thierry Champion 76 60; Carl-Uwe Steeb d Frederic Fontang 75 46 63; Karel Novacek d Jean-Philippe Fleurian 62 63; Guillermo Perez-Roldan d

Eric Jelen 62 62; Goran Prpic d Mats Wilander 63 61; Horacio de la Pena d Aki Rahunen 63 62; Eduardo Bengoechea d Andrei Cherkasov 64 46 64; Alexander Volkov d Marian Vajda 57 75 62; Cedric Pioline d Fabrice Santoro 36 61 64; Henri Leconte d Franco Davin 64 60; Andrei Chesnokov d Magnus Larsson 62 62. **Rd 16:** Jaite d Arias 62 61; Furlan d Arrese 64 75; Mancini d Gomez 62 36 61; Novacek d Steeb 36 75 64; Prpic d Perez-Roldan 61 46 61; de la Pena d Bengoechea 64 36 60; Pioline d Volkov 64 63; Leconte d Chesnokov 63 75. **QF:** Jaite d Furlan 62 61; Novacek d Mancini 63 76; Prpic d de la Pena 75 62; Pioline d Leconte 62 64. **SF:** Jaite d Novacek 46 64 76; Prpic d Pioline 61 63. **F:** Jaite d Prpic 36 76 63.
DOUBLES: Rikard Bergh/Jan Gunnarsson d Vojtech Flegl/Niklas Utgren 64 46 63.

15-21 APRIL: KAL CUP KOREA TENNIS CHAMPIONSHIPS, SEOUL $165,000 Winner: PATRICK BAUR
Rd 32: Jan Siemerink d Nick Brown 64 26 62; Karsten Braasch d Andrew Sznajder 61 61; Girts Dzelde d Paul Wekesa 64 64; Shuzo Matsuoka d Patrik Kuhnen 75 46 62; Richard Krajicek d Jan Apell 61 64; Dan Goldie d Eduardo Masso 26 61 63; Scott Melville d Sandon Stolle 61 75; Patrick Baur d Alexander Mronz 76 60; Gilad Bloom d Milan Srejber 60 61; Eui-Jong Chang d Jae-Sik Kim 36 60 61; Jeff Tarango d Kelly Evernden 64 64; Seung-Ho Ji d Jim Grabb 76 57 64; Bryan Shelton d Grant Connell 64 16 76; Luis Herrera d Jacco Eltingh 57 63 63; Menho Oosting d Han-Cheol Shin 16 63 64; Alex Antonitsch d Brian Garrow 60 64. **Rd 16:** Siemerink d Braasch 36 76 63; Matsuoka d Dzelde 62 61; Krajicek d Goldie 76 60; Baur d Melville 62 61; Bloom d Chang 64 61; Tarango d Ji 26 62 61; Herrera d Shelton 63 63; Antonitsch d Oosting 60 62. **QF:** Matsuoka d Siemerink 46 62 64; Baur d Krajicek 75 67 62; Tarango d Bloom 61 76; Herrera d Antonitsch 61 62. **SF:** Baur d Matsuoka 76 62; Tarango d Herrera 26 75 62. **F:** Baur d Tarango 64 17 76.
DOUBLES: Alex Antonitsch/Gilad Bloom d Kent Kinnear/Sven Salumaa 64 64.

22-28 APRIL: VOLVO MONTE CARLO OPEN $1,000,000 Winner: SERGI BRUGUERA
Rd 64: Stefan Edberg bye; Magnus Larsson d David Rikl 63 61; Magnus Gustafsson d Udo Riglewski 67 62 64; Guillermo Perez-Roldan d Thierry Tulasne 60 64; Sergi Bruguera d Renzo Furlan 63 67 63; Cristiano Caratti d Henri Leconte 75 26 61; Alberto Mancini d Jimmy Arias 62 76; Emilio Sanchez bye; Andre Agassi bye; Horst Skoff d Jean-Philippe Fleurian 46 64 62; Juan Aguilera d Peter Lundgren 61 64; Claudio Pistolesi d Marc Rosset 76 57 63; Veli Paloheimo d Thomas Muster 67 62 61; Mark Koevermans d Luiz Mattar 63 62; Dimu Pescariu d Franco Davin 64 10 Ret.; Jonas Svensson bye; Goran Ivanisevic bye; Jordi Arrese d Bjorn Borg 62 63; Carl-Uwe Steeb d Thierry Champion 26 64 63; Omar Camporese d Andres Gomez 63 36 61; Goran Prpic d Karel Novacek 62 63; Richard Fromberg d Martin Jaite 63 62; Paul Haarhuis d Christian Bergstrom 63 62; Guy Forget bye; Andrei Chesnokov bye; Mats Wilander d Mark Woodforde 60 63; Ronald Agenor d Nicklas Kulti 26 76; Andrei Cherkasov d Eric Jelen 60 62; Alexander Volkov d Horacio de la Pena 57 63 75; Fabrice Santoro d Thierry Guardiola 63 61; Javier Sanchez d Marcelo Filippini 61 61; Boris Becker bye. **Rd 32:** Larsson d Edberg 57 63 76; Gustafsson d Perez-Roldan 64 63; Bruguera d Caratti 61 75; Mancini d E Sanchez 63 63; Skoff d Agassi 60 67 63; Pistolesi d Aguilera 63 16 75; Paloheimo d Koevermans 75 64; Svensson d Pescariu 63 46 64; Ivanisevic d Arrese 76 76; Steeb d Camporese 64 63; Prpic d Fromberg 61 64; Forget d Haarhuis 75 64; Chesnokov d Wilander 76 62; Cherkasov d Agenor 76 63; Volkov d Santoro 26 61 64; Becker d J Sanchez 67 63 63. **Rd 16:** Gustafsson d Larsson 76 64; Bruguera d Mancini 61 64; Skoff d Pistolesi 62 75; Svensson d Paloheimo 61 46 63; Steeb d Ivanisevic 26 60 62; Prpic d Forget 62 60; Chesnokov d Cherkasov 61 60; Becker d Volkov 36 61 61. **QF:** Bruguera d Gustafsson 75 75; Skoff d Svensson 63 63; Prpic d Steeb 64 62; Becker d Chesnokov 61 63. **SF:** Bruguera d Skoff 61 64; Becker d Prpic 63 63. **F:** Bruguera d Becker 57 64 76 76.
DOUBLES: Luke Jensen/Laurie Warder d Paul Haarhuis/Mark Koevermans 57 76 64.

22-28 APRIL: EPSON SINGAPORE SUPER TENNIS $250,000 Winner: JAN SIEMERINK
Rd 32: Todd Woodbridge d Jeff Tarango 62 40 Ret.; Christo van Rensburg d Patrick Baur 63 46 64; Jim Grabb d Andrew Sznajder 64 62; Jason Stoltenberg d Richard Krajicek 62 62; Leander Paes d Wally Masur 62 57 75; Glenn Michibata d Patrik Kuhnen 76 64; Gilad Bloom d Eduardo Masso 75 75; Jacco Eltingh d Scott Davis 16 64 63; Alex Antonitsch d Kely Jones 62 63; Grant Connell d Jonathon Canter 64 26 64; Thomas Hogstedt d Brian Garrow 62 62; Slobodan Zivojinovic d Kevin Curren 67 63 64; Shuzo Matsuoka d Gary Muller 63 63; Dan Goldie d John Fitzgerald 46 63 61; Luis Herrera d Bryan Shelton 63 64; Jan Siemerink d Mark Kratzmann 36 76 62. **Rd 16:** Woodbridge d van Rensburg 61 57 76; Stoltenberg d Grabb 64 62; Michibata d Paes 64 76; Bloom d Eltingh 64 62; Connell d Antonitsch 64 64; Hogstedt d Zivojinovic 64 76; Matsuoka d Goldie 62 62; Siemerink d Herrera 76 76. **QF:** Stoltenberg d Woodbridge 62 76; Bloom d Michibata 63 63; Connell d Hogstedt 75 64; Siemerink d Matsuoka 64 64. **SF:** Bloom d Stoltenberg 36 64 63; Siemerink d Connell 62 62. **F:** Siemerink d Bloom 64 63.
DOUBLES: Grant Connell/Glenn Michibata d Stefan Kruger/Christo van Reneburg 64 57 76.

29 APRIL-5 MAY: XX TROFEO GRUPO ZETA VILLA DE MADRID, MADRID OPEN, MADRID $500,000 Winner: JORDI ARRESE
Rd 32: Renzo Furlan d Emilio Sanchez 46 76 63; Thierry Champion d Eduardo Masso 60 36 63; Jose Francisco Altur d J Antonio Rodriguez 64 61; Jordi Arrese d Jose A Conde 63 62; Karel Novacek d Diego Nargiso 63 76; Cassio Motta d Jimmy Connors 76 16 61; Mats Wilander d Henrik Jan Davids 62 64; Franco Davin d Jan Gunnarsson 61 64; Marcelo Filippini d Francisco Clavet 60 64; Jaime Oncins d Patrick Baur 63 61; Jacco Eltingh d Milan Srejber 63 76; Andres Gomez d Ctislav Dosedel 60 62; Martin Sinner d Luiz Mattar 64 64; German Lopez d Roberto Azar 76 67 76; Javier Sanchez d Tarik Benhabiles 76 64; Sergi Bruguera d Tomas Carbonell 64 60. **Rd 16:** Champion d Furlan 36 61 61; Arrese d Altur 64 67 76; Novacek d Motta 63 75; Davin d Wilander 63 26 60; Filippini d Oncins 62 36 76; Eltingh d Gomez 63 57 31 Ret.; Lopez d Sinner 64 75; J Sanchez d Bruguera 36 61 64. **QF:** Arrese d Champion 64 32 Ret.; Novacek d Davin 63 36 61; Filippini d Eltingh 64 62; J Sanchez d Lopez 76 64. **SF:** Arrese d Novacek 64 63; Filippini d J Sanchez 75 61. **F:** Arrese d Filippini 75 61.
DOUBLES: Gustavo Luza/Cassio Motta d Luiz Mattar/Jaime Oncins 60 75.

29 APRIL-5 MAY: BMW OPEN, MUNICH $250,000 Winner: MAGNUS GUSTAFSSON
Rd 32: Ivan Lendl d Alexander Mronz 62 62; Goran Prpic d Mark Woodforde 63 62; Eduardo Bengoechea d Horacio de la Pena 46 75 61; Todd Witsken d Alexander Volkov 16 75 61; Anders Jarryd d Jonas Svensson 63 61; Goran Prpic d John McEnroc 62 62; Horst Skoff d Amos Mansdorf 64 62; Magnus Gustafsson d Michael Stich 57 64 63; Christian Bergstrom d Thomas Muster 61 26 64; Marian Vajda d Carl-Uwe Steeb 76 62; Lars Jonsson d Andrej Medvedev 63 75; Dinu Pescariu d John McEnroc 62 62; Guillermo Perez-Roldan d Juan Aguilera 63 60; David Engel d Paul Vojtischek 63 63; Eric Jelen d Ronald Agenor 36 64 60; Goran Ivanisevic d Jens Woehrmann 76 61. **Rd 16:** Lendl d Prpic 36 64 62; Witsken d Bengoechea 64 36 64; Riglewski d Jarryd 46 64 76; Gustafsson d Skoff 60 46 64; Bergstrom d Vajda 62 64; Jonsson d Pescariu 61 64; Perez-Roldan d Engel 75 62; Ivanisevic d Jelen 64 46 63. **QF:** Lendl d Witsken 36 64 75; Gustafsson d Riglewski 62 75; Bergstrom d Jonsson 46 62 62; Perez-Roldan d Ivanisevic 76 61. **SF:** Gustafsson d Lendl 64 75; Perez-Roldan d Bergstrom 60 60. **F:** Gustafsson d Perez-Roldan 36 63 43 Ret.
DOUBLES: Patrick Galbraith/Todd Witsken d Anders Jarryd/Danie Visser 75 64.

29 APRIL-5 MAY: USTA MEN'S CLAY COURTS OF TAMPA $250,000 Winner: RICHEY RENEBERG
Rd 32: Richey Reneberg d Lawson Duncan 76 62; Bruno Oresar d Bart Wuyts 63 61; Bryan Shelton d Todd Martin 26 63 75; Malivai Washington d Chuck Adams 63 62; Niclas Kroon d Jaime Yzaga 64 63; Pablo Arraya d Andrew Sznajder 64 36 61; Henrik Holm d Thomas Hogstedt 46 63 64; Kelly Evernden d Brad Pearce 63 62; Mikael Pernfors d David Pate 63 62; Christian Saceanu d Diego Perez 67 76 63; Jimmy Brown d Pedro Rebolledo 60 62; Petr Korda d Rich Leach 63 62; Stefano Pescosolido d Martin Wostenholme 46 76 64; Chris Garner d Mark Kaplan 36 63 10 Ret.; Javier Frana d Danilo Marcelino 64 61; Jimmy Arias d Jim Pugh 62 63. **Rd 16:** Reneberg d Oresar 63 64; Washington d Shelton 76 75; Arraya d Kroon 57 64 76; Evernden d Holm W/O; Pernfors d Saceanu 64 62; Korda d Brown 64 26 76; Garner d Pescosolido 76 76; Frana d Arias 67 63 63. **QF:** Reneberg d Washington 63 63; Arraya d Evernden 67 64 61; Korda d Pernfors 63 62; Garner d Frana 46 76 76. **SF:** Reneberg d Arraya 63 61; Korda d Garner 64 64. **F:** Reneberg d Korda 46 62.
DOUBLES: Ken Flach/Robert Seguso d David Pate/Richey Reneberg 67 64 61.

6-12 MAY: PANASONIC GERMAN OPEN, HAMBURG $1,000,000 Winner: KAREL NOVACEK
Rd 64: Stefan Edberg bye; Alexander Mronz d Patrik Kuhnen 62 75; Ronald Agenor d Nicklas Kulti 64 76; Aaron Krickstein d Marc Rosset 46 62 63; Michael Stich d Tomas Carbonell 16 63 75; Paul Haarhuis d Tom Nijssen 36 64 76; Francisco Clavet d Amos Mansdorf 76 62; Emilio Sanchez bye; Pete Sampras bye; Horst Skoff d Thomas Muster 75 62; Omar Camporese d Rudiger Haas 76 64; Karel Novacek d Carl-Uwe Steeb 64 76; Franco Davin d Andres Gomez 64 63 Mark Koevermans d Marian Vajda 63 62; Martin Jaite d Eric Jelen 75 63; Sergi Bruguera bye; Jim Courier bye; Horacio de la Pena d Christian Bergstrom 62 36 62; Jordi Arrese d Juan Aguilera 62 75; Goran Prpic d Andrei Chesnokov 64 63; Alexander Volkov d Gilad Bloom 61 76; Arnaud Boetsch d Anders Jarryd 64 61; Luiz Mattar d Udo Riglewski 61 64; Goran Ivanisevic bye; Jonas Svensson bye; Cristiano Caratti d Claudio Pistolesi 63 63; Magnus Gustafsson d David Engel 64 62; Andrei Cherkasov d Henri Leconte 76 63; Magnus Larsson d Wayne Ferreira 62 36 63; Yannick Noah d Richard Fromberg 76 60; Renzo Furlan d Marcelo Filippini 63 63; Ivan Lendl bye. **Rd 32:** Edberg d Mronz 63 61; Agenor d Krickstein 75 06 62; Stich d Haarhuis 75 60; Clavet d Sanchez 63 46 64; Sampras d Skoff 63 46 64; Novacek d Camporese 63 62; Koevermans d Davin 64 64; Bruguera d Jaite 63 61; de la Pena d Courier 67 62 64; Prpic d Arrese 63 63; Volkov d Boetsch 76 76; Ivanisevic d Mattar 61 76; Caratti d Svensson 62 62; Gustafsson d Cherkasov 36 64 64; Noah d Larsson 46 16 63; Furlan d Lendl 75 64. **Rd 16:** Edberg d Agenor 62 61; Stich d Clavet 61 64; Novacek d Sampras 64 64; Koevermans d Bruguera 64 64; Prpic d de la Pena 63 64; Ivanisevic d Volkov 61 63; Gustafsson d Caratti 75 36 62; Noah d Furlan 16 64 63. **QF:** Stich d Edberg 62 76; Novacek d Koevermans 46 64 62; Prpic d Ivanisevic 75 30 Ret.; Gustafsson d Noah 61 64. **SF:** Novacek d Stich 63 76; Gustafsson d

---

Prpic 61 16 76. **F:** Novacek d Gustafsson 63 63 57 06 61.
DOUBLES: Sergio Casal/Emilio Sanchez d Cassio Motta/Danie Visser 46 63 62.

6-12 MAY: USAIR/US MEN'S CLAY COURT CHAMPIONSHIPS, CHARLOTTE $250,000 Winner: JAIME YZAGA
Rd 32: Michael Chang d Niclas Kroon 60 75; Bryan Shelton d Stefano Pescosolido 62 62; Jimmy Brown d Andrew Sznajder 61 36 64; Jaime Yzaga d Chris Garner 76 63; David Wheaton d Chuck Adams 64 63; Petr Korda d Jim Pugh 61 63; Malivai Washington d Rick Leach 61 76; Christian Saceanu d Scott Davis 61 36 60; Jimmy Arias d Thomas Hogstedt 63 63; Diego Perez d Jeff Tarango 64 62; Martin Wostenholme d Mikael Pernfors 64 64; Richey Reneberg d Raul Viver 64 75; Brad Pearce d David Pate 36 61 63; Javier Frana d Brian Garrow 76 63; Diego Nargiso d Kelly Evernden 62 76; Pablo Arraya d Derrick Rostagno 76 63. **Rd 16:** Chang d Shelton 67 64 75; Yzaga d Brown 64 64; Wheaton d Korda 63 64; Washington d Saceanu 63 64; Arias d Perez 61 64; Reneberg d Wostenholme 46 60 63; Frana d Pearce 64 62; Arraya d Nargiso 26 64 76. **QF:** Yzaga d Chang 76 61; Washington d Wheaton 67 61 62; Arias d Reneberg 64 62; Frana d Arraya 64 Ret. **SF:** Yzaga d Washington 75 62; Arias d Frana 36 63 75. **F:** Yzaga d Arias 36 63 75.
DOUBLES: Rick Leach/Jim Pugh d Bret Garnett/Greg van Emburgh 62 36 63.

13-19 MAY: XLVII CAMPIONATI INTERNAZIONALI D'ITALIA, ROME $1,280,000 Winner: EMILIO SANCHEZ
Rd 64: Cedric Pioline d Marc Rosset 75 63; Cristiano Caratti d Martin Jaite 46 75 76; Richard Fromberg d Patrick McEnroe 46 76 62; Alexander Volkov d Jan Siemerink 67 63 63; Emilio Sanchez d Todd Woodbridge 61 61; Horst Skoff d Luiz Mattar 61 61; Wayne Ferreira d Tomas Carbonell 64 26 64; Mark Woodforde d Brad Gilbert 36 62 64; Paul Haarhuis d Goran Ivanisevic 36 75 63; Thomas Muster d Amos Mansdorf 64 62; Goran Prpic d Marcelo Filippini 60 26 61; Jakob Hlasek d Paolo Cane 36 62 64; Andrei Cherkasov d Alex Antonitsch 63 62; Stefano Pescosolido d Richard Krajicek 61 62; Nicklas Kulti d Omar Camporese 75 46 64; Jim Courier d Jordi Arrese 64 46 63; Sergi Bruguera d Carlos Costa 36 62 76; Yannick Noah d Alexander Mronz 61 63; Aaron Krickstein d Claudio Pistolesi 46 76 76; Christian Bergstrom d Guillermo Perez-Roldan 67 64 61; Magnus Gustafsson d Mats Wilander 76 61; Henri Leconte d Frederic Fontang 62 46 62; Fabrice Santoro d Magnus Larsson 64 61; Pete Sampras d Vladimir Gabrichidze 76 46 62; Jonas Svensson d Franco Davin 64 36 64; Alberto Mancini d Ronald Agenor 64 62; Juan Aguilera d Pat Cash 36 64 61; Mark Koevermans d Michael Stich 46 64 64; Massimo Cierro d Karel Novacek 60 64; Horacio de la Pena d Peter Lundgren 62 62; Renzo Furlan d Jaime Yzaga 64 63; Eric Jelen d Andre Agassi 63 76. **Rd 32:** Caratti d Pioline 64 75; Fromberg d Volkov 75 63; Sanchez d Skoff 64 63; Ferreira d Woodforde 76 64; Muster d Haarhuis 62 64; Prpic d Hlasek 61 75; Cherkasov d Pescosolido 67 62 76; Courier d Kulti 60 63; Bruguera d Noah 61 63; Miniussi d Krickstein 62 64; Leconte d Gustafsson 60 63; Santoro d Sampras 42 46 75; Mancini d Svensson 46 75 75; Koevermans d Aguilera 62 62; de la Pena d Cierro 75 61; Jelen d Furlan 26 63 76. **Rd 16:** Fromberg d Caratti 75 60; Sanchez d Ferreira 62 62; Prpic d Muster 36 63 62; Cherkasov d Courier 46 62 62; Bruguera d Miniussi 61 62; Santoro d Leconte 64 57 76; Mancini d Koevermans 60 46 76; de la Pena d Jelen 76 61. **QF:** Sanchez d Fromberg 62 62; Prpic d Cherkasov 76 75; Bruguera d Santoro 64 76; Mancini d de la Pena 64 62. **SF:** Sanchez d Prpic 64 62; Mancini d Bruguera 63 61. **F:** Sanchez d Mancini 63 61 30 (4040) Ret.
DOUBLES: Omar Camporese/Goran Ivanisevic d Luke Jensen/Laurie Warder 62 63.

13-19 MAY: YUGOSLAV OPEN-UMAG, UMAG $250,000 Winner: DIMITRI POLIAKOV
Rd 32: Richey Reneberg d Andrei Medvedev 26 62 63; Martin Stringari d Emanuel Rasberger 63 64; Nuno Marques d Francesco Cancellotti 36 63 64; Petr Korda d Thierry Champion 64 36 63; Jaime Oncins d David Wheaton 64 63; Bruno Oresar d Andrei Merinov 62 62; Tarik Benhabiles d Aki Rahunen 16 63 62; Javier Sanchez d Joao Cunha-Silva 62 46 62; Francisco Clavet d Guillaume Raoux 36 61 64; Jacco Eltingh d Lars Jonsson 64 75; Dimitri Poliakov d Roberto Azar 63 76; Jan Gunnarsson d Gilad Bloom 76 36 75; Carl-Uwe Steeb d Martin Sinner 61 75; Marian Vajda d Christian Saceanu 46 64 64; Jean-Philippe Fleurian d Jose-Antonio Fernandez 62 75; Rodolphe Gilbert d Derrick Rostagno 60 64. **Rd 16:** Reneberg d Stringari 57 62 62; Korda d Marques 62 61; Oresar d Oncins 64 46 63; Sanchez d Benhabiles 60 63; Clavet d Eltingh 62 76; Poliakov d Gunnarsson 60 67 62; Vajda d Steeb 36 63 62; Fleurian d Gilbert 63 62. **QF:** Korda d Reneberg 75 64; Sanchez d Oresar 72 76; Poliakov d Clavet 26 62; Fleurian d Vajda 63 62. **SF:** Sanchez d Korda 06 76 75; Poliakov d Fleurian 46 64 62. **F:** Poliakov d Sanchez 64 64.
DOUBLES: Gilad Bloom/Javier Sanchez d Richey Reneberg/David Wheaton 76 26 61.

20-26 MAY PEUGEOT ATP WORLD TEAM CUP, DUSSELDORF $1,277,500 Winner: SWEDEN
Red Group: Sweden v Argentina: Magnus Gustafsson d Franco Davin 64 76; Stefan Edberg d Horacio de la Pena 64 62; de la Pena/Javier Frana d Edberg/Gustafsson 26 64 64. **Soviet Union v Spain:** Emilio Sanchez d Andrei Cherkasov d 63 36 76; Alexander Volkov d Juan Aguilera 64 76; E. Sanchez/Sergio Casal d Cherkasov/Volkov 63 62. **Sweden v Spain:** Gustafsson d Aguilera 63 63; Edberg d E. Sanchez 61 64; Edberg/Gustafsson d E. Sanchez/Casal 75 61. **Soviet Union v Argentina:**

Cherkasov d de la Pena 36 62 62; Volkov d Davin 60 62; de la Pena/Frana d Cherkasov/Volkov 64 36 63. **Sweden v Soviet Union:** Cherkasov d Edberg 64 61; Gustafsson d Volkov 62 62; Cherkasov/Volkov d Edberg/Gustafsson 60 60. **Argentina v Spain:** E. Sanchez d Guillermo Perez-Roldan 76 63; Davin d Aguilera 62 64; E. Sanchez/Casal d de la Pena/Frana 63 61. **Blue Group: Germany v Switzerland:** Jakob Hlasek d Michael Stich 64 64; Eric Jelen d Marc Rosset 63 61; Hlasek/Rosset d Stich/Udo Riglewski 46 61 64. **Yugoslavia v USA:** Goran Ivanisevic d Brad Gilbert 76 63; Aaron Krickstein d Goran Prpic 76 36 64; Ivanisevic/Slobodan Zivojinovic d Rick Leach/Jim Pugh 63 57 76. **Yugoslavia v Germany:** Stich d Ivanisevic 63 64; Prpic d Jelen 64 62; Ivanisevic/Zivojinovic d Stich/Riglewski 63 67 75. **Switzerland v USA:** Hlasek d Gilbert 60 64; Krickstein d Rosset 63 62; Hlasek/Rosset d Leach/Pugh 16 63 76. **Yugoslavia v Switzerland:** Ivanisevic d Hlasek 64 63; Prpic d Rosset 63 64; Hlasek/Rosset d Ivanisevic/Zivojinovic 36 61 76; **USA v Germany:** Stich d Gilbert 63 64; Krickstein d Carl-Uwe Steeb 64 60; Leach/Pugh d Riglewski/Stich 75 67 75. **Final: Sweden v Yugoslavia:** Gustafsson d Prpic 62 36 64; Edberg d Ivanisevic 64 75; Prpic/Zivojinovic d Edberg/Gustafsson 36 63 64.

20-26 MAY: INTERNAZIONALI DI TENNIS CASSA DI RISPARMIO, BOLOGNA $250,000 Winner: PAOLO CANE
Rd 32: Jeff Tarango d Derrick Rostagno 64 61; Nuno Marques d Federico Mordegan 63 62; Jaime Oncins d Tomas Carbonell 76 62; Marian Vajda d Vladimir Gabrichidze 60 60; Thomas Muster d Christian Saceanu 64 64; Shuzo Matsuoka d Felipe Rivera 63 62; Paolo Cane d Jason Stolenberg 63 61; Javier Sanchez d Jacco Eltingh 46 62 64; Eduardo Masso d Francisco Clavet 62 75; Wayne Ferreira d Pat Cash 76 63; Francesco Cancelotti d Tarik Benhabiles 63 63; Jan Gunnarsson d Richard Fromberg 63 61; Luiz Mattar d Alexander Mronz 36 62 61; Pedro Rebolledo d Martin Sinner 61 62; Joao Cunha-Silva d Patrick Baur 60 16 64; Omar Camporese d Diego Nargiso 61 36 62. **Rd 16:** Tarango d Marques 46 61 63; Oncins d Vajda 62 62; Muster d Matsuoka 76 16 63; Cane d Sanchez 63 75; Masso d Ferreira 76 33 Ret.; Gunnarsson d Cancellotti 62 60; Mattar d Rebolledo 75 63; Camporese d Cunha-Silva 62 63. **QF:** Tarango d Oncins 46 63 62; Cane d Muster 76 75; Gunnarsson d Masso 60 62; Camporese d Mattar 62 61. **SF:** Cane d Tarango 64 64; Gunnarsson d Camporese 76 64. **F:** Cane d Gunnarsson 57 63 75.
DOUBLES: Luke Jensen/Laurie Warder d Luiz Mattar/Jaime Oncins 64 76.

27 MAY-9 JUNE: FRENCH OPEN, PARIS $3,482,000 Winner: JIM COURIER
Rd 128: Stefan Edberg d Bart Wuyts 62 62 63; Horst Skoff d David Wheaton 62 67 36 62 64; Patrik Kuhnen d Guillaume Raoux 46 62 64 64; Andrei Chesnokov d Mark Koevermans 75 62 67 26 63; Dinu Pescariu d Felipe Rivera 57 75 60 40 Ret.; Jaime Yzaga d Thierry Tulasne 61 46 64 62; Pat Cash d Sandor Hoszaly 64 76 63; Andrei Cherkasov d John McEnroe 26 64 75 76; Jim Courier d Derrick Rostagno 63 63 60; Wayne Ferreira d Carl-Uwe Steeb 64 61 64; Ctislav Dosedel d Renzo Furlan 63 60 62; Magnus Larsson d Nuno Marques 61 63 62; Todd Martin d Luis Herrera 63 67 64 64; Gary Muller d Grant Connell 64 46 64 67 60; Paul Haarhuis d Richey Reneberg 63 63 61; Goran Ivanisevic d Frederic Fontang 64 76 63 61; Martin Jaite d Marcelo Ingaramo 46 64 57 75 64; Franco Davin d Christian Bergstrom 63 64 61; Henri Leconte d Rodolphe Gilbert 62 61 61; Marian Vajda d Niclas Kroon 36 63 61 63; Nicklas Kulti d Patrick Baur 64 36 64 62; Arnaud Boetsch d Luiz Mattar 64 63 61; Diego Perez d Mark Woodforde 61 67 61 63; Gabriel Markus d Andrew Sznajder 61 75 64; Michael Stich d Brad Pearce 63 63 75; Richard Krajicek d Jose Francisco Altur 60 64 61; Carlos Costa d Jacco Eltingh 62 63 63; Tarik Benhabiles d Jim Grabb 46 46 64 62 63; Fabrice Santoro d Alexander Mronz 64 75 61; Mats Wilander d Leonardo Lavalle 64 63 62; Thierry Champion d Aki Rahunen 76 75 16 61; Pete Sampras d Thomas Muster 46 46 64 61 64; Sergi Bruguera d Scott Davis 62 62 61; Omar Camporese d Udo Riglewski 64 62 62; Cristiano Miniussi d Juan-Carlos Baguena 64 36 26 63 63; Marcelo Filippini d Richard Fromberg 64 36 61 62; Christiano Caratti d German Lopez 26 26 63 63 64; Tomas Carbonell d Jan Gunnarsson 57 62 63 61; Jakob Hlasek d David Pate 64 61 75; Emilio Sanchez d Anders Jarryd 62 63 62; Magnus Gustafsson d Karel Novacek 62 36 51 Ret.; Aaron Krickstein d Eduardo Masso 67 64 26 61 75; Goran Prpic d Michael Robertson 76 63 63; Alberto Mancini d Eric Jelen 75 64 62; Patrick McEnroe d Gilad Bloom 75 64 76; Jason Stoltenberg d Olivier Soules 62 76 75; Petr Korda d Jean-Philippe Fleurian 64 63 64; Andre Agassi d Mark Rosset 36 75 64 62; Guy Forget d Malivai Washington 75 26 75 16 75; Jimmy Arias d Pedro Rebolledo 60 36 60 62; Veli Paloheimo d Jeff Tarango 62 62 61; Marcos Ondruska d Juan Aguilera 36 75 63 62; Ronald Agenor d Shuzo Matsuoka 63 67 63; Jimmy Connors d Todd Witsken 63 63 75; Lars Jonsson d Horacio de la Pena 76 63 20 Ret.; Michael Chang d Jan Siemerink 62 60 63; Cedric Pioline d Brad Gilbert 64 26 61 64; Francisco Clavet d Kelly Evernden 64 60 62; Olivier Delaitre d Guillermo Perez-Roldan 62 61 61; Peter Lundgren d Alexander Volkov 63 76 67 75; Wally Masur d Joao Cunha-Silva 76 61 64; Jaime Oncins d Javier Sanchez 57 64 64 63; Todd Woodbridge d Christian Saceanu 64 76 64; Boris Becker d Jordi Arrese 62 75 62. **Rd 64:** Edberg d Skoff 64 57 76 63; Chesnokov d Kuhnen 46 63 36 63 86; Yzaga d Pescariu 62 60; Cherkasov d Cash 67 61 63 36 75; Courier d Ferreira 62 63 64; Larsson d Dosedel 75 62 64; Martin d Muller 61 62 64; Haarhuis d Ivanisevic 61 64 61; Davin d Jaite 64 63 62; Vajda d Leconte 36 64 76 64; Boetsch d Kulti 63 63 63; Markus d Perez 26 26 64 64 63; Stich d Krajicek 67 76 63 62; Costa d Benhabiles 75 61 62; Santoro d Wilander 62 63 62; Champion d

Sampras 63 61 61; Camporese d Bruguera 16 26 64 10 Ret.; Miniussi d Filippini 16 62 44 Ret.; Carbonell d Caratti 61 75 36 61; Hlasek d E Sanchez 63 46 62 76; Gustafsson d Krickstein 61 46 64 62; Mancini d Prpic 16 75 64 16 62; McEnroe d Stoltenberg 76 63 64; Agassi d Korda 61 62 62; Forget d Arias 63 62 57 76; Ondruska d Paloheimo 36 61 61 26 60; Connors d Agenor 64 62 36 06 64; Chang d Jonsson 76 46 63 63; Clavet d Pioline 62 63 76; Delaitre d Lundgren 62 67 64 62; Masur d Oncins 61 76 75; Becker d Woodbridge 57 16 64 64 64. **Rd 32:** Edberg d Chesnokov 61 64 63; Cherkasov d Yzaga 75 36 63 63; Courier d Larsson 63 46 46 75 62; Martin d Haarhuis 62 46 63 64; Davin d Vajda 62 26 64 36 64; Boetsch d Markus 57 76 63 62; Stich d Costa 36 75 76 62; Santoro d Champion 62 60 64; Miniussi d Camporese 26 63 61 63; Hlasek d Carbonell 76 46 64 63; Mancini d Gustafsson 63 36 62 62; Agassi d McEnroe 62 62 60; Forget d Ondruska 61 64 36 63; Chang d Connors 46 75 62 46 015 Ret.; Clavet d Delaitre 46 62 63 64; Becker d Masur 63 63 62. **Rd 16:** Edberg d Cherkasov 76 64 63; Courier d Martin 62 63 63; Davin d Boetsch 76 46 63 61; Stich d Santoro 63 61 62; Hlasek d Miniussi 46 63 57 75 62; Agassi d Mancini 63 63 57 61; Chang d Clavet 61 61 46 63; Becker d Clavet 76 62 63. **QF:** Courier d Edberg 64 26 63 64; Stich d Davin 64 64 64; Agassi d Hlasek 63 61 61; Becker d Chang 64 64 62. **SF:** Courier d Stich 62 67 62 64; Agassi d Becker 75 63 36 61. **F:** Courier d Agassi 36 64 26 61 64.
DOUBLES: John Fitzgerald/Anders Jarryd d Rick Leach/Jim Pugh 60 76.

10-16 JUNE: THE STELLA ARTOIS GRASS COURT CHAMPIONSHIPS, LONDON $500,000 Winner: STEFAN EDBERG
Rd 64: Stefan Edberg d Arnaud Boetsch d Dan Goldie 46 75 62; Jason Stoltenberg d Mark Kratzmann 62 63; Peter Lundgren d Veli Paloheimo 64 64; Kevin Curren d Gianluca Pozzi 36 61 63; Pat Cash d Felix Barrienton 61 64; Wayne Ferreira d Jaime Morgan 61 62; Todd Woodbridge bye; Pete Sampras bye; Mark Keil d Patrick Baur 26 63 62; Jeremy Bates d David Pate 64 62; Malivai Washington d Scott Davis 76 64; Christo van Rensburg d Wally Masur 62 76; Ramesh Krishnan d Luiz Mattar 61 67 63; John Fitzgerald d Chris Bailey 64 62; Derrick Rostagno bye; David Wheaton bye; Byron Black d Jim Grabb 62 76; Javier Frana d Glenn Michibata 64 62; Patrik Kuhnen d Mats Wilander 64 64; Todd Witsken d Luis Herrera 75 62; Guillaume Raoux d Niclas Kroom 62 61; Danny Sapsford d Alex Antonitsch 63 21 Ret.; Michael Chang d Thomas Hogstedt 61 55 Ret.; Jaime Oncins d Andrew Castle 36 63 75; Eric Jelen d Jeff Tarango 63 57 119; Rodolphe Gilbert d Mark Woodforde 64 57 108; Shuzo Matsuoka d Gary Muller 76 76; Grant Connell d Martin Laurendeau 76 26 64; Ivan Lendl bye. **Rd 32:** Edberg d Boetsch 64 63; Stoltenberg d Lundgren 61 64; Cash d Curren 64 61; Woodbridge d Ferreira 76 57 64; Keil d Sampras 62 76; Washington d Bates 75 61; van Rensburg d Krishnan 62 67 63; Fitzgerald d Rostagno 64 62; Wheaton d Black 61 36 63; Kuhnen d Frana 67 64 63; Raoux d Witsken 64 62; Chang d Sapsford 63 63; Jarryd d Pearce 63 36 63; Oncins d Jelen 36 62 63; Matsuoka d Gilbert 63 62; Connell d Lendl 57 63 64. **Rd 16:** Edberg d Stoltenberg 64 64; Cash d Woodbridge 62 61; Washington d Keil 67 63 62; Fitzgerald d van Rensburg 67 64 64; Wheaton d Kuhnen 64 75; Chang d Raoux 75 62; Jarryd d Oncins 62 61; Connell d Matsuoka 64 75. **QF:** Edberg d Cash 63 64; Washington d Fitzgerald 75 64; Wheaton d Chang 63 63; Jarryd d Connell 62 61. **SF:** Edberg d Washington 64 62; Wheaton d Jarryd 63 64. **F:** Edberg d Wheaton 62 63.
DOUBLES: Todd Woodbridge/Mark Woodforde d Grant Connell/Glenn Michibata 64 76.

10-16 JUNE: THE CONTINENTAL GRASS COURT CHAMPIONSHIPS, ROSMALEN, THE NETHERLANDS $250,000 Winner: CHRISTIAN SACEANU
Rd 32: Aldrei Olhovskiy d Guy Forget 63 46 61; Kelly Evernden d Patrick McEnroe 63 67 63; Todd Nelson d Danilo Marcelino 76 67 75; Christian Saceanu d Marc Rosset 63 63; Jakob Hlasek d Jacco Eltingh 36 75 75; Jan Siemerink d Johan Kriek 75 62; Amos Mansdorf d Jan Gunnarsson 36 64 64; Alexander Volkov d Joey Rive 61 64; Richey Reneberg d Nicklas Kulti 26 64 62; Diego Nargiso d Fernando Roese 63 62; Arne Thoms d Bryan Shelton 76 63; Michiel Schapers d Goran Prpic 64 63; Henrik Holm d Cristiano Caratti 76 62; Richard Krajicek d Chuck Adams 62 62; Paul Haarhuis d Glenn Layendecker 64 61; Michael Stich d Simon Youl 76 63. **Rd 16:** Olhovskiy d Evernden 36 63 64; Saceanu d Nelson 63 62; Hlasek d Siemerink 76 75; Mansdorf d Volkov 67 63 63; Nargiso d Reneberg 76 76; Schapers d Thoms 46 63 62; Krajicek d Holm 63 46 63; Stich d Haarhuis 63 63. **QF:** Saceanu d Olhovskiy 63 63; Hlasek d Mansdorf 64 63; Schapers d Nargiso 76 75; Stich d Krajicek 64 76. **SF:** Saceanu d Hlasek 63 36 76; Schapers d Stich 64 76. **F:** Saceanu d Schapers 61 36 75.
DOUBLES: Henrik Jan Davids/Paul Haarhuis d Richard Krajicek/Jan Siemerink 63 76.

10-16 JUNE: TORNEO INTERNAZIONALE "CITTA' DI FIRENZE", FLORENCE $250,000 Winner: THOMAS MUSTER
Rd 32: Horst Skoff d Cedric Pioline 64 62; Bart Wuyts d Andrei Medvedev 60 46 63; Gabriel Markus d Carl-Uwe Steeb 61 42 Ret.; Renzo Furlan d Udo Riglewski 76 62; Eduardo Masso d Jordi Arrese 62 57 61; Javier Sanchez d Claudio Pistolesi 76 26 64; Lars Jonsson d Stefano Pescosolido 46 20 Ret.; Magnus Larsson d Silvio Moine 61 64; Richard Fromberg d Andrea Gaudenzi 36 63 63; Carlos Costa d Roberto Azar 63 64; Jimmy Arias d Nuno Marques 36 61 64; Andres Vysand d Mark Koevermans 62 63; Fabrice Santoro d Aki Rahunen 63 62; Francisco Roig d Franco Davin 16 61 61; Thomas Muster d Pedro Rebolledo 16 64 60; Thierry Champion d Omar Camporese 46 64 63. **Rd 16:** Skoff d Wuyts 63 57 61; Markus d

Furlan 26 76 62; Masso d Sanchez 63 76; Larsson d Jonsson 36 63 76; Costa d Fromberg 63 57 64; Arias d Vysand 64 62; Santoro d Roig 75 62; Muster d Champion 46 63 62. **QF:** Skoff d Markus 61 67 62; Masso d Larsson 63 46 61; Costa d Arias 64 61; Muster d Santoro 67 61 61. **SF:** Skoff d Masso 64 64; Muster d Costa 67 61 63. **F:** Muster d Skoff 62 67 64.
DOUBLES: Lars Jonsson/Magnus Larsson d Juan C Baguena/Carlos Costa 36 61 61.

17-23 JUNE: IP CUP, GENOVA, ITALY $250,000 Winner: CARL-UWE STEEB
Rd 32: Ronald Agenor d Jose Francisco Altur 63 26 64; Andrei Medvedev d Nuno Marques 75 20 Ret.; Bart Wuyts d Pedro Rebolledo 76 76; Carl-Uwe Steeb d Tarik Benhabiles 64 46 62; Fabrice Santoro d Massimo Cierro 61 61; Cedric Pioline d Andrea Gaudenzi 61 64; Thomas Muster d Thierry Champion 46 60 63; Stefano Pescosolido d Javier Sanchez 57 63 61; Renzo Furlan d Andres Vysand 62 61; Roberto Azar d Ctislav Dosedel 63 36 62; Carlos Costa d Frederic Fontang 62 60; Jordi Arrese d Joao Cunha-Silva 63 76; Jean-Philippe Fleurian d Markus Naewie 61 75; Lars Jonsson d Claudio Pistolesi 63 62; Eduardo Masso d Francesco Cancellotti 62 75; Mark Koevermans d Gabriel Markus 62 67 61. **Rd 16:** Agenor d Medvedev 36 60 76; Steeb d Wuyts 63 26 61; Pioline d Santoro 64 61; Muster d Pescosolido 64 63; Azar d Furlan 26 64 63; Arrese d Costa 36 62 63; Fleurian d Jonsson 46 75 64; Masso d Koevermans 64 64. **QF:** Steeb d Agenor 61 64; Muster d Pioline 46 76 62; Arrese d Azar 64 75; Masso d Fleurian 75 61. **SF:** Steeb d Muster 75 64; Arrese d Masso 76 63. **F:** Steeb d Arrese 63 64.
DOUBLES: Marco Aurelio Gorriz/Alfonso Mora d Massimo Ardinghi/Massimo Boscatto 57 75 63.

17-22 JUNE: DIRECT LINE INSURANCE MANCHESTER OPEN $250,000 Winner: GORAN IVANISEVIC
Rd 32: Petr Sampras d Christian Bergstrom 75 46 62; Malivai Washington d Nicolas Pereira 76 67 63; Wally Masur d Jim Grabb 64 36 63; Derrick Rostagno d Christian Saceanu 46 61 75; Gilad Bloom d Brad Gilbert 62 62; Veli Paloheimo d Jan Siemerink 76 62; Peter Lundgren d Mark Petchey 61 57 62; Amos Mansdorf d Goran Prpic 36 63 63; Alexander Volkov d Luiz Mattar 62 76; Gary Muller d Chris Pridham 62 75; Todd Witsken d Eric Jelen 76 61; Cristiano Caratti d John McEnroe 76 76; Arne Thoms d Horst Skoff 64 76; Omar Camporese d Richard Krajicek 36 62 64; Jeremy Bates d Paul Haarhuis 64 76; Goran Ivanisevic d Andrew Castle 75 76.
Rd 16: Sampras d Washington 76 46 62; Masur d Rostagno 64 64; Paloheimo d Bloom 67 64 75; Mansdorf d Lundgren 76 76; Muller d Volkov 76 76; Witsken d Caratti 63 64; Thoms d Camporese 26 76 75; Ivanisevic d Bates 63 64. **QF:** Sampras d Masur 75 62; Paloheimo d Mansdorf 36 63 64; Muller d Witsken 36 76 62; Ivanisevic d Thoms 75 63. **SF:** Sampras d Paloheimo 64 75; Ivanisevic d Muller 76 76. **F:** Ivanisevic d Sampras 64 64.
DOUBLES: Omar Camporese/Goran Ivanisevic d Nick Brown/Andrew Castle 64 63.

24 JUNE-7 JULY: THE LAWN TENNIS CHAMPIONSHIPS, WIMBLEDON $3,460,5000 Winner: MICHAEL STICH
Rd 128: Stefan Edberg d Marc Rosset 64 64 64; David Pate d Patrick Baur 46 67 64 62 63; Wayne Ferreira d Juan Aguilera 64 63 63; Christo van Rensburg d Todd Witsken 61 76 46 64; Horst Skoff d Guillaume Raoux 64 64 63; Jean-Philippe Fleurian d Alexander Mronz 64 60 63; Sandon Stolle d Mark Kratzmann 67 63 67 76 64; John McEnroe d Jaime Oncins 61 62 64; Goran Ivanisevic d Andrew Castle 76 76 61; Nick Brown d Mark Keil 64 75 61; Pat Cash d Jeff Tarango 62 63 63; Thierry Champion d Chris Wilkinson 64 62 36 64; Jimmy Connors d Veli Paloheimo 62 60 75; Aaron Krickstein d Stefano Pescosolido 61 63 67 67 75; Derrick Rostagno d Renzo Furlan 60 63 64; Pete Sampras d Danilo Marcelino 61 62 62; Jim Courier d Rodolphe Gilbert 64 62 76; Jim Grabb d Nuno Marques 75 67 64 61; Gianluca Pozzi d Brad Pearce 46 63 62 62; Arnaud Boetsch d Broderick Dyke 76 63; Javier Frana d Luis Herrera 36 26 63 63 63; Kevin Curren d Fernando Roese 63 63 61; Javier Sanchez d Johan Kriek 64 64 67 63; Karel Novacek d Udo Riglewski 76 63 64; Richey Reneberg d Andrei Cherkasov 64 63 64; Martin Laurendeau d Danny Sapsford 63 76 36 63; Alexander Volkov d Bart Wuyts 61 62 62; Anders Jarryd d Niclas Kroon 63 64 36 63; Omar Camporese d Claudio Pistolesi 61 63 26 63; Glenn Michibata d Jason Stoltenberg 57 64 36 76 64; Diego Nargiso d Mark Woodforde 64 76 76; Michael Stich d Dan Goldie 64 61 62; Andre Agassi d Grant Connell 46 61 67 75 63; Goran Prpic d Jan Siemerink 64 36 63 36 108; Magnus Larsson d Paul Haarhuis 64 16 63 61; Gary Muller d Jordi Arrese 62 63 63; Christian Saceanu d Scott Davis 64 76 64; Jacco Eltingh d Richard Vogel 76 67 76 67 63; Patrick McEnroe d Emilio Sanchez 63 76 61; Jakob Hlasek d Slobodan Zivojinovic 62 36 63 62; Todd Woodbridge d Pablo Arraya 26 62 63 61; Lars Jonsson d Marian Vajda 75 63 75; Jan Gunnarsson d Pedro Rebolledo 61 75 62; Cedric Pioline d Glenn Layendecker 46 63 64 76; David Wheaton d Petr Korda 76 67 64 62; Malivai Washington d Mark Koevermans 63 62 61; Ivan Lendl d Kelly Evernden 62 75 76; Guy Forget d Gilad Bloom 26 76 75 67 64; Magnus Gustafsson d Francisco Clavet 76 63 63; Henri Leconte d Tomas Carbonell 63 61 76; Jaime Yzaga d Nicklas Kulti 62 75 57 61; Mark Petchey d Jim Pugh 46 46 63 63 64; Patrik Kuhnen d Aki Rahunen 64 63 64; Jeremy Bates d Jose Francisco Altur 64 64 62; Tim Mayotte d Michael Chang 76 46 61 76 62; Brad Gilbert d Daniel Orsanic 75 61 62; Wally Masur d Amos Mansdorf 63 16 76 64; Henrik Holm d Cristiano Caratti 76 63 64; Christian Bergstrom d Eduardo Masso 61 75 63; Luis Mattar d Shuzo Matsuoka 64 46 67 75 75; Andrei Olhovskiy d Eric Jelen 36 63 63

76; Peter Lundgren d Richard Fromberg 64 76 62; Boris Becker d Carl-Uwe Steeb 64 62 64. **Rd 64:** Edberg d Pate 62 62 63; van Rensberg d Ferreira 64 76 62; Fleurian d Skoff 62 60 63; J McEnroe d Stolle 76 67 60 76; Brown d Ivanisevic 46 63 76 63; Champion d Cash 75 67 46 61 1210; Connors d Krickstein 63 62 63; Rostagno d Sampras 64 36 76 64; Courier d Grabb 64 75 26 46 63; Boetsch d Pozzi 46 76 76 64; Frana d Curren 76 62 62; Novacek d J Sanchez 60 61 76; Laurendeau d Reneberg 36 64 67 64 62; Volkov d Jarryd 62 36 64 36 86; Camporese d Michibata 75 62 61; Stich d Nargiso 63 64 67 62; Agassi d Prpic 76 36 64 62; Krajicek d Larsson 63 64 63; Saceanu d Muller 76 64 76; Eltingh d P McEnroe 76 26 16 64 1210; Woodbridge d Hlasek 63 16 75 63; Gunnarsson d Jonsson 62 63 26 76; Wheaton d Pioline 64 67 63 63; Lendl d Washington 46 26 64 64 75; Forget d Gustafsson 64 63 64; Leconte d Yzaga 64 62 63; Kuhnen d Petchey 62 64 63; Mayotte d Bates 63 36 64 76; B Gilbert d Masur 76 26 63 57 64; Bergstrom d Holm 75 60 64; Olhovskiy d Mattar 26 76 64 46 63; Becker d Lundgren 76 75 75. **Rd 32:** Edberg d van Rensburg 61 63 62; J McEnroe d Fleurian 62 76 61; Champion d Brown 76 16 75 63; Rostagno d Connors 76 61 61; Courier d Boetsch 62 62 60; Novacek d Frana 64 64 57 64; Volkov d Laurendeau 62 61 61; Stich d Camporese 76 62 67 64; Agassi d Krajicek 76 63 76; Eltingh d Saceanu 63 46 64 75; Gunnarsson d Woodbridge 76 46 63 64; Wheaton d Lendl 63 36 76 63; Forget d Leconte 36 46 61 41 ret; Mayotte d Kuhnen 36 62 76 64; Bergstrom d B Gilbert 63 62 36 63; Becker d Olhovskiy 61 64 36 63. **Rd 16:** Edberg d J McEnroe 76 61 64; Champion d Rostagno 67 62 61 36 63; Courier d Novacek 63 64 62; Stich d Volkov 46 63 75 16 75; Agassi d Eltingh 63 36 63 64; Wheaton d Gunnarsson 64 63 61; Forget d Mayotte 67 75 62 64; Becker d Bergstrom 64 67 61 76. **QF:** Edberg d Champion 63 62 75; Stich d Courier 63 76 62; Wheaton d Agassi 62 06 36 76 62; Becker d Forget 67 76 62 76. **SF:** Stich d Edberg 46 76 76 76; Becker d Wheaton 64 76 75. **F:** Stich d Becker 64 76 64.
DOUBLES: John Fitzgerald/Anders Jarryd d Javier Frana/Leonardo Lavalle 63 64 67 61.

8-14 JULY: RADO SWISS OPEN, GSTAAD $305,000 Winner: EMILIO SANCHEZ
Rd 32: Sergi Bruguera d Wally Masur 75 64; Ronald Agenor d Guillermo Perez-Roldan 64 64; Andres Gomez d Carl-Uwe Steeb 75 63; Goran Prpic d Fabrice Santoro 76 16 64; Goran Ivanisevic d Javier Sanchez 57 75 61; David Wheaton d Marc Rosset 46 76 62; Horacio de la Pena d Francisco Clavet 63 61; Horst Skoff d Jakob Hlasek 64 76; Emilio Sanchez d Sasa Hirszon 62 64; Aaron Krickstein d Jordi Arrese 76 63; Martin Jaite d Petr Korda 61 62; Guy Forget d Marian Vajda 62 26 63; Karel Novacek d Andrei Chesnokov 60 62; Claudio Mezzadri d Omar Camporese 62 62; Daniel Vacek d Roberto Jabali 76 60; Michael Stich d Cyril Suk 61 62. **Rd 16:** Bruguera d Agenor 64 60; Gomez d Prpic 46 76 64; Ivanisevic d Wheaton 64 64; de la Pena d Skoff 61 61; E Sanchez d Krickstein 63 62; Jaite d Forget 76 75; Novacek d Mezzadri 63 62; Stich d Vacek 64 60. **QF:** Bruguera d Gomez 76 76; Ivanisevic d de la Pena 64 62; E Sanchez d Jaite 64 75; Novacek d Stich 63 64. **SF:** Bruguera d Ivanisevic 61 75; E Sanchez d Novacek 62 61. **F:** E Sanchez d Bruguera 61 64 64.
DOUBLES: Gary Muller/Danie Visser d Guy Forget/Jakob Hlasek 76 64.

8-14 JULY: SWEDISH OPEN, BASTAD $250,000 Winner: MAGNUS GUSTAFSSON
Rd 32: Magnus Larsson d Andrei Cherkasov 63 62; Lars Wahlgren d Marco Aurelio Gorriz 63 36 63; Claudio Pistolesi d Thierry Champion 64 60; Alberto Mancini d Jonas Bjorkman 63 61; Alexander Volkov d Veli Paloheimo 63 63; Mikael Pernfors d Juan Aguilera 63 63; Lars Jonsson d Tomas Carbonell 63 64; Marcelo Filippini d Bart Wuyts 20 Ret.; Nicklas Kulti d Johan Anderson 46 62 63; Christian Bergstrom d Aki Rahunen 61 62; Jan Gunnarsson d Thomas Enqvist 64 61; Eduardo Masso d Anders Jarryd 63 61; Pablo Arraya d Mark Koevermans 36 61 75; David Engel d Cedric Pioline 16 75 64; Niclas Kroon d Patrik Kuhnen 75 46 64; Magnus Gustafsson d Nuno Marques 60 75. **Rd 16:** Larsson d Wahlgren 60 63; Mancini d Pistolesi 36 63 62; Volkov d Pernfors 46 64; Jonsson d Filippini 61 62; Bergstrom d Kulti 62 61; Gunnarsson d Masso 75 76; Arraya d Engel 76 46 64; Gustafsson d Kroon 64 67 61. **QF:** Mancini d Larsson 46 63 64; Volkov d Jonsson 62 61; Bergstrom d Gunnarsson 36 62 62; Gustafsson d Arraya 61 62. **SF:** Mancini d Volkov 06 63 62; Gustafsson d Bergstrom 46 63 62. **F:** Gustafsson d Mancini 61 62.
DOUBLES: Ronnie Bathman/Rikard Bergh d Magnus Gustafsson/Anders Jarryd 64 64.

8-14 JULY: MILLER LITE HALL OF FAME TENNIS CHAMPIONSHIPS, NEWPORT, RHODE ISLAND $175,000 Winner: BRYAN SHELTON
Rd 32: Peter Lundgren d Jimmy Brown 62 60; Todd Martin d Joey Rive 75 63; Martin Wostenholme d Alex Nizet 75 62; Paul Annacone d Henrik Holm 46 64 76; Bryan Shelton d Patrick Baur 75 16 75; Jonathan Stark d Bruce Steel 64 64; Johan Kriek d Bret Garnett 62 64; Christo van Rensburg d Simon Youl 61 36 63; Gianluca Pozzi d Dan Goldie 57 63 64; Mark Kratzmann d Daniel Orsanic 76 63; Alex Reichel d Francisco Montana 76 16 75; Jacco Eltingh d Keith Evans 63 76; Javier Frana d Tom Mercer 75 62; Jared Palmer d Brett Steven 62 76; Glenn Layendecker d Jamie Morgan 16 76 76; Christian Saceanu d Neil Borwick 63 75. **Rd 16:** Martin d Lundgren 75 26 63; Wostenholme d Annacone 64 64; Shelton d Stark 64 64; van Rensburg d Kriek 61 46 76; Kratzmann d Pozzi 64 46 64; Eltingh d Reichel 63 62; Frana d Palmer 61 63; Layendecker d Saceanu 61 63. **QF:** Martin d Wostenholme 61 61; Shelton d van Rensburg 64 46 63; Kratzmann d Eltingh 64 67 64; Frana d Layendecker 63 64. **SF:** Shelton d

Martin 75 64; Frana d Kratzmann 62 46 75. **F:** Shelton d Frana 36 64 64.
DOUBLES: Gianluca Pozzi/Brett Steven d Javier Frana/Bruce Steel 64 64.

15-21 JULY: MERCEDES CUP, STUTTGART $1,000,000 Winner:
MICHAEL STICH
Rd 64: Michael Stich bye; Fabrice Santoro d Udo Riglewski 60 61; Javier
Sanchez d Magnus Larsson 63 60; Jordi Arrese bye; Horst Skoff bye;
Horacio de la Pena d Kevin Curren 64 64; Richard Krajicek d Franco Davin
62 64; Magnus Gustafsson bye; Goran Ivanisevic bye; Andres Gomez d
Renzo Furlan 26 62 61; Francisco Clavet d Thomas Muster 61 63; Omar
Camporese bye; Alexander Volkov bye; Jens Woehrmann d Jan Siemerink
76 46 63; Cedric Pioline d Yannick Noah 63 62; Karel Novacek bye;
Andrei Cherkasov bye; Alberto Mancini d Paul Haarhuis 64 62; Carlos
Costa d Mark Koevermans 63 67 60; Guillermo Perez-Roldan bye; Ronald
Agenor bye; Marc Rosset d Markus Naewie 62 64; German Lopez d
Thierry Champion 67 63 62; Emilio Sanchez bye; Goran Prpic bye;
Marcelo Filippini d Nicklas Kulti 62 46 75; Eric Jelen d Carl-Uwe Steeb 06
63 62; Jonas Svensson bye; Martin Jaite bye; Lars Koslowski d Francisco
Roig 76 76; Wally Masur d Marian Vajda 46 63 63; Guy Forget bye. **Rd 32:**
Stich d Santoro 63 76; J Sanchez d Arrese 46 61 64; Skoff d de la Pena 60
63; Krajicek d Gustafsson 76 57 76; Gomez d Ivanisevic 46 63 76; Clavet d
Camporese 75 60; Volkov d Woehrmann 62 63; Pioline d Novacek 61 16
63; Mancini d Cherkasov 46 64 62; Perez-Roldan d Costa 63 62; Agenor d
Rosset 61 36 63; Lopez d E Sanchez 76 76; Prpic d Filippini 76 62; Jelen d
Svensson 76 61; Koslowski d Jaite 63 64; Forget d Masur 57 76 76. **Rd 16:**
Stich d J Sanchez 63 63; Krajicek d Skoff 63 63; Clavet d Gomez 63 63;
Pioline d Volkov 62 46 63; Mancini d Perez-Roldan 75 62; Lopez d Agenor
62 63; Prpic d Jelen 63 26 62; Koslowski d Forget 76 76. **QF:** Stich d
Krajicek 64 36 76; Clavet d Pioline 63 67 61; Mancini d Lopez 63 63;
Koslowski d Prpic 62 26 75. **SF:** Stich d Clavet 62 62; Mancini d
Koslowski 46 61 63. **F:** Stich d Mancini 16 76 64 62.
DOUBLES: Wally Masur/Emilio Sanchez d Omar Camporese/Goran
Ivanisevic 46 63 64.

15-21 JULY: SOVRAN BANK CLASSIC, WASHINGTON DC $600,000
Winner: ANDRE AGASSI
Rd 64: Andre Agassi bye; David Pate d Kenny Thorne 63 46 76; Chuck
Adams d John Ross 57 63 76; Patrick Baur d Guillaume Raoux 64 76; Peter
Lundgren d Jamie Morgan 64 62; Johan Carlsson d Chris Garner 67 62 64;
Shuzo Matsuoka d Jeff Tarango 64 62; Todd Witsken bye; Richey
Reneberg d Glenn Layendecker d Tommy Ho 26 63 76; Grant Stafford d
Martin Laurendeau 63 64; Scott Davis d Daniel Orsanic 64 76; Malivai
Washington d Javier Frana 63 67 61; Chris Pridham d Fernando Roese 76
61; Mark Knowles d Brad Pearce 64 60; Jaime Yzaga bye; Derrick
Rostagno bye; Simon Youl d Dan Goldie 76 64; Bret Garnett d Robert
Seguso 46 64 62; Petr Korda d Nicolas Pereira 46 63 62; Grant Connell d
Martin Wostenholme 67 64 64; Andrew Sznajder d Henrik Holm 57 75 75;
John Sullivan d Jimmy Brown 63 62; Brad Gilbert bye; Aaron Krickstein
bye; Markus Zoecke d Neil Borwick 76 64; Alexander Mronz d Ctislav
Dosedel 63 75; Jimmy Arias d Mark Woodforde 64 57 64; Luis Herrera d
Jacco Eltingh 75 76; Jim Grabb d Ivan Baron 63 63; Brian Garrow d Jared
Palmer 63 63; John McEnroe bye. **Rd 32:** Agassi d Pate 64 63; Adams d
Baur 64 64; Carlsson d Lundgren 16 62 64; Matsuoka d Witsken 63 61;
Reneberg d Layendecker 57 63 64; Stafford d Davis 57 75 60; Washington
d Pridham 63 63; Yzaga d Knowles 75 61; Rostagno d Youl 63 46 64;
Korda d Garnett 76 76; Connell d Sznajder 63 75; Gilbert d Sullivan 46 62
62; Zoecke d Krickstein 67 62 76; Arias d Mronz 64 75; Herrera d Grabb
64 36 63; McEnroe d Garrow 63 75. **Rd 16:** Agassi d Adams 62 62;
Carlsson d Matsuoka 76 76; Reneberg d Stafford 76 60; Yzaga d
Washington 64 64; Korda d Rostagno 61 64; Gilbert d Connell 63 62;
Zoecke d Arias 63 64; Herrera d McEnroe 36 62 62. **QF:** Agassi d Carlsson
75 62; Yzaga d Reneberg 63 64; Korda d Gilbert 76 76; Zoecke d Herrera
46 63 63. **SF:** Agassi d Yzaga 63 62; Korda d Zoecke 62 64. **F:** Agassi d
Korda 63 64.
DOUBLES: Scott Davis/David Pate d Ken Flach/Robert Seguso 64 62.

22-28 JULY: PLAYER'S LTD INTERNATIONAL CANADIAN OPEN,
MONTREAL $1,200,000 Winner: ANDREI CHESNOKOV
Rd 64: Ivan Lendl bye; Gilad Bloom d Brad Pearce 64 61; Jeff Tarango d
Andrew Sznajder 64 63; Wally Masur d Mark Woodforde 63 64; Richey
Reneberg d Tim Mayotte 63 61; Jim Grabb d Jamie Morgan 46 64 76;
Alexander Mronz d Scott Davis 64 63; Brad Gilbert bye; Pete Sampras bye;
Shuzo Matsuoka d Arnaud Boetsch 67 76 63; Chris Garner d Patrick Baur
46 64 76Patrick McEnroe d Todd Witsken 61 61; Andrei Chesnokov d Dan
Goldie 61 62; Sebastian Lareau d Ian Aler 36 76 64; Stefano Pescosolido d
Henrik Holm 75 64; Michael Chang bye; Jakob Hlasek bye; Neil Borwick d
Johan Kriek 64 63; Simon Youl d Luis Herrera 63 67 76; Chris Pridham d
Cristiano Caratti 63 36 75; Guillaume Raoux d Jaime Yzaga 63 16 63;
Martin Laurendeau d Jimmy Brown 62 75; Petr Korda d Gianluca Pozzi 36
63 76; Amos Agassi d John McEnroe d Jimmy Arias d Grant Connell
76 76; Thomas Hogstedt d Jean-Philippe Fleurian 63 62; Derrick Rostagno
d David Pate 36 75 62; Amos Mansdorf d Ramesh Krishnan 62 62; Peter
Lundgren d Ctislav Dosedel 64 64; Malivai Washington d Markus
Zoecke 64 64; Jim Courier bye. **Rd 32:** Lendl d Bloom 46 64 64; Masur d
Tarango 76 61 64; Grabb d Reneberg 67 62 75; Gilbert d Mronz 63 75;
Matsuoka d Sampras 26 74 76; P McEnroe d Garner 62 64; Chesnokov d
Lareau 46 61 63; Pescosolido d Chang 76 36 63; Hlasek d Borwick 26 64
64; Youl d Pridham 16 63 75; Raoux d Laurendeau 36 75 60; Korda d
Agassi 76 62; J McEnroe d Arias 61 62; Rostagno d Hogstedt 63 61;

Mansdorf d Lundgren 64 67 61; Courier d Washington 75 63. **Rd 16:** Lendl
d Masur 63 36 64; Grabb d Gilbert 46 63 64; Matsuoka d P McEnroe 64 63;
Chesnokov d Pescosolido 64 64; Hlasek d Youl 76 64; Korda d Raoux 62
63; Rostagno d J McEnroe 62 16 76; Courier d Mansdorf 63 36 63.
QF: Lendl d Grabb 76 67 75; Chesnokov d Matsuoka 62 36 75; Korda d
Hlasek 76 64; Courier d Rostagno 63 63. **SF:** Chesnokov d Lendl 76 75;
Korda d Courier 36 76 62. **F:** Chesnokov d Korda 36 64 63.
DOUBLES: Patrick Galbraith/Todd Witsken d Grant Connell/Glenn
Michibata 64 36 61.

22-28 JULY: INTERNATIONAL CHAMPIONSHIP OF THE
NETHERLANDS, HILVERSUM $250,000 Winner: MAGNUS
GUSTAFSSON
Rd 32: Sergi Bruguera d Diego Perez 64 64; Mark Koevermans d Paul
Haarhuis 76 62; Renzo Furlan d Marcelo Filippini 36 62 61; Omar
Camporese d Martin Jaite 61 63; Thomas Muster d Andrei Cherkasov 63
63; Tomas Carbonell d Ronald Agenor 61 63; Jordi Arrese d Olivier
Delaitre 60 62; Horst Skoff d Jacco Eltingh 64 63; Goran Prpic d Karsten
Braasch 64 76; Marc Rosset d Richard Krajicek 64 64; Lars Jonsson d
Horacio de la Pena 36 64 60; Magnus Gustafsson d Francisco Clavet 76 76;
Thierry Champion d Guillermo Perez-Roldan 64 36 76; Franco Davin d Jan
Siemerink 64 63; Cedric Pioline d Francisco Roig 64 62; Karel Novacek d
Alberto Mancini 57 63 61. **Rd 16:** Koevermans d Bruguera 75 64; Furlan d
Camporese 16 76 62; Muster d Carbonell 67 61 61; Arrese d Skoff 36 76
62; Rosset d Prpic 76 36 64Gustafsson d Jonsson 75 75; Davin d Champion
36 64 64; Novacek d Pioline 64 64. **QF:** Koevermans d Furlan 61 61;
Arrese d Muster 64 61; Gustafsson d Rosset 67 62 64; Novacek d Davin 76
26 62. **SF:** Arrese d Koevermans 63 36 64; Gustafsson d Novacek 76 63.
F: Gustafsson d Arrese 57 76 26 61 60.
DOUBLES: Richard Krajicek/Jan Siemerink d Francisco Clavet/Magnus
Gustafsson 75 64.

29 JULY-5 AUGUST: PHILIPS HEAD CUP, KITZBUHEL $375,000
Winner: KAREL NOVACEK
Rd 64: Sergi Bruguera bye; Claudio Pistolesi d Henrik Holm 61 64;
Marcus Zillner d Wojtek Kowalski 46 64 63; Marcelo Filippini bye;
Horacio de la Pena bye; German Lopez d Pablo Arraya 76 63; Patrik
Kuhnen d Michael Geserer 61 75; Francisco Clavet bye; Karel Novacek
bye; Karsten Braasch d Arnaud Boetsch 26 64 62; Tarik Benhabiles d
Andres Vysand 36 64 62; Marian Vajda bye; Javier Sanchez bye; Dimitri
Poliakov d Tomas Carbonell 64 63; Rodolphe Gilbert d Christian
Saceanu 64 61; Horst Skoff bye; Alberto Mancini d Olivier Delaitre d
Reinhard Wawra 76 61; Thomas Buchmayer d Francisco Roig 64 06 62;
Thierry Champion bye; Thomas Muster bye; Johan Anderson d Martin
Strelba 46 76 76; Diego Nargiso d Aki Rahunen 62 62; Magnus Gustafsson
bye; Martin Jaite bye; Eric Jelen d Udo Riglewski 76 76; Gerald Mandl d
Andrei Olhovskiy 64 64; Christian Bergstrom bye; Cedric Pioline bye;
Richard Vogel d Cassio Motta 62 63; Eric Winogradsky d Thierry
Guardiola 64 67 63; Emilio Sanchez bye. **Rd 32:** Bruguera d Pistolesi 36 62
61; Zillner d Filippini 57 63 63; de la Pena d Lopez 63 60; Clavet d Kuhnen
16 64 64; Novacek d Braasch 62 63; Vajda d Benhabiles 63 63; J Sanchez d
Poliakov 75 62; Skoff d Gilbert 62 61; Mancini d Delaitre 76 76; Champion
d Buchmeyer 36 64 76; Muster d Anderson 63 61; Gustafsson d Nargiso 64
75; Jaite d Jelen 63 67 62; Bergstrom d Mandl 76 67 76; Vogel d Pioline 76
62; E Sanchez d Winogradsky 76 64. **Rd 16:** Zillner d Bruguera 61 16 62;
Clavet d de la Pena 64 62; Novacek d Vajda 61 76; Skoff d J Sanchez 64
63; Champion d Mancini 62 62; Gustafsson d Muster 75 26 64; Jaite d
Bergstrom 64 63; E Sanchez d Vogel 63 46 62. **QF:** Clavet d Zillner 62 63;
Novacek d Skoff 75 06 75; Gustafsson d Champion 46 63 61; Jaite d
E Sanchez 63 63. **SF:** Novacek d Clavet 63 67 62; Gustafsson d Jaite 62
62. **F:** Novacek d Gustafsson 76 76 62.
DOUBLES: Tomas Carbonell/Francisco Roig d Pablo Arraya/Dimitri
Poliakov 67 62 64.

29 JULY-4 AUGUST: VOLVO TENNIS LOS ANGELES $250,000
Winner: PETE SAMPRAS
Rd 32: Stefan Edberg d Ramesh Krishnan 64 63; Peter Lundgren d David
Pate 75 62; Jason Stoltenberg d Paul Annacone 61 63; Aaron Krickstein d
Dan Goldie 76 76; Brad Gilbert d Javier Frana 63 75; Jean-Philippe
Fleurian d Jim Pugh 46 75 61; Steve Bryan d Brad Pearce 16 61 61; Todd
Woodbridge d Wayne Ferreira 63 76; Scott Davis d Cristiano Caratti 63 62;
Gary Muller d Jonathan Stark 75 75; Stefano Pescosolido d Mark
Woodforde 64 64; Michael Chang d Mikael Pernfors 26 61 76; Amos
Mansdorf d Thomas Hogstedt 64 63; Gianluca Pozzi d Mark Kaplan 62 64;
Shuzo Matsuoka d Jeff Tarango 63 61; Pete Sampras d Gilad Bloom 60 62.
Rd 16: Edberg d Lundgren 63 64; Krickstein d Stoltenberg 63 36 63;
Gilbert d Fleurian 76 60; Bryan d Woodbridge 64 62; Davis d Muller 76 36
63; Pescosolido d Chang 46 62 64; Mansdorf d Pozzi 64 63; Sampras d
Matsuoka 63 64. **QF:** Edberg d Krickstein 64 75; Gilbert d Bryan 61 63;
Pescosolido d Davis 76 63; Sampras d Mansdorf 63 64. **SF:** Gilbert d Edberg
76 67 64; Sampras d Pescosolido 63 61. **F:** Sampras d Gilbert 62 67 63.
DOUBLES: Javier Frana/Jim Pugh d Glenn Michibata/Brad Pearce 75 26 64.

29 JULY-4 AUGUST: CAMPIONATI INTERNAZIONALI DI TENNIS
DE SAN MARINO $250,000 Winner: GUILLERMO PEREZ-ROLDAN
Rd 32: Guillermo Perez-Roldan d Diego Perez 60 61; Menno Oosting d
Olli Rahnasto 60 61; Libor Nemecek d Fernando Luna 62 61; Carlos Costa
d Jose Francisco Altur 64 76; Franco Davin d Massimo Ardinghi 61 61;
Paolo Cane d Joao Cunha-Silva 76 63; Paolo Pambianco d Ctislav Dosedel

233

76 46 62; Renzo Furlan d Christian Miniussi 63 61; Roberto Azar d Massimo Cierro 63 61; Daniel Orsanic d Vaclav Roubicek 62 62; Marco Aurelio Gorriz d Tomas Zdrazila 64 62; Nicklas Kulti d John Sobel 61 61; Nuno Marques d Marcelo Ingaramo 63 75; Claudio Mezzadri d Mario Visconti 76 63; Frederic Fontang d Mihnea Nastase 63 64; Jordi Arrese d Pedro Rebolledo 57 62 62. **Rd 16:** Perez-Roldan d Oosting 26 60 76; Costa d Nemecek 62 62; Davin d Cane 76 75; Furlan d Pambianco 64 62; Azar d Orsanic 64 26 64; Kulti d Gorriz 63 62; Mezzadri d Marques 63 63; Fontang d Arrese 63 60. **QF:** Perez-Roldan d Costa 57 62 61; Furlan d Davin 62 63; Azar d Kulti 63 62; Fontang d Mezzadri 64 60. **SF:** Perez-Roldan d Furlan 62 62; Fontang d Azar 62 62. **F:** Perez-Roldan d Fontang 63 61.
DOUBLES: Jordi Arrese/Carlos Costa d Christian Miniussi/Diego Perez 63 36 63.

5-11 AUGUST: THRIFTWAY ATP CHAMPIONSHIP, CINCINATTI
$1,300,000 Winner: GUY FORGET
Rd 64: Boris Becker bye; Jean-Philippe Fleurian d Jim Grabb 75 46 63; Malivai Washington d Richard Fromberg 63 64; Aaron Krickstein d Richey Reneberg 76 36 76; Andrei Cherkasov d Todd Woodbridge 76 61; Peter Lundgren d Andrei Chesnokov 76 46 63; Andres Gomez d Stefano Pescosolido 57 64 76; David Wheaton bye; Ivan Lendl bye; Patrick McEnroe d Kevin Curren 63 75; Chris Garner d Cristiano Caratti 62 76; Derrick Rostagno d Gilad Bloom 62 63; Jakob Hlasek d Jimmy Arias 61 61; Gianluca Pozzi d Todd Witsken 64 62; Marcos Ondruska d Mark Woodforde 63 63; Guy Forget bye; Andre Agassi bye; Petr Korda d Grant Connell 63 61; Jaime Yzaga d Fernando Roese 63 61; Brad Gilbert d Brad Pearce 75 63; Michael Chang d Rodolphe Gilbert 46 62 61; Danie Visser d Ronald Agenor 64 36 76; Mikael Pernfors d David Pate 73 76; Jim Courier bye; Pete Sampras bye; Wally Masur d Gary Muller 67 64 76; Wayne Ferreira d Ramesh Krishnan 61 63; Jason Stoltenberg d Emilio Sanchez 63 64; Anders Jarryd d Jonas Svensson 67 75 64; Amos Mansdorf d Scott Davis 64 64; Grant Stafford d Steve Devries 64 63; Stefan Edberg bye.
Rd 32: Becker d Fleurian 61 63; Washington d Krickstein 61 64; Cherkasov d Lundgren 64 62; Wheaton d Gomez 75 62; Lendl d McEnroe 61 63; Rostagno d Garner 46 63 64; Pozzi d Hlasek 64 75; Forget d Ondruska 62 62; Agassi d Korda 75 26 62; B Gilbert d Yzaga 62 75; Chang d Visser 61 63; Courier d Pernfors 63 61; Sampras d Masur 76 64; Ferreira d Stoltenburg 62 36 63; Mansdorf d Jarryd 64 61; Edberg d Stafford 62 60.
Rd 16: Becker d Washington 64 64; Cherkasov d Wheaton 63 62; Rostagno d Lendl 76 36 63; Forget d Pozzi 64 64; B Gilbert d Agassi 76 67 64; Courier d Chang 75 62; Sampras d Ferreira 64 64; Edberg d Mansdorf 61 62. **QF:** Becker d Cherkasov 76 63; Forget d Rostagno 76 64; Courier d B Gilbert 63 63; Sampras d Edberg 63 63. **SF:** Forget d Becker 76 46 63; Sampras d Courier 62 75. **F:** Forget d Sampras 26 76 64.
DOUBLES Ken Flach/Robert Seguso d Grant Connell/Glenn Michibata 67 64 75.

5-11 AUGUST: CZECHOSLOVAK OPEN, PRAGUE $350,000 Winner:
KAREL NOVACEK
Rd 32: Magnus Gustafsson d Lukas Thomas 63 62; Carlos Costa d Marcelo Filippini 61 62; Libor Pimek d Pedro Rebolledo 64 61; Arnaud Boetsch d Nicklas Kulti 61 64; Horst Skoff d Radomir Vasek 61 61; Dimitri Poliakov d Milan Trneny 36 63 62; Carl-Uwe Steeb d Roberto Azar 64 64; Guillermo Perez-Roldan d Josef Francisco Altur 64 64; Jordi Arrese d Franco Davin 62 62; Thomas Muster d Diego Nargiso 64 62; Karel Kucera d Paul Vojtischek 75 63; Magnus Larsson d Goran Prpic 62 62; Horacio de la Pena d Pablo Arraya 67 60 62; Juan Aguilera d Jan Kodes 63 64; Renzo Furlan d Andrei Olhovskiy 76 57 64; Karel Novacek d Veli Paloheimo 64 63. **Rd 16:** Gustafsson d Costa 64 61; Boetsch d Pimek 62 63; Skoff d Poliakov 64 61; Perez-Roldan d Steeb 64 62; Muster d Arrese 62 63; Larsson d Kucera 61 60; de la Pena d Aguilera 62 63Novacek d Furlan 46 64 76. **QF:** Gustafsson d Boetsch 62 62; Perez-Roldan d Skoff 36 64 76; Muster d Larsson 63 60; Novacek d de la Pena 60 64. **SF:** Gustafsson d Perez-Roldan 75 67 62; Novacek d Muster 61 26 75. **F:** Novacek d Gustafsson 76 62.
DOUBLES: Vojtech Flegl/Cyril Suk d Libor Pimek/Daniel Vacek 64 62.

12-18 AUGUST: GTE/US MEN'S HARDCOURT CHAMPIONSHIPS,
INDIANAPOLIS $1,000,000 Winner: PETE SAMPRAS
Rd 64: Boris Becker bye; David Pate d Andrew Sznajder 64 75; Nuno Marques d Buff Farrow 64 64; Christian Bergstrom d Wayne Ferreira 63 63; Jakob Hlasek d Grant Connell 76 63; Robbie Weiss d Byron Black 63 60; Jason Stoltenberg d Javier Sanchez 75 64; Emilio Sanchez bye; Andre Agassi bye; Kent Kinnear d Jose Francisco Altur 63 67 76; Cedric Pioline d Neil Borwick 63 61; Fabrice Santoro d Tomas Carbonell 64 62; Steve Bryan d Anders Jarryd 76 61; Clement N'Goran d Kelly Evernden 67 75 76; Aaron Krickstein d Jonathan Stark 63 46 64; David Wheaton bye; Pete Sampras bye; Grant Stafford d Peter Lundgren 46 63 62; Stefano Pescosolido d Rick Leach 63 63; Patrick McEnroe d Brad Pearce 75 61; Brett Steven d Ronald Agenor 46 64 76; Richard Fromberg d Scott Davis 64 62; Tim Mayotte d Jimmy Brown 64 64; Guy Forget bye; Andrei Cherkasov bye; Todd Witsken d Ramesh Krishnan 61 46 61; Shuzo Matsuoka d David Witt 75 36 63; Alexander Volkov d Gary Muller 36 62 63; Francisco Clavet d Guillaume Raoux 75 62; Rodolphe Gilbert d Todd Martin 67 64 64; Jim Pugh d Kevin Curren 76 57 63; Jim Courier bye.
Rd 32: Becker d Pate 63 62; Bergstrom d Marques 76 63; Hlasek d Weiss 75 36 75; Stoltenberg d E Sanchez 75 62; Agassi d Kinnear 76 75; Santoro d Pioline 64 57 62; Bryan d N'Goran 62 36 76; Wheaton d Krickstein 64 75; Sampras d Stafford 64 62; McEnroe d Pescosolido 76 ret; Fromberg d

Steven 62 62; Mayotte d Forget 76 61; Cherkasov d Witsken 26 76 62; Volkov d Matsuoka 76 62; Clavet d Gilbert 63 63; Courier d Pugh 64 64. **Rd 16:** Becker d Bergstrom 62 62; Hlasek d Stoltenberg 63 64; Santoro d Agassi 26 75 62; Wheaton d Bryan 63 75; Sampras d McEnroe 63 64; Fromberg d Mayotte 61 75; Cherkasov d Volkov 76 75; Courier d Clavet 62 61. **QF:** Becker d Hlasek 75 62; Wheaton d Santoro 61 64; Sampras d Fromberg 76 62; Courier d Cherkasov 62 75. **SF:** Becker d Wheaton 76 64; Sampras d Courier 63 76. **F:** Sampras d Becker 76 36 63.
DOUBLES: Ken Flach/Robert Seguso d Kent Kinnear/Sven Salumaa 76 64.

12-18 AUGUST: VOLVO INTERNATIONAL TENNIS, NEW HAVEN
$1,000,000 Winner: PETR KORDA
Rd 64: Stefan Edberg bye; Malivai Washington d Jimmy Connors 64 62; Gilad Bloom d Pablo Arraya 67 61 40 Ret.; Richard Krajicek d Christo van Rensburg 36 63 64; Derrick Rostagno d Brian Garrow 63 64; Alex O'Brien d Johan Kriek 75 62; Paul Haarhuis d Tommy Ho 63 60; Andrei Chesnokov bye; John McEnroe bye; Luiz Mattar d Andres Gomez 62 63; Fernando Roese d Jimmy Arias 64 64; Brian Shelton d Todd Woodbridge 76 63; Jan Siemerink d Andrew Castle 61 64; Ctislav Dosedel d Todd Nelson 75 26 62; Gianluca Pozzi d Thomas Hogstedt 60 10 Ret.; Goran Ivanisevic bye; Richey Reneberg bye; Paul Annacone d Chuck Adams 36 76 63; Javier Frana d Marian Vajda 62 62; Petr Korda d Jean-Philippe Fleurian 63 63; Omar Camporese d Wally Masur 46 64 64; Luis Herrera d Jaime Oncins 63 62; Danilo Marcelino d Leander Paes 64 75; Brad Gilbert bye; Jonas Svensson d Mark Kaplan d Dan Goldie 36 63 76; Amos Mansdorf d Mark Petchey 62 62; Michael Chang d Mikael Pernfors 63 57 62; Marc Rosset d Mark Woodforde 64 62; Olivier Delaitre d Chris Garner 64 76; Arnaud Boetsch d Jim Grabb 61 46 64; Ivan Lendl bye. **Rd 32:** Edberg d Washington 64 62; Krajicek d Bloom 75 63; Rostagno d O'Brien 62 62; Haarhuis d Chesnokov 76 36 75; McEnroe d Mattar 46 63 64; Roese d Shelton 75 26 64; Siemerink d Dosedel 63 61; Ivanisevic d Pozzi 76 46 62; Reneberg W/O; Korda d Frana 76 63; Camporese d Herrera 64 76; Marcelino d Gilbert 64 46 64; Svensson d Kaplan 64 63; Chang d Mansdorf 75 62; Rosset d Delaitre 63 61; Lendl d Boetsch 62 62. **Rd 16:** Krajicek d Edberg 46 63 63; Rostagno d Haarhuis 63 75; McEnroe d Roese 60 63; Ivanisevic d Siemerink 62 64; Korda d Reneberg 63 76; Camporese d Marcelino 62 62; Chang d Svensson 63 36 63; Rosset d Lendl 64 64. **QF:** Rostagno d Krajicek 36 21 Ret.; Ivanisevic d McEnroe 64 62; Korda d Camporese 64 61; Rosset d Chang 62 63. **SF:** Ivanisevic d Rostagno 64 75; Korda d Rosset 64 63. **F:** Korda d Ivanisevic 64 62.
DOUBLES: Petr Korda/Wally Masur d Jimmy Brown/Scott Melville 75 60.

19-25 AUGUST: NORSTAR BANK HAMLET CHALLENGE CUP,
LONG ISLAND $250,000 Winner: IVAN LENDL
Rd 32: Stefan Edberg d Chris Garner 61 61; Peter Lundgren d Rodolphe Gilbert 26 61 61; Jimmy Connors d Todd Martin 63 64; Nicklas Kulti d Alberto Mancini 76 62; Magnus Larsson d David Wh· en 61 67; Olivier Delaitre d Ronald Agenor 16 76 62; Jean-Philippe Fleurian d Marc Rosset 61 62; Thierry Champion d Goran Ivanisevic 62 62; Fabrice Santoro d Jonas Svensson 76 75; Luiz Mattar d Marian Vajda 75 62; Patricio Arnold d Amos Mansdorf 76 64; John McEnroe d Gilad Bloom 64 46 61; Omar Camporese d Jaime Oncins 62 62; Patrick McEnroe d Jan Siemerink 64 63; Eric Jelen d Diego Nargiso 75 67 60; Ivan Lendl d Carl-Uwe Steeb 64 36 63. **Rd 16:** Edberg d Lundgren 63 63; Connors d Kulti 16 64 60; Delaitre d Larsson 60 26 61; Champion d Fleurian 57 64 75; Mattar d Santoro 60 64; J McEnroe d Arnold 61 63; Camporese d P McEnroe 63 36 63; Lendl d Jelen 62 60. **QF:** Edberg d Connors 63 46 64; Delaitre d Champion 64 64; J McEnroe d Mattar 63 61; Lendl d Camporese 76 63. **SF:** Edberg d Delaitre 61 76; Lendl d J McEnroe 63 75. **F:** Lendl d Edberg 63 62.
DOUBLES: Eric Jelen/Carl-Uwe Steeb d Ken Flach/Diego Nargiso 06 64 76.

19-25 AUGUST: OTB INTERNATIONAL TENNIS OPEN,
SCHENECTADY $150,000 Winner: MICHAEL STICH
Rd 32: Michael Stich d Mark Woodforde 76 63; Tomas Carbonell d Patrik Kuhnen 46 63 75; Andres Gomez d Jacco Eltingh 64 60; Todd Woodbridge d Christian Bergstrom 61 62; Andrei Cherkasov d Jeff Tarango 62 63; Richard Fromberg d Jimmy Arias 64 62; Chuck Adams d Ramesh Krishnan 63 64; Horst Skoff d Wayne Ferreira 63 67 62; Alexander Volkov d Dimitri Poliakov 62 61; Javier Sanchez d Cedric Pioline 62 64; Bart Wuyts d Guillaume Raoux 63 21 def.; Emilio Sanchez d David Adams 64 64; Francisco Clavet d Stephane Simian 75 76; Mark Knowles d Nicolas Pereira 64 76; Paul Haarhuis d Jason Wetter 63 62; Sergi Bruguera d Jason Stoltenberg 46 62 63. **Rd 16:** Stich d Carbonell 61 62; Woodbridge d Gomez 67 64 75; Cherkasov d Fromberg 62 75; Skoff d C Adams 57 62 76; Volkov d J Sanchez 06 76 75; E Sanchez d Wuyts 76 62; Clavet d Knowles 63 60; Bruguera d Haarhuis 64 36 75. **QF:** Stich d Woodbridge 64 62; Skoff d Cherkasov 67 63 76; E Sanchez d Volkov 61 75; Clavet d Bruguera 61 64. **SF:** Stich d Skoff 75 61; E Sanchez d Clavet 75 61. **F:** Stich d E Sanchez 62 64.
DOUBLES: Javier Sanchez/Todd Woodbridge d Andres Gomez/Emilio Sanchez 36 76 76.

26 AUGUST-2 SEPTEMBER: UNITED STATES TENNIS OPEN
CHAMPIONSHIPS, NEW YORK $3,099,300 Winner: STEFAN EDBERG
Rd 128: Boris Becker d Martin Jaite 76 64 64; Alexander Volkov d Luis Herrera 76 63 36 64; Paul Haarhuis d Eric Jelen 26 62 61 36 62; Andrei Chesnokov d Mikael Pernfors 62 62 63; Grant Stafford d Jim Pugh 63 67 76 36 63; Carl-Uwe Steeb d Chuck Adams 62 75 63; Christian Bergstrom d

Francisco Montana 67 46 63 60 63; Arnaud Boetsch d Petr Korda 61 63 36 62; Karel Novacek d Scott Davis 63 57 61 63; Nuno Marques d Glenn Michibata 63 64 76; Jimmy Connors d Patrick McEnroe 46 67 64 62 64; Michiel Schapers d Jose Francisco Altur 46 64 62 61; Guillaume Raoux d Marc Rosset 57 63 63 46 63; Francisco Clavet d Richey Reneberg 76 67 64 62; Jaime Yzaga d Tim Mayotte 75 75 75; Aaron Krickstein d Andre Agassi 75 76 62; Jim Courier d Nicklas Kulti 63 64 64; Jimmy Arias d Peter Lundgren 75 75 36 63; Thierry Champion d Claudio Pistolesi 36 46 63 62 62; Anders Jarryd d Pablo Arraya 61 63 63; Wally Masur d Philip Williamson 46 63 63 62; Michael Joyce d Patrick Crow 36 76 64 64; Andrew Castle d Bart Wuyts 06 75 64 75; Emilio Sanchez d David Witt 64 64 36 63; David Wheaton d Richard Fromberg 60 46 76 63; Horst Skoff d Kelly Evernden 46 76 64 62; Todd Martin d Gary Muller 63 76 62; Danny Sapsford d Andrei Olhovskiy 75 61; Stephane Simian d Jean-Philippe Fleurian 61 67 36 64 62; Kevin Curren d Fabrice Santoro 36 26 63 63 63; Wayne Ferreira d Cedric Pioline 76 46 62 26 63; Pete Sampras d Christo van Rensburg 60 63 63; Ivan Lendl d Richard Krajicek 36 26 64 76 60; Patrik Kuhnen d Simon Youl 76 76 64 62; Christian Saceanu d Marian Vadja 26 76 64 64; Todd Woodbridge d Bertrand Madsen 62 60 62; Cristiano Caratti d Gilad Bloom 46 36 62 62 64; Luiz Mattar d Rick Leach 63 36 76 62; Goran Prpic d Brad Gilbert 26 64 61 16 64; Goran Ivanisevic d Henrik Holm 67 63 63 76; Jonas Svensson d Andrei Cherkasov 76 62 62; Jakob Hlasak d Roberto Azar 63 75 63; Derrick Rostagno d Patrick Baur 60 62 63; Rodolphe Gilbert d Jared Palmer 61 62 57 16 76; Omar Camporese d Amos Mansdorf 57 64 75 36 63; Malivai Washington d Jaime Oncins 62 62 61; Jimmy Brown d Alberto Mancini 62 34 67 62; Michael Stich d Jacco Eltingh 76 61 60; Guy Forget d Marcos Ondruska 75 63 61; Jan Siemerink d Dimitri Poliakov 57 75 36 64 64; Gabriel Markus d Diego Nargiso 76 76 76; Stefano Pescosolido d David Pate 76 67 26 62 63; Magnus Larsson d Andres Gomez 46 63 76 26 61; Javier Frana d David Engel 63 64 64; Javier Sanchez d Alexander Mronz 62 63 31 Retd.; Sergi Bruguera d Tomas Carbonell 36 46 63 76 63; John McEnroe d Glenn Layendecker 64 63 63; Martin Laurendeau d Ronald Agenor 75 76 36 75; Todd Witsken d Veli Paloheimo 63 57 64 61; Michael Chang d Mark Woodforde 63 60 62; Jim Grabb d Mark Koevermans 64 76 62; Jason Stoltenberg d Grant Connell 64 76 62; Jeff Tarango d Ramesh Krishnan 62 61 67 57 63; Stefan Edberg d Brian Shelton 64 26 76 61. **Rd 64:** Becker d Volkov 60 76 61; Haarhuis d Chesnokov 61 46 62 76; Steeb d Stafford 60 76 61; Boetsch d Bergstrom 62 63 21 ret.; Novacek d Marques 67 76 64 36 63; Connors d Schapers 62 63 62; Clavet d Raoux 61 61 64; Krickstein d Yzaga 61 36 61 32 ret.; Courier d Arias 63 62 62; Jarryd d Champion 75 62 11 ret.; Masur d Joyce 64 63 36 63; E Sanchez d Castle 63 62 62; Wheaton d Skoff 61 62 62; Martin d Sapsford 62 63 36 46 62; Simian d Curren 63 67 76 64; Sampras d Ferreira 61 62 22 ret. Lendl d Kuhnen 63 62 64; Woodbridge d Saceanu 62 63 63; Mattar d Caratti 36 63 60 76; Ivanisevic d Prpic 61 62 62; Hlasek d Svensson 64 75 67 63; Rostagno d R Gilbert 76 61 63; Washington d Camporese 46 61 61 64; Stich d Brown W/O; Siemerink d Forget 46 63 62 76; Markus d Pescosolido 62 16 46 76 62; Larsson d Frana 46 64 62 64; J Sanchez d Bruguera 76 63 60; J McEnroe d Laurendeau 63 64 62; Chang d Witsken 63 60 62; Grabb d Stoltenberg 75 64 46 75; Edberg d Tarango 63 75 60. **Rd 32:** Haarhuis d Becker 63 64 62; Steeb d Boetsch 36 63 64 64; Connors d Novacek 63 64 64; Krickstein d Clavet 64 64 67 76; Courier d Jarryd 63 62 62; E Sanchez d Masur 64 76 76; Wheaton d Martin 76 46 63 64; Sampras d Simian 76 64 67 63. Lendl d Woodbridge 36 63 64 63; Ivanisevic d Mattar 63 62 62; Rostagno d Hlasek 67 76 76 76; Stich d Washington 57 75 62 46 63; Markus d Siemerink 64 64 16 67 76; J Sanchez d Larsson 76 60 63; Chang d J McEnroe 44 76 26 63; Edberg d Grabb 76 46 63 64. **Rd 16:** Haarhuis d Steeb 62 63 64; Connors d Krickstein 36 76 16 63 76; Courier d E Sanchez 64 64 63; Sampras d Wheaton 36 62 62 64. Lendl d Ivanisevic 75 64 36 76; Stich d Rostagno 62 36 61 76; J Sanchez d Markus 64 62 63; Edberg d Chang 75 75 63. **QF:** Connors d Haarhuis 46 76 64 62; Courier d Sampras 62 76 76. Lendl d Stich 63 36 46 76 61; Edberg d J Sanchez 63 62 63. **SF:** Courier d Connors 63 63 62. Edberg d Lendl 63 63 64. **F:** Edberg d Courier 62 64 60.
DOUBLES: John Fitzgerald/Anders Jarryd d Scott Davis/David Pate 63 36 63 63.

9-15 SEPTEMBER! GRAND PRIX PASSING SHOT, BORDEAUX $300,000 Winner: GUY FORGET
Rd 32: Guy Forget d Rodolphe Gilbert 62 61; Patrik Kuhnen d Tomas Zdrazila 64 64; Laurent Prades d Jose Francisco Altur 57 64 64; Lars Jonsson d Christian Saceanu 64 16 63; Fabrice Santoro d Dimitri Poliakov 63 26 64; Carlos Costa d Martin Wostenholme 75 76; Pierre Bouteyre d Tomas Hogstedt 76 76; Cedric Pioline d Ctislav Dosedel 63 16 63; Tomas Carbonell d Andrei Olhovskiy 64 64; Arnaud Boetsch d Nuno Marques 62 61; Udo Riglewski d Stephane Simian 64 64; Thierry Champion d Guillaume Raoux 62 61; Alexander Mronz d Francisco Roig 57 62 76; Tarik Benhabiles d Henri Leconte 36 62 75; Olivier Delaitre d Gabriel Markus 57 62 63; Jonas Svensson d Cyril Suk 26 61. **Rd 16:** Forget d Kuhnen 63 62; Jonsson d Prades 67 62 63; Santoro d Costa 76 62; Pioline d Bouteyre 63 64; Boetsch d Carbonell 64 61; Champion d Riglewski 61 61; Mronz d Benhabiles 36 63 64; Delaitre d Svensson 76 63. **QF:** Forget d Jonsson 63 61; Pioline d Santoro 63 36 64; Champion d Boetsch 62 76; Delaitre d Mronz 46 63 60. **SF:** Forget d Pioline 63 61; Delaitre d Champion 63 61. **F:** Forget d Delaitre 61 63.
DOUBLES: Arnaud Boetsch/Guy Forget d Patrik Kuhnen/Alexander Mronz 62 62.

7-15 SEPTEMBER: ABERTO DE REPUBLICA, BRASILIA $250,000 ANDRES GOMEZ
Rd 64: Karel Novacek bye; Sandon Stolle d Ricardo Camargo 67 62 75; Jose Daher d William Kyriakos 61 61; Ramesh Krishnan bye; Bryan Shelton bye; Tommy Ho d Oliver Fernandez 36 64 75; Mauro Menezes d Cesar Kist 26 63 64; Fernando Roese bye; Francisco Clavet bye; Kent Kinnear d Yahiya Doumbia 76 46 61; Mark Keil d Andrew Sznajder 57 76 76; Todd Martin bye; David Rikl bye; Martin Damm d Bertrand Madsen 75 64; Fernando Meligeni d Rodrigo Faria 64 61; Javier Sanchez bye; Javier Frana bye; Felipe Rivera d Cassio Motta 76 36 61; Nelson Aerts d Maurice Ruah 63 36 75; Andres Gomez bye; Chris Pridham bye; Roger Smith d Nduka Odizor 64 64; Robbie Weiss d John Stimpson 64 62; Martin Jaite bye; Danilo Marcelino bye; Roberto Jabali d Martin Laurendeau 26 76 64; Ricardo Acioly d Pedro Rebolledo 76 62; Pablo Arraya bye; Francisco Montana bye; Joao Zwetsch d Fabio Silberberg 62 76; Marcelo Saliola d Alexandre Hocevar 62 62; Emilio Sanchez bye. **Rd 32:** Stolle d Novacek 64 76; Krishnan d Daher 75 61; Shelton d Ho 63 64; Roese d Menezes 64 62; Clavet d Kinnear 76 62; Martin d Keil 63 64; Damm d Rikl 63 36 63; J Sanchez d Meligeni 67 64 63; Frana d Rivera 57 63 61; Gomez d Aerts 46 63 63; Smith d Pridham 76 64; Jaite d Weiss 64 26 76; Marcelino d Jabali 64 64; Arraya d Acioly 63 76; Montana d Zwetsch 61 62; Saliola d E Sanchez 76 57 62. **Rd 16:** Stolle d Krishnan 26 62 76; Shelton d Roese 75 76; Martin d Clavet 64 76; J Sanchez d Damm 76 64; Gomez d Frana 67 64 64; Jaite d Smith 63 76; Marcelino d Arraya 76 75; Montana d Saliola 64 63. **QF:** Shelton d Stolle 75 64; J Sanchez d Martin 62 62; Gomez d Jaite 63 63; Marcelino d Montana 62 61. **SF:** J Sanchez d Shelton 16 76 76; Gomez d Marcelino 64 76. **F:** Gomez d J Sanchez 64 36 63.
DOUBLES: Kent Kinnear/Roger Smith d Ricardo Acioly/Mauro Menezes 64 63.

9-15 SEPTEMBER: BARCLAY OPEN, GENEVA $250,000 Winner: THOMAS MUSTER
Rd 32: Sergi Bruguera d Bart Wuyts 63 62; Claudio Mezzadri d Thierry Tulasne 63 75; Thomas Muster d Marian Vajda 63 75; Guillaume Perez-Roldan d Marcelo Filippini 76 63; Goran Prpic d Gilad Bloom 46 64 64; Christian Miniussi d Renzo Furlan 64 75; Eduardo Masso d Jan Gunnarsson 63 63; Andrei Medvedev d Marc Rosset 62 61; Alberto Mancini d Luiz Mattar 63 64; Horacio de la Pena d Franco Davin 76 76; Miguel Merz d Patrick Baur 36 76 75; Horst Skoff d German Lopez 62 60; Carsten Arriens d Omar Camporesi 63 64; Jaime Oncins d Juan Gisberg 64 75; Veli Paloheimo d Ronald Agenor 76 46 64; Jordi Arrese d Andrei Cherkasov 44 46 61. **Rd 16:** Bruguera d Mezzadri 76 16 61; Muster d Perez-Roldan 46 61 62; Miniussi d Prpic 67 60 75; Medvedev d Masso 57 76 61; de la Pena d Mancini 61 36 64; Skoff d Merz 62 60; Oncins d Arriens 75 57 75; Arrese d Paloheimo 62 76 75. **QF:** Muster d Bruguera 46 64 64; Medvedev d Miniussi d Medvedev 76 76; Skoff d Arrese 76 62. **F:** Muster d Skoff 62 64.
DOUBLES: Sergi Bruguera/Marc Rosset d Per Henricsson/Lars Jonsson 36 63 62.

23-29 SEPTEMBER: SWISS INDOORS, BASEL $750,000 Winner: JAKOB HLASEK
Rd 32: Christian Bergstrom d Michael Stich 63 63; Johan Carlsson d Alexander Mronz 75 57 63; Patrick McEnroe d Claudio Mezzadri 67 75 60; John McEnroe d Thierry Guardiolo 62 64; Petr Korda d Andres Jarryd 36 64 63; Jimmy Connors d Laurent Prades 63 61; Paolo Cane d Thomas Enqvist 46 63 76; Amos Mansdorf d Andrei Cherkasov 75 63; Jakob Hlasek d Jan Gunnarsson 63 62; Carl-Uwe Steeb d Jean-Philippe Fleurian 60 76; Kevin Curren d Marc Rosset 26 76 61; Sergi Bruguera d David Engel 26 75 76; Alexander Volkov d Guillaume Raoux 63 64; Tomas Carbonell d Christian Saceanu 75 63; Niclas Kulti d Cristiano Caratti 61 64; Karel Novacek d Paul Haarhuis 62 16 63. **Rd 16:** Bergstrom d Carlsson 63 62; J McEnroe d P McEnroe 62 64; Connors d Korda 63 64; Mansdorf d Cane 75 64; Hlasek d Steeb 76 63; Curren d Bruguera 64 36 63; Volkov d Carbonell 64 64; Novacek d Kulti 64 67 76. **QF:** J McEnroe d Bergstrom 76 64; Connors d Mansdorf 63 62; Hlasek d Curren 76 64; Volkov d Novacek 61 67 63. **SF:** J McEnroe d Connors 61 63; Hlasek d Volkov 76 67 76. **F:** Hlasek d J McEnroe 76 60 63.
DOUBLES: Jakob Hlasek/Patrick McEnroe d Petr Korda/John McEnroe 36 76 76.

23-29 SEPTEMBER: 39TH INTERNATIONAL CHAMPIONSHIP OF SICILY $300,000 Winner: FREDERIC FONTANG
Rd 32: Emilio Sanchez d Diego Perez 64 60; Martin Jaite d Jacco Eltingh 62 62; Roberto Azar d Stefano Pescosolido 75 36 76; Thomas Muster d Ronald Agenor 60 64; Diego Nargiso d Horst Skoff 76 62; Rodolphe Gilbert d Martin Schaffl 63 62; Marian Vajda d Marcelo Filippini 36 62; Guillermo Perez-Roldan d Francisco Roig 63 75. Claudio Pistolesi d Andres Vysand 62 62; Yannick Noah d Carlos Costa 16 75 64; Jose Antonio Conde d Arnaud Boetsch 75 76; Jordi Arrese d Javier Sanchez 64 26 75; German Lopez d Francisco Clavet 62 64; Massimo Cierro d Bart Wuyts 62 62; Frederic Fontang d Andrei Medvedev 46 63 64; Renzo Furlan d Goran Prpic 64 76. **Rd 16:** E Sanchez d Jaite 26 76 64; Muster d Azar 61 63; Nargiso d Gilbert 64 46 61; Vajda d Perez-Roldan 62 64; Noah d Pistolesi 76 63; Arrese d Conde 64 64; Cierro d Lopez 63 42 Ret.; Fontang d Furlan 62 63. **QF:** E Sanchez d Muster 63 76; Vajda d Nargiso 26 76 63; Arrese d Noah 62 46 64; Fontang d Cierro 61 76. **SF:** E Sanchez d Vajda 61 62; Fontang d Arrese 63 26 76. **F:** Fontang d E Sanchez 16 63 63.
DOUBLES: Jacco Eltingh/Tom Kempers d Emilio Sanchez/Javier Sanchez 36 63 63.

23-29 SEPTEMBER: QUEENSLAND OPEN, BRISBANE $250,000
Winner: GIANLUCA POZZI
Rd 32: Brad Gilbert d Thomas Hogstedt 62 61; Niclas Kroon d Simon Youl
46 76 76; Jamie Morgan d Danilo Marcelino 76 62; Jason Stoltenberg d
Gary Muller 67 62 62; Todd Woodbridge d Jeff Tarango 63 76; Gianluca
Pozzi d Sandon Stolle 76 46 64; Jim Grabb d Lars Wahlgren 61 61; Shuzo
Matsuoka d Peter Lundgren 64 64; Wayne Ferreira d Johan Anderson 76 26
63; Daniel Orsanic d Brett Richardson 16 61 75; Mark Woodforde d Andrei
Olhovskiy 61 63; Aaron Krickstein d John Fitzgerald 63 76; Richard
Fromberg d Mark Kratzmann 75 63; Jason Cask d Neil Borwick 26 62 64;
Robbie Weiss d Dimitri Poliakov 62 63; Andrei Chesnokov d Patrick Rafter
64 61. **Rd 16:** Gilbert d Kroon 62 61; Stoltenberg d Morgan 63 61; Pozzi d
Woodbridge 64 06 61; Grabb d Matsuoka 75 57 63; Ferreira d Orsanic 64
63; Krickstein d Woodforde 63 75; Fromberg d Cask 60 61; Chesnokov d
Weiss 36 62 60. **QF:** Stoltenberg d Gilbert 63 61; Pozzi d Grabb 63 16 63;
Krickstein d Ferreira 64 63; Chesnokov d Fromberg 64 64. **SF:** Pozzi d
Stoltenberg 63 61; Krickstein d Chesnokov 75 64. **F:** Pozzi d Krickstein 63 76.
DOUBLES: Todd Woodbridge/Mark Woodforde d John Fitzgerald/Glenn
Michibata 76 63.

30 SEPTEMBER-6 OCTOBER: UNCLE TOBY'S AUSTRALIAN
INDOOR TENNIS CHAMPIONSHIPS, SYDNEY $1,000,000 Winner:
BRAD GILBERT
Rd 64: Stefan Edberg bye; Peter Lundgren d Gary Muller 76 63; Mark
Woodforde d Grant Doyle 62 61; Wally Masur bye; Andrei Chesnokov
bye; Gianluca Pozzi d Paolo Cane 75 16 61; Niclas Kroon d Thomas
Hogstedt 76 76; Michael Chang bye; Andre Agassi bye; Jason Stoltenberg
d Ctislav Dosedel 75 63; Jeff Tarango d Robbie Weiss 46 60 63; Malivai
Washington bye; Richey Reneberg bye; Sandon Stolle d Tomas Zdrazila 36
64 64; Simon Youl d Richard Fromberg 46 62 63; Goran Ivanisevic bye;
David Wheaton bye; Neil Borwick d Jamie Morgan 61 75; Grant Connell d
Chris Wilkinson 67 63 76; Aaron Krickstein bye; Todd Woodbridge bye;
Jim Grabb d Andrei Olhovskiy 75 63; Todd Nelson d Shuzo Matsuoka 36
63 64; Pete Sampras bye; Derrick Rostagno d Danilo Marcelino d Luis
Herrera 62 61; John Fitzgerald d Johan Anderson 62 63; Brad Gilbert bye;
Wayne Ferreira bye; Dimitri Poliakov d David Pate 60 36 63; Scott Davis d
Daniel Orsanic 61 60; Ivan Lendl bye. **Rd 32:** Edberg d Lundgren 63 64;
Woodforde d Masur 62 46 76; Pozzi d Chesnokov 61 64; Chang d Kroon
63 64; Agassi d Stoltenberg 62 62; Washington d Tarango 76 62; Reneberg
d Stolle 46 75 76; Ivanisevic d Youl 64 63; Wheaton d Borwick 62 63;
Connell d Krickstein 64 76; Woodbridge d Grabb 63 46 62; Sampras d
Nelson 46 61 64; Marcelino d Rostagno 64 64; Gilbert d Fitzgerald 62 62;
Ferreira d Poliakov 64 75; Lendl d Davis 64 67 75. **Rd 16:** Edberg d
Woodforde 64 62; Chang d Pozzi 61 62; Agassi d Washington 63 61;
Ivanisevic d Reneberg 63 62; Wheaton d Connell 75 62; Sampras d
Woodbridge 62 61; Gilbert d Marcelino 61 62; Ferreira d Lendl 64 26 63.
QF: Edberg d Chang 64 75; Ivanisevic d Agassi 75 76; Sampras d Wheaton
63 46 64; Gilbert d Ferreira 61 64. **SF:** Edberg d Ivanisevic 46 76 76;
Gilbert d Sampras 16 75 63. **F:** Gilbert d Edberg 62 62 62.
DOUBLES: Jim Grabb/Richey Reneberg d Luke Jensen/Laurie Warder.

30 SEPTEMBER-6 OCTOBER: GRAND PRIX DE TOULOUSE $300,000
Winner: GUY FORGET
Rd 32: Guy Forget d Johan Carlsson 64 64; Thierry Champion d Yannick
Noah 57 75 63; Thomas Enqvist d Libor Pimek 61 62; Marc Rosset d
Fabrice Santoro 61 63; Jacob Hlasek d Thierry Guardiola 61 62; Richard
Krajicek d Frederic Fontang 62 60; Tomas Carbonell d Guillaume Raoux
67 64 63; John McEnroe d Arnaud Boetsch 36 62 60; Alexander Volkov d
Nicklas Kulti 36 62 62; Tom Nijssen d Christian Saceanu 67 75 64; Cedric
Pioline d Kevin Curren 64 76 63; Ronald Agenor d Jonas Svensson 64 76;
Patrick McEnroe d Cristiano Caratti 36 75 62; Christian Bergstrom d Jean-
Philippe Fleurian 67 61 61; Alexander Mronz d Patrick Baur 64 46 61;
Amos Mansdorf d Magnus Gustafsson 64 61. **Rd 16:** Forget d Champion
61 36 63; Rosset d Enqvist 64 76; Krajicek d Hlasek 62 64; J McEnroe d
Carbonell 61 64; Volkov d Nijssen 75 46 64; Pioline d Agenor 75 76;
Bergstrom d P McEnroe 63 75; Mansdorf d Mronz 75 46 62. **QF:** Forget d
Rosset 36 63 63; Krajicek d J McEnroe 64 64; Volkov d Pioline 57 76 62;
Mansdorf d Bergstrom 64 64. **SF:** Forget d Krajicek 76 36 64; Mansdorf d
Volkov 75 57 61. **F:** Forget d Mansdorf 62 76.
DOUBLES: Tom Nijssen/Cyril Suk d Jeremy Bates/Kevin Curren 46 63 76.

30 SEPTEMBER-6 OCTOBER: ATHENS INTERNATIONAL $150,000
Winner: SERGI BRUGUERA
Rd 32: Sergi Bruguera d Patrik Kuhnen 62 75; Wojtek Kowalski d Milen
Velev 64 63; Jens Woehrmann d Marian Vajda 63 62; Renzo Furlan d
Martin Jaite 61 36 63; Thomas Muster d Jacco Eltingh 64 63; Francisco
Yunis d Juan-Carlos Baguena 62 36 76; Bart Wuyts d George Kalovelonis
64 36 63; Guillermo Perez-Roldan d Tasos Bavelas 63 61; Francisco Clavet
d Eduardo Masso 76 63; Roberto Azar d Andrea Gaudenzi 64 60; Lars
Jonsson d Marcelo Filippini 62 06 63; Javier Sanchez d Bernd Karbacher
64 76; Jordi Arrese d Torben Theine 76 61; Gabriel Markus d Claudio
Pistolesi 62 36 61; Mark Koevermans d T J Middleton 61 62; Markus
Zoecke d Goran Prpic 76 36 64. **Rd 16:** Bruguera d Kowalski 62 61; Furlan
d Woehrmann 75 60; Muster d Yunis 64 63; Perez-Roldan d Wuyts 61 62;
Clavet d Azar 46 64 60; Jonsson d Sanchez 64 36 64; Arrese d Markus 26
63 64; Koevermans d Zoecke 60 62. **QF:** Bruguera d Furlan 62 62; Muster
d Perez-Roldan 63 36 76; Clavet d Jonsson 76 61; Arrese d Koevermans 26
63 64. **SF:** Bruguera d Muster 16 62 60; Arrese d Clavet 75 62. **F:** Bruguera
d Arrese 75 63.

DOUBLES: Jacco Eltingh/Mark Koevermans d Menno Oosting/Olli
Rahnasto 57 76 75.

7-13 OCTOBER: SEIKO SUPER TENNIS, TOKYO $1,000,000 Winner:
STEFAN EDBERG
Rd 64: Stefan Edberg bye; David Pate d John Sobel 63 64; Gary Muller d
Ctislav Dosedel 75 76; Frederic Fontang bye; Andrei Chesnokov bye; Paolo
Cane d Hidehiko Tanizawa 63 64; Mark Woodforde d Peter Lundgren 61
63; Michael Chang bye; Andrei Agassi bye; Luis Herrera d Danilo
Marcelino 36 61 64; Jeff Tarango d Nicklas Kroon 62 16 75; Wayne
Ferreira bye; Malivai Washington bye; Simon Youl d Thomas Hogstedt 76
61; Dimitri Poliakov d Jamie Morgan 63 75; Goran Ivanisevic bye; David
Wheaton bye; Jim Grabb d Bong-Soo Kim 62 63; Gianluca Pozzi d Andrei
Olhovskiy 63 75; Todd Woodbridge bye; Wally Masur bye; Glenn
Michibata d Rick Leach 62 64; Scott Davis d Neil Borwick 76 76; Ivan
Lendl bye; Derrick Rostagno bye; Jason Stoltenberg d Grant Connell 75 63;
Johan Anderson d Ryuso Tsujino 64 75; Richey Reneberg bye; Shuzo
Matsuoka bye; Robbie Weiss d Tasufumi Yamamoto 62 63; Jan
Gunnarsson d Daniel Orsanic 63 64; Boris Becker bye. **Rd 32:** Edberg d
Pate 62 64; Fontang d Muller 76 63; Chesnokov d Cane 75 63; Chang d
Woodforde 61 64; Agassi d Herrera 75 61; Tarango d Ferreira 76 64;
Washington d Youl 64 76; Ivanisevic d Poliakov 64 62; Wheaton d Grabb
76 36 62; Pozzi d Woodbridge 76 63; Masur d Michibata 60 63; Lendl d
Davis 62 63; Rostagno d Stoltenberg 36 63 62; Reneberg d Anderson 64
76; Matsuoka d Weiss 26 62 76; Becker d Gunnarsson 62 64. **Rd 16:** Edberg
d Fontang 62 75; Chang d Chesnokov 64 76; Agassi d Tarango 64 76;
Ivanisevic d Washington 76 67 64; Wheaton d Pozzi 60 62; Lendl d Masur
64 67 62; Rostagno d Reneberg 36 63 64; Becker d Matsuoka 26 63 64.
QF: Edberg d Chang 62 62; Ivanisevic d Agassi 63 64; Lendl d Wheaton
76 75; Rostagno d Becker 76 46 63. **SF:** Edberg d Ivanisevic 46 76 75;
Rostagno d Lendl 76 62. **F:** Edberg d Rostagno 63 16 62.
DOUBLES: Jim Grabb/Richey Reneberg d Scott Davis/David Pate 75 26 76.

7-13 OCTOBER: HOLSTEN INTERNATIONAL, BERLIN $300,000
Winner: PETR KORDA
Rd 32: Michael Stich d Carl-Uwe Steeb 62 36 75; Jan Siemerink d Eric
Jelen 75 76; Fabrice Santoro d Johan van Merck 63 36 63; Anders Jarryd d
Johan Kriek 63 62; Petr Korda d Ronald Agenor 63 16 63; Udo Riglewski d
Danie Visser 76 67 64; Guillaume Raoux d Rodolphe Gilbert 75 61;
Alexander Volkov d Christian Saceanu 67 63 76; Jonas Svensson d Patrick
Baur 63 64; Arnaud Boetsch d Christian Bergstrom 64 62; Jean-Philippe
Fleurian d Kelly Jones 36 76 64; Sergi Bruguera d Markus Zoecke 63 16
63; Tim Mayotte d Cristiano Caratti 63 63; Patrik Kuhnen d Alexander
Mronz 63 64; Cedric Pioline d Thierry Champion 64 46 63; Kevin Curren d
Karel Novacek 76 63. **Rd 16:** Stich d Siemerink 62 63; Jarryd d Santoro 63
67 63; Korda d Riglewski 76 63; Volkov d Raoux 46 64 62; Boetsch d
Svensson 62 61; Fleurian d Bruguera 64 63; Kuhnen d Mayotte 36 75 64;
Pioline d Curren 63 63. **QF:** Jarryd d Stich 64 76; Korda d Volkov 63 57
61; Boetsch d Fleurian 60 63; Kuhnen d Pioline 76 63. **SF:** Korda d Jarryd
63 16 62; Boetsch d Kuhnen 63 62. **F:** Korda d Boetsch 63 64.
DOUBLES: Petr Korda/Karel Novacek d Jan Siemerink/Daniel Vacek 36
75 75.

7-12 OCTOBER: RIKLIS ISRAEL TENNIS CENTER CLASSIC, TEL
AVIV $150,000 Winner: LEONARDO LAVALLE
Rd 32: Andrei Cherkasov d Shamar Perkis 75 64; Chuck Adams d Ofer
Sela 63 64; Chris Pridham d Martin Wostenholme 64 63; Leonardo Lavalle
d Jacco Eltingh 46 63 64; Jan Apell d Mark Koevermans 61 60; Peter
Nyborg d Ohad Weinberg 62 64; Raviv Weidenfeld d Vaclav Roubicek 63
76; Bryan Shelton d Lars Jonsson 63 76; Olivier Delaitre d Brett Steven 62
46 61; David Rikl d Tomas Zdrazila 26 64 63; Henrik Holm d Martin
Laurendeau 16 64 64; Christo van Rensberg d Amos Mansdorf 63 62;
Javier Frana d Michiel Schapers 63 63; Johan Carlsson d Vladimir
Gabrichidze 36 64 62; Gilad Bloom d Martin Strelba 62 63; Martin Jaite d
Alex Antonitsch 63 61. **Rd 16:** Cherkasov d Adams 63 76; Lavalle d
Pridham 64 76; Nyborg d Apell 75 46 64; Shelton d Weidenfeld 63 61;
Delaitre d Rikl 63 75; van Rensburg d Holm 76 61; Carlsson d Frana 63 64;
Bloom d Jaite 63 64. **QF:** Lavalle d Cherkasov 75 67 63; Shelton d Nyborg
76 64; van Rensburg d Delaitre 63 63; Bloom d Carlsson 63 75. **SF:** Lavalle
d Shelton 64 76; van Rensburg d Bloom 63 26 63. **F:** Lavalle d van
Rensburg 62 36 63.
DOUBLES: David Rikl/Michiel Schapers d Javier Frana/Leonardo Lavalle
62 67 73.

14-20 OCTOBER: GRAND PRIX DE TENNIS DE LYON $500,000
Winner: PETE SAMPRAS
Rd 32: Olivier Delaitre d Guy Forget 16 64 63; Cedric Pioline d Tomas
Carbonell 75 67 63; Johan Kriek d Stefano Pescosolido 76 63; Fabrice
Santoro d Marc Rosset 61 63; Sergi Bruguera d Arnaud Boetsch 36 63 64;
Guillaume Raoux d Jean-Philippe Fleurian 63 62; Christo van Rensburg d
Frederic Fontang 60 76; Kevin Curren d Derrick Rostagno 67 76 76;
Alberto Mancini d Christian Saceanu 26 75 76; Nicklas Kulti d Veli
Paloheimo 62 64; Eric Winogradsky d Steve Devries 61 36 63; Brad Gilbert
d Alexander Mronz 63 75; Jonas Svensson d Patrick Kuhnen 16 63 76;
Ronald Agenor d Yahiya Doumbia 67 75 75; Thierry Champion d Yannick
Noah 64 64; Pete Sampras d Tom Nijssen 63 62. **Rd 16:** Delaitre d Pioline
62 76; Kriek d Santoro 64 64; Bruguera d Raoux 76 76; Curren d van
Rensburg 61 62; Mancini d Kulti 26 76 64; Gilbert d Winogradsky 75 61;
Svensson d Agenor 67 63 61; Sampras d Champion 61 63. **QF:** Delaitre d

Kriek 62 76; Bruguera d Curren 60 76; Gilbert d Mancini 62 62; Sampras d Svensson 62 62. **SF:** Delaitre d Bruguera 64 64; Sampras d Gilbert 61 62. **F:** Sampras d Delaitre 61 61.
DOUBLES: Tom Nijssen/Cyril Suk d Steve Devries/David Macpherson 76 63.

14-20 OCTOBER: CA TENNIS TROPHY, VIENNA $250,000 Winner: MICHAEL STICH
Rd 32: Michael Stich d Leonardo Lavalle 63 64; Patrick McEnroe d Gary Muller 75 63; Eric Jelen d Gerald Mandl 64 62; Anders Jarryd d Claudio Pistolesi 61 62; Petr Korda d Alexis Hombrecher 46 61 62; Lars Jonsson d Marian Vajda 16 76 64; Aaron Krickstein d Thomas Hogstedt 63 62; Andrei Cherkasov d Amos Mansdorf 76 67 76; Alexander Volkov d Markus Zoecke d David Engel 64 63; Richard Krajicek d Thomas Buchmayer 67 76 64; Javier Frana d Goran Prpic 61 61; Horst Skoff d Roberto Azar 76 46 63; Patrick Baur d Alex Antonitsch 63 63; Jan Siemerink d Paul Vojtisek 64 63; Jakob Hlasek d Cristiano Caratti 62 62. **Rd 16:** Stich d McEnroe 63 64; Jarryd d Jelen 76 63; Korda d Jonsson 62 64; Krickstein d Cherkasov 63 64; Steeb d Volkov 62 67 63; Frana d Krajicek 76 46 76; Skoff d Baur 57 63 61; Siemerink d Hlasek 67 76 63. **QF:** Stich d Jarryd 62 61; Korda d Krickstein 46 62 61; Steeb d Frana 76 75; Siemerink d Skoff 63 61. **SF:** Stich d Korda 46 26 62; Siemerink d Steeb 63 64. **F:** Stich d Siemerink 64 64 64.
DOUBLES: Anders Jarryd/Gary Muller d Jakob Hlasek/Patrick McEnroe 64 75

21-27 OCTOBER: STOCKHOLM OPEN $1,100,000 Winner: BORIS BECKER
Rd 64: Stefan Edberg bye; Peter Lundgren d Mark Koevermans 63 62; Patrick McEnroe d Horst Skoff 67 63 63; Brad Gilbert bye; Karel Novacek bye; Wally Masur d Jan Gunnarsson 64 64; Richey Reneberg d Alexander Volkov 64 62; Sergi Bruguera bye; Michael Stich bye; Aaron Krickstein d Libor Pimek 62 26 76; Jan Siemerink d Thierry Champion 75 63; Jakob Hlasek d Goran Ivanisevic 76 61; Magnus Larsson d Rikard Berg 62 61; Ronald Agenor d Marc Rosset 64 63; Guy Forget bye; Ivan Lendl bye; Todd Woodbridge d Thomas Enqvist 76 63; Christian Bergstrom d Andrei Cherkasov 63 75; Petr Korda bye; Derrick Rostagno bye; Anders Jarryd d Henrik Holm 63 76; Carl-Uwe Steeb d Alberto Mancini 67 63 64; Jim Courier bye; Pete Sampras bye; Thomas Hogstedt d Jonas Svensson 75 46 61; David Engel d Nicklas Kulti 57 64 62; David Wheaton bye; Goran Prpic bye; Jimmy Connors d Martin Jaite 63 76; Omar Camporese d Rick Leach 64 62; Boris Becker bye. **Rd 32:** Edberg d Lundgren 63 64; Gilbert d McEnroe 62 62; Novacek d Masur 64 67 64; Reneberg d Bruguera 76 16 61; Krickstein d Stich 67 76 60; Hlasek d Siemerink 46 76 63; Ivanisevic d Larsson 75 67 75; Forget d Agenor 63 63; Lendl d Woodbridge 75 62; Korda d Bergstrom 67 76 63; Rostagno d Jarryd 30 Ret.; Courier d Steeb 64 64; Sampras d Hogstedt 76 67 63; Engel d Wheaton 46 64 76; Prpic d Connors 76 67 61; Becker d Camporese 46 75 63. **Rd 16:** Edberg d Gilbert 62 63; Reneberg d Novacek 26 63 63; Krickstein d Hlasek 36 62 63; Ivanisevic d Forget 76 76; Korda d Lendl 57 61 64; Courier d Rostagno 75 61; Sampras d Engel 67 62 64; Becker d Prpic 76 61. **QF:** Edberg d Reneberg 63 26 63; Krickstein d Ivanisevic 76 10 Ret.; Courier d Korda 64 64; Becker d Sampras 75 75. **SF:** Edberg d Krickstein 62 62; Becker d Courier 67 63 64. **F:** Becker d Edberg 36 64 16 62 62.
DOUBLES: John Fitzgerald/Anders Jarryd d Tom Nijssen/Cyril Suk 75 62.

21-27 OCTOBER: BLISS OPEN, GUARUJA, BRAZIL $150,000 Winner: JAVIER FRANA
Rd 32: Luis Mattar d Thomas Muster 63 62; Francisco Roig d Shuzo Matsuoka 64 63; Bart Wuyts d Mark Knowles 46 52 Ret.; Frederic Fontang d Marcelo Filippini 57 61 64; Paul Haarhuis d Eduardo Masso 62 61; Maurice Ruah d Cassio Motta 60 63; Javier Frana d Danilo Marcelino 76 63; Guillermo Perez-Roldan d Jaime Oncins 64 26 76; Francisco Clavet d Gabriel Markus 46 64 30 Ret.; Carlos Costa d Luiz Herrera 76 36 64; Andres Gomez d Roberto Azar 64; Patrick Baur d Javier Sanchez 75 63; Olivier Delaitre d Jacco Eltingh 63 63; German Lopez d Carsten Arriens 67 64 62; Markus Zoecke d Daniel Nestor 63 64; Jordi Arrese d Jean-Philippe Fleurian 57 63 62. **Rd 16:** Roig d Mattar 62 57 64; Wuyts d Fontang 62 63; Ruah d Haarhuis 57 64 64; Frana d Perez-Roldan 62 76; Costa d Clavet 76 36 63; Gomez d Baur 63 62; Lopez d Delaitre 64 61; Zoecke d Arrese 61 67 63. **QF:** Roig d Wuyts 46 61 64; Frana d Ruah 46 64 76; Costa d Gomez 46 61 63; Zoecke d Lopez 63 46 75. **SF:** Frana d Roig 16 63 60; Zoecke d Costa 64 62. **F:** Frana d Zoecke 26 63 63.
DOUBLES: Jacco Eltingh/Paul Harrhuis d Bret Garnett/Todd Nelson 63 75.

28 OCTOBER-3 NOVEMBER: 6e OPEN DE LA VILLE DE PARIS $2,000,000 Winner: GUY FORGET
Rd 64: Stefan Edberg bye; Thomas Hogstedt d Jim Grabb 36 75 76; Rodolphe Gilbert d Anders Jarryd 26 75 75; Michael Chang d Petr Korda bye; Jason Stoltenberg d Alberto Mancini 36 75 76; Wally Masur d Carl-Uwe Steeb 76 46 64; Sergi Bruguera bye; Wayne Ferreira bye; Arnaud Boetsch d Andrei Chesnokov 64 62; Alexander Volkov d Marc Rosset 63 64; Brad Gilbert bye; Goran Ivanisevic d John McEnroe d Christian Bergstrom 61 76; Andrei Cherkasov d Richey Reneberg 64 75; Pete Sampras bye; Guy Forget bye; Patrick McEnroe d Martin Jaite 63 76; Yannick Noah d Fabrice Santoro 75 63; Derrick Rostagno bye; Jakob Hlasek bye; Omar Camporese d Thierry Champion 76 16 64; Jimmy Connors d Ronald Agenor 57 64 62; Jim Courier bye; Karel Novacek bye; Malivai Washington d Todd Woodbridge 76 62; Nicklas Kulti d Cedric

Pioline 76 62; David Wheaton bye; Goran Prpic bye; Jan Svensson d Richard Krajicek 63 62; Horst Skoff d Jan Siemerink 62 06 64; Boris Becker bye. **Rd 32:** Edberg d Hogstedt 60 67 63; Chang d R Gilbert 76 36 76; Korda d Stoltenberg 36 64 76; Bruguera d Masur 46 76 62; Boetsch d Ferreira 75 63; Volkov d B Gilbert 62 26 63; Ivanisevic d J McEnroe 64 64; Sampras d Cherkasov 76 62; Forget d P McEnroe 63 62; Rostagno d Noah 63 63; Camporese d Hlasek 76 62; Courier d Connors 64 64; Novacek d Washington 64 64; Kulti d Wheaton 63 63; Svensson d Prpic 62 63; Becker d Skoff 62 64. **Rd 16:** Chang d Edberg 26 61 64; Korda d Bruguera 62 64; Volkov d Boetsch 75 62; Sampras d Ivanisevic 63 67 76; Forget d Rostagno 46 63 61; Camporese d Courier 76 63; Novacek d Kulti 63 62; Svensson d Becker W/O. **QF:** Chang d Korda 75 61; Sampras d Volkov 62 63; Forget d Camporese 61 36 63; Svensson d Novacek 64 62. **SF:** Sampras d Chang 26 64 63; Forget d Svensson 75 64. **F:** Forget d Sampras 76 46 57 64 64.
DOUBLES: John Fitzgerald/Anders Jarryd d Kelly Jones/Rick Leach 36 63 62.

28 OCTOBER-3 NOVEMBER: KOLYNOS CUP, BUZIOS $175,000 Winner: JORDI ARRESE
Rd 32: Markus Zoecke d Emilio Sanchez 76 62; Daniel Nestor d Danilo Marcelino 64 62; Jaime Oncins d Jean-Philippe Fleurian 76 63; Olivier Delaitre d Andres Vysand 61 46 62; Thomas Muster d Mark Koevermans 63 76; Andres Gomez d Jacco Eltingh 75 62; Francisco Roig d Maurice Ruah 62 63; Paul Haarhuis d Luiz Mattar 76 63; Francisco Clavet d Eduardo Masso 60 61; Fernando Roese d Patrick Baur 75 76; Luis Herrera d Nicolas Pereira 75 63; Javier Sanchez d Tomas Carbonell 64 64; Guillermo Perez-Roldan d Javier Frana 64 60; Carlos Costa d Bart Wuyts 76 46 62; Jose Daher d Gabriel Markus 46 64 63; Jordi Arrese d Shuzo Matsuoka 61 63. **Rd 16:** Zoecke d Nestor 63 62; Oncins d Delaitre 76 64; Muster d Gomez 64 64; Roig d Haarhuis 62 61; Clavet d Roese 62 62; J Sanchez d Herrera 26 62 75; Perez-Roldan d Costa 64 67 61; Arrese d Daher 76 16 64. **QF:** Oncins d Zoecke 64 62; Roig d Muster 46 63 63; J Sanchez d Clavet 67 64 62; Arrese d Perez-Roldan 67 75 31 Ret. **SF:** Oncins d Roig 64 64; Arrese d J Sanchez 62 76. **F:** Arrese d Oncins 16 64 60.
DOUBLES: Sergio Casal/Emilio Sanchez d Javier Frana/Leonardo Lavalle 46 63 64.

4-10 NOVEMBER: DIET PEPSI INDOOR CHALLENGE, BIRMINGHAM $500,000 Winner: MICHAEL CHANG
Rd 32: Michael Chang d Marian Vajda 61 62; Grant Connell d Chris Bailey 67 76 63; Pat Cash d Stefano Pescosolido 63 76; Ronald Agenor d Kevin Curren 36 75 62; Richey Reneberg d Lars Jonsson 46 63 63; Gary Muller d David Engel 61 36 63; Patrik Kuhnen d Frederic Fontang 62 63; Wayne Ferreira d Nicklas Kulti 62 62; Thierry Champion d Jan Gunnarsson 62 62; Jeremy Bates d Christian Saceanu 46 76 64; Gianluca Pozzi d Rodolphe Gilbert 67 64 63; Malivai Washington d Peter Lundgren 63 36 75; Magnus Larsson d Wally Masur 63 62; Tom Nijssen d Jeff Tarango 62 64; Guillaume Raoux d Jacco Eltingh 62 63; Alexander Mronz d John McEnroe 63 46 63. **Rd 16:** Chang d Connell 57 63 61; Agenor d Cash 46 64 62; Reneberg d Muller 76 63; Ferreira d Kuhnen 64 63; Champion d Bates 67 75 61; Washington d Pozzi 60 75; Nijssen d Larsson 76 62; Raoux d Mronz 76 62. **QF:** Chang d Agenor 42 Ret.; Reneberg d Ferreira 64 64; Champion d Washington 64 64; Raoux d Nijssen 75 63. **SF:** Chang d Reneberg 46 61 62; Raoux d Champion 63 64. **F:** Chang d Raoux 63 62.
DOUBLES: Jacco Eltingh/Paul Wekesa d Ronnie Bathman/Rikard Bergh 75 75.

4-10 NOVEMBER: BAYER KREMLIN CUP, MOSCOW $330,000 Winner: ANDREI CHERKASOV
Rd 32: Karel Novacek d Udo Riglewski 76 62; Carl-Uwe Steeb d Amos Mansdorf 63 76; Marco Aureli Gorriz d Henrik Jan Davids 26 63 62; Thomas Hogstedt d Horst Skoff 63 60; Andrei Cherkasov d Florian Krumrey 63 64; Andrew Medvedev d Todd Woodbridge 75 63; Jason Stoltenberg d Richard Krajicek 36 63 64; Marc Rosset d Sergi Soulie 64 63; Jan Siemerink d Eric Jelen 61 64; Chuck Adams d Lars Koslowski 63 46 64; Rudiger Haas d Sergei Skakun 61 62; Jakob Hlasek d Branislav Stankovic 46 63 76; Alexander Volkov d Diego Nargiso 63 36 63; Dimitri Poliakov d Arnaud Boetsch 60 41 Ret.; Jim Grabb d Tim Mayotte 36 75 75; Mark Woodforde d Petr Korda 06 62 63. **Rd 16:** Steeb d Novacek 63 75; Gorriz d Hogstedt W/O; Cherkasov d Medvedev 61 62; Rosset d Stoltenberg 75 63; Siemerink d Adams 63 63; Hlasek d Haas 63 64; Volkov d Poliakov 75 63; Grabb d Woodforde 76 62. **QF:** Gorriz d Steeb 26 62 76; Cherkasov d Rosset 46 61 75; Hlasek d Siemerink 67 62 62; Volkov d Grabb 76 46 63. **SF:** Cherkasov d Gorriz 63 64; Hlasek d Volkov 64 62. **F:** Cherkasov d Hlasek 76 36 76.
DOUBLES: Eric Jelen/Carl-Uwe Steeb d Andrei Cherkasov/Alexander Volkov 64 76.

4-10 NOVEMBER: BANESPA OPEN, SAO PAULO $250,000 Winner: CHRISTIAN MINUSSI
Rd 32: Emilio Sanchez d Carlos Costa 76 64; Eduardo Masso d Fabio Silberberg 36 76 62; Cassio Motta d Oliver Fernandez 76 64; Francisco Clavet d Bart Wuyts 63 64; Francisco Roig d Jordi Arrese 62 62; Danilo Marcelino d Luis Herrera 61 46 62; Jaime Oncins d Marcelo Filippini 75 62; Tomas Carbonell d Paul Haarhuis 62 64; Christian Miniussi d Javier Frana 64 63; German Lopez d Roberto Azar 76 64; Gabriel Markus d Patrick Baur 64 16 64; Javier Sanchez d Luiz Mattar 67 76 12 Ret.; Felipe Rivera d Martin Jaite 63 64; Jean-Philippe Fleurian d Shuzo Matsuoka 64

62; Andres Gomez d Mark Koevermans 61 63; Markus Zoecke d Alberto Mancini 63 63. **Rd 16:** Masso d E Sanchez W/O; Clavet d Motta 62 62; Marcelino d Roig 63 64; Oncins d Carbonell 67 62 61; Miniussi d Lopez W/O; Markus d J Sanchez 64 26 64; Rivera d Fleurian 76 36 63; Gomez d Zoecke 62 64. **QF:** Clavet d Masso 61 61; Oncins d Marcelino 63 76; Miniussi d Markus 46 60 64; Gomez d Rivera 64 64. **SF:** Oncins d Clavet 64 63; Miniussi d Gomez 64 64. **F:** Miniussi d Oncins 26 63 64.
DOUBLES: Andres Gomez/Jaime Oncins d Jorge Lozano/Cassio Motta 75 64.

11-17 NOVEMBER: ATP TOUR WORLD CHAMPIONSHIP, FRANKFURT $2,250,000 Winner: PETE SAMPRAS
Ilie Nastase Group: Jim Courier, Ivan Lendl, Guy Forget, Karel Novacek. **John Newcombe Group:** Boris Becker, Michael Stich, Pete Sampras, Andre Agassi. **Round Robin:** Courier d Novacek 67 75 64; Lendl d Forget 62 64; Agassi d Becker 63 75; Forget d Novacek 63 76; Sampras d Stich 62 76; Lendl d Courier 62 63; Sampras d Agassi 63 16 63; Becker d Stich 76 63; Lendl d Novacek 62 62; Courier d Forget 76 64; Becker d Sampras 64 67 61; Agassi d Stich 75 63. **SF:** Courier d Agassi 63 75; Sampras d Lendl 62 63. **F:** Sampras d Courier 36 76 63 64.

18-24 NOVEMBER: ATP TOUR WORLD DOUBLES FINAL, JOHANNESBURG $1,000,000 Winners: JOHN FITZGERALD AND ANDERS JARRYD
Hewitt-McMillan Group: John Fitzgerald/Anders Jarryd, Grant Connell/Glenn Michibata, Patrick Galbraith/Todd Witsken, Tom Nijssen/Cyril Suk. **Forbes-Segal Group:** Scott Davis/David Pate, Ken Flach/Robert Seguso, Todd Woodbridge/Mark Woodforde, Luke Jensen/Laurie Warder. **Round Robin:** Connell/Michibata d Galbraith/Witsken 63 36 75; Jensen/Warder d Davis/Pate 64 63; Fitzgerald/Jarryd d Nijssen/Suk 63 64; Flach/Seguso d Woodbridge/Woodforde 76 76; Galbraith/Witsken d Nijssen/Suk 76 62; Fitzgerald/Jarryd d Connell/Michibata 76 64; Flach/Seguso d Jensen/Warder 76 63; Woodbridge/Woodforde d Davis/Pate 67 64 64; Connell/Michibata d Nijssen/Suk 46 76 76; Woodbridge/Woodforde d Jensen/Warder 76 36 64; Flach/Seguso d Davis/Pate 64 64; Fitzgerald/Jarryd d Galbraith/Witsken 61 26 76. **SF:** Flach/Seguso d Connell/Michibata 76 76; Fitzgerald/Jarryd d Woodbridge/Woodforde 75 62. **F:** Fitzgerald/Jarryd d Flach/Seguso 64 64 26 64.

Singles Rankings

IBM / ATP TOUR
SINGLES RANKING AT 25 NOVEMBER 1991

RANK	NAME	POINTS
1	EDBERG, STEFAN	3515
2	COURIER, JIM	3205
3	BECKER, BORIS	2822
4	STICH, MICHAEL	2675
5	LENDL, IVAN	2565
6	SAMPRAS, PETE	2494
7	FORGET, GUY	2392
8	NOVACEK, KAREL	1599
9	KORDA, PETR	1550
10	AGASSI, ANDRE	1519
11	BRUGUERA, SERGI	1504
12	GUSTAFSSON, MAGNUS	1462
13	ROSTAGNO, DERRICK	1392
14	SANCHEZ, EMILIO	1388
15	CHANG, MICHAEL	1363
16	IVANISEVICH, GORAN	1352
17	WHEATON, DAVID	1289
18	PRPIC, GORAN	1178
19	GILBERT, BRAD	1129
20	HLASEK, JAKOB	1109
21	CHERKASOV, ANDREI	1099
22	MANCINI, ALBERTO	1067
23	ARRESE, JORDI	960
24	CAMPORESE, OMAR	929
25	VOLKOV, ALEXANDER	910
26	SIEMERINK, JAN	885
27	RENEBERG, RICHEY	883
28	MCENROE, JOHN	866
29	SVENSSON, JONAS	865
30	CLAVET, FRANSISCO	837
31	CHESNOKOV, ANDREI	835
32	SANCHEZ, JAVIER	833
33	SKOFF, HORST	825
34	KRICKSTEIN, AARON	803
35	MUSTER, THOMAS	780
36	MCENROE, PATRICK	778
37	HAARHUIS, PAUL	773
38	CARATTI, CHRISTIANO	769
39	STEEB, CARL-UWE	746
40	KRAJICEK, RICHARD	744
41	DELAITRE, OLIVIER	737
42	PEREZ-ROLDAN, GUILLERMO	736
43	SANTORO, FABRICE	715
44	BERGSTROM, CHRISTIAN	709
45	JARRYD, ANDERS	701
46	JAITE, MARTIN	697
47	CHAMPION, THIERRY	653
48	CONNORS, JIMMY	650
49	WASHINGTON, MALIVAI	645
50	FERREIRA, WAYNE	637
51	PIOLINE, CEDRIC	609
52	FURLAN, RENZO	607
53	YZAGA, JAIME	606
54	BOESCH, ARNAUD	606
55	COSTA, CARLOS	559
56	ZOEKE, MARKUS	558
57	MASUR, WALLY	545
58	CURREN, KEVIN	538
59	FONTANG, FREDERIC	538
60	ROSSET, MARC	537
61	LARSSON, MAGNUS	525
62	MANSDORF, AMOS	519
63	ARIAS, JIMMY	518
64	ONCINS, JAIME	517
65	MARKUS, GABRIEL	516
66	FRANA, JAVIER	510
67	MATSUOKA, SHUZO	504
68	GOMEZ, ANDRES	500
69	PESCOSOLIDO, STEFANO	499
70	KOEVERMANS, MARK	498
71	SHELTON, BRYAN	495
72	POZZI, GIANLUCA	486
73	FLEURIAN, JEAN-PHILIPPE	485
74	AGENOR, RONALD	485
75	STOLTENBERG, JASON	482
76	SACEANU, CHRISTIAN	478
77	WOODBRIDGE, TODD	468
78	JONSSON, LARS	465
79	KULTI, NIKLAS	462
80	LOPEZ, GERMAN	455
81	MINIUSSI, CHRISTIAN	436
82	CONNELL, GRANT	428
83	GRABB, JIM	428
84	VAN RENSBURG, CHRISTO	427
85	SCHAPERS, MICHIEL	426
86	KUHNEN, PATRIK	421
87	KOSLOWSKI, LARS	417
88	WUYTS, BART	417
89	CAHILL, DARREN	412
90	AZAR, ROBERTO	408
91	GILBERT, RODOLPHE	408
92	GUNNARSSON, JAN	407
93	FROMBERG, RICHARD	401
94	MASSO, EDUARDO	400
95	CARBONELL, TOMAS	398
96	BAUR, PATRICK	391
97	PALOHEIMO, VELI	389
98	VAJDA, MARIAN	386
99	ROESE, FERNANDO	384
100	DE LA PENA, HORACIO	383
101	WOODFORDE, MARK	382
102	NARGISO, DIEGO	370
103	POLIAKOV, DIMITRI	361
104	RAOUX, GUILLAUME	361
105	MRONZ, ALEXANDER	358
106	TARANGO, JEFF	357
107	FILIPPINI, MARCELO	356
108	MULLER, GARY	353
109	ADAMS, CHUCK	347
110	ELTINGH, JACCO	346
111	DAVIN, FRANCO	344
112	MATTAR, LUIZ	344
113	CASH, PAT	343
114	MAYOTTE, TIM	338
115	ANTONITSCH, ALEX	336
116	PISTOLESI, CLAUDIO	328
117	JELEN, ERIC	324
118	GORRIZ, MARCO AURELIO	322
119	STRELBA, MARTIN	316
120	ARRAYA, PABLO	302
121	CANE, PAOLO	301
122	BLACK, BYRON	301
123	MARCELINO, DANILO	292
124	BLOOM, GILAD	291
125	CIERRO, MASSIMO	286
126	MEZZADRI, CLAUDIO	285
127	HOGSTEDT, THOMAS	283
128	ROIG, FRANCISCO	281
129	HOLM, HENRIK	275

130	BRAASCH, KARSTEN	274
131	PRIDHAM, CHRIS	265
132	LAVALLE, LEONARDO	257
133	MARTIN, TODD	256
134	BRYAN, STEVE	256
135	LAYENDECKER, GLENN	255
136	WITSKEN, TODD	255
137	MONTANA, FRANCISCO	255
138	HERRERA, LUIS	254
139	OLHOVSKIY, ANDREI	253
140	ONDRUSKA, MARCOS	252
141	LUNDGREN, PETER	252
142	YOUL, SIMON	251
143	ZIVOJINOVIC, SLOBODAN	250
144	DAMM, MARTIN	248
145	ANDERSON, JOHAN	247
146	PEREIRA, NICOLAS	245
147	GARNER, CHRIS	244
148	MARQUES, NUNO	243
149	ENGEL, DAVID	242
150	GUARDIOLA, THIERRY	239
151	CUHNA-SILVA, JOAO	236
152	WOSTENHOLME, MARTIN	234
153	NAEWIE, MARKUS	231
154	LAURENDEAU, MARTIN	228
155	DAVIS, SCOTT	227
156	GABRICHIDZE, VLADIMIR	224
157	WILANDER, MATS	220
158	PATE, DAVID	220
159	LECONTE, HENRI	219
160	BROWN, JIMMY	218
161	RIKL, DAVID	218
162	BATES, JEREMY	215
163	FERNANDEZ, OLIVER	214
164	KRISHNAN, RAMESH	214
165	ROUBICEK, VACLAV	212
166	THOMS, ARNE	211
167	PESCARIU, DINU	208
168	RIGLEWSKI, UDO	206
169	STOLLE, SANDON	203
170	APELL, JAN	201
171	BORWICK, NEIL	201
172	ZILLNER, MARCUS	200
173	RACKL, MARKUS	196
174	MORGAN, JAMIE	196
175	ZDRAZILA, TOMAS	196
176	DAHER, JOSE	193
177	PEREZ, DIEGO	192
178	BENHABILES, TARIK	191
179	STRINGARI, MARTIN	190
180	CARLSSON, JOHAN	189
181	RIVERA, FELIPE	189
182	STAFFORD,GRANT	188
183	NYBORG, PETER	188
184	ALTUR, JOSE FRANSISCO	188
185	GOLDIE, DAN	186
186	VIVER, RAUL ANTONIO	185
187	LOBO, LUIS	185
188	ORSANIC, DANIEL	183
189	BRUNO, NICOLA	179
190	NOAH, YANNICK	172
191	DAUFRESNE, XAVIER	172
192	SOULES, OLIVIER	171
193	KROON, NICLAS	168
194	SIMIAN, STEPHANE	167
195	EVERNDEN, KELLY	165
196	BECERRA, NICOLAS	164
197	SZNAJDER, ANDREW	160
198	VALERI, MASSIMO	158
199	SAAD, ROBERTO	158
200	SINNER, MARTIN	158

Doubles Rankings

IBM / ATP TOUR
DOUBLES RANKINGS AT 25 NOVEMBER 1991

RANK	NAME	POINTS
1	FITZGERALD, JOHN	3452
2	JARRYD, ANDERS	3346
3	PATE, DAVID	2354
4	DAVIS, SCOTT	2336
5	FLACH, KEN	2183
6	SEGUSO, ROBERT	2121
7	WOODBRIDGE, TODD	2086
8	MICHIBATA, GLENN	2066
9	GALBRAITH, PATRICK	1900
10	CONNELL, GRANT	1877
11	WOODFORDE, MARK	1814
12	WARDER, LAURIE	1792
13	SANCHEZ, EMILIO	1784
14	LEACH, RICK	1708
15	WITSKEN, TODD	1687
16	JENSEN, LUKE	1680
17	HAARHUIS, PAUL	1557
18	SUK, CYRIL	1511
19	NORVAL, PIET	1486
20	CASAL, SERGIO	1459
21	FRANA, JAVIER	1452
22	GRABB, JIM	1414
23	IVANISEVIC, GORAN	1383
24	FERREIRA, WAYNE	1380
25	NIJSSEN, TOM	1370
26	LAVALLE, LEONARDO	1359
27	STICH, MICHAEL	1343
28	MCENROE, PATRICK	1330
29	RIGLEWSKI, UDO	1327
30	PUGH, JIM	1307
31	CAMPORESE, OMAR	1299
32	KOEVERMANS, MARK	1278
33	MASUR, WALLY	1224
34	MULLER, GARY	1217
35	VISSER, DANIE	1210
36	SANCHEZ, JAVIER	1205
37	JONES, KELLY	1193
38	DEVRIES, STEVE	1116
39	HLASEK, JAKOB	1100
40	MACPHERSON, DAVID	1074
41	RENEBERG, RICHEY	1021
42	SALUMAA, SVEN	1019
43	BATES, JEREMY	1012
44	BROAD, NEIL	997
45	STOLTENBERG, JASON	992
46	BERGH, RIKARD	991
47	WHEATON, DAVID	969
48	BROWN, NICK	916
49	KINEAR, KENT	905
50	ONCINS, JAIME	903
51	CURREN, KEVIN	894
52	PEARCE, BRAD	890
53	MOTTA, CASSIO	878
54	ELTINGH, JACCO	872
55	BATHMAN, RONNIE	862
56	GOMEZ, ANDRES	859
57	VACEK, DANIEL	847
58	SCHAPERS, MICHIEL	843
59	PIMEK, LIBOR	835
60	SIEMERINK, JAN	795
61	BECKMAN, CHARLES	795
62	KRATZMANN, MARK	789
63	KORDA, PETER	777
64	COURIER, JIM	776
65	MATTAR, LUIZ	772
66	MELVILLE, SCOTT	738
67	CARBONELL, TOMAS	734
68	FLEGL, VOJTECH	723
69	NARGISO, DIEGO	686
70	KRUGER, STEFAN	664
71	PEREZ, DIEGO	657
72	BROWN, JEFF	655
73	NOVACEK, KAREL	651
74	KRAJICEK, RICHARD	649
75	PEREIRA, NICOLAS	646
76	DAVIDS, HENRIK JAN	642
77	JELEN, ERIC	638
78	GUNNARSSON, JAN	633
79	LUZA, GUSTAVO	633
80	WEKESA, PAUL	627
81	CANNON, SHELBY	622
82	LOZANO, JORGE	617
83	MINIUSSI, CHRISTIAN	616
84	FORGET, GUY	603
85	EDBERG, STEFAN	598
86	GARROW, BRIAN	595
87	TALBOT, BYRON	590
88	BLOOM, GILAD	588
89	OOSTING, MENNO	587
90	SVANTESSON, TOBIAS	585
91	BECKER, BORIS	584
92	VAN EMBURGH, GREG	582
93	JONSSON, OLA	569
94	ALBANO, PABLO	564
95	OLHOVSKIY, ANDREI	563
96	BRUGUERA, SERGI	557
97	YOUL, SIMON	557

98	DYKE, BRODERICK	549
99	SMITH, ROGER	540
100	SAMPRAS, PETE	537
101	COSTA, CARLOS	525
102	ACIOLY, RICARDO	517
103	ADAMS, DAVID	516
104	DAMM, MARTIN	513
105	VOGEL, RICHARD	504
106	LECONTE, HENRI	503
107	GARNETT, BRET	501
108	SHELTON, BRYAN	499
109	RIKL, DAVID	497
110	LUNDGREN, PETER	489
111	ODIZOR, NDUKA	476
112	VAN RENSBURG, CHRISTO	473
113	LAYENDECKER, GLENN	469
114	BOSCATTO, MASSIMO	467
115	BORWICK, NEIL	453
116	POZZI, GIANLUCA	451
117	MONTANA, FRANCISCO	440
118	SCHERMAN, TED	438
119	PRPIC, GORAN	434
120	PESCOSOLIDO, STEFANO	426
121	MENEZES, MAURO	424
122	DELAITRE, OLIVIER	421
123	GORRIZ, MARCO AURELIO	421
124	ZDRAZILA, TOMAS	421
125	PATRIDGE, SCOTT	420
126	GUSTAFSSON, MAGNUS	412
127	BAHRAMI, MANSOUR	410
128	POLIAKOV, DIMITRI	408
129	CIHAK, JOSEF	407
130	BAGUENA, JUAN CARLOS	402
131	SOBEL, JOHN	402
132	EVERNDEN, KELLY	400
133	CAHILL, DARREN	393
134	KEMPERS, TOM	391
135	DE LA PENA, HORACIO	389
136	NELSON, TODD	389
137	HENRICSSON, PER	389
138	STARK, JONATHAN	387
139	RAHNASTO, OLLI	379
140	PALMER, JARED	372
141	AERTS, NELSON	370
142	STEEB, CARL-UWE	368
143	BENHABILES, TARIK	367
144	THORNE, KENNY	366
145	DZELDE, GIRTS	366
146	CLAVET, FRANCISCO	365
147	KEIL, MARK	362
148	HOLM, HENRIK	359
149	CASTLE, ANDREW	357
150	MCENROE, JOHN	355

Prize Money

IBM / ATP TOUR
PRIZE MONEY LEADERS

RANK	NAME	US$ PRIZE
1	EDBERG, STEFAN	2,363,575
2	SAMPRAS, PETE	1,908,413
3	COURIER, JIM	1,748,171
4	LENDL, IVAN	1,438,983
5	STICH, MICHAEL	1,217,636
6	BECKER, BORIS	1,216,568
7	FORGET, GUY	1,072,252
8	AGASSI, ANDRE	980,611
9	JARRYD, ANDERS	752,514
10	SANCHEZ, EMILIO	672,071
11	NOVACEK, KAREL	647,540
12	FITZGERALD, JOHN	616,493
13	KORDA, PETR	573,970
14	HLASEK, JAKOB	573,642
15	IVANISEVIC, GORAN	562,795
16	GUSTAFSSON, MAGNUS	538,792
17	BRUGUERA, SERGI	527,320
18	WHEATON, DAVID	479,239
19	CHANG, MICHAEL	455,870
20	PRPIC, GORAN	411,068
21	VOLKOV, ALEXANDER	404,046
22	ROSTAGNO, DERRICK	399,739
23	CAMPORESE, OMAR	397,149
24	CHERKASOV, ANDREI	382,327
25	WOODBRIDGE, TODD	358,679
26	SVENSSON, JONAS	347,659
27	GILBERT, BRAD	343,803
28	DAVIS, SCOTT	338,781
29	CHESNOKOV, ANDREI	337,810
30	SANCHEZ, JAVIER	335,562
31	RENEBERG, RICHEY	333,121
32	PATE, DAVID	330,191
33	MCENROE, PATRICK	328,112
34	CONNELL, GRANT	326,046
35	MCENROE, JOHN	321,209
36	HAARHUIS, PAUL	312,082
37	FERREIRA, WAYNE	302,205
38	MASUR, WALLY	301,158
39	MANCINI, ALBERTO	290,375
40	WOODFORDE, MARK	289,050
41	FLACH, KEN	284,573
42	SIEMERINK, JAN	280,559
43	ROSSET, MARC	278,258
44	SEGUSO, ROBERT	272,553
45	CLAVET, FRANCISCO	259,384
46	WITSKEN, TODD	255,963
47	STEEB, CARL-UWE	253,273
48	ARRESE, JORDI	252,860
49	MICHIBATA, GLENN	249,445
50	GRABB, JIM	243,346
51	SKOFF, HORST	237,088
52	FRANA, JAVIER	232,306
53	KRAJICEK, RICHARD	231,590
54	CHAMPION, THIERRY	229,336
55	KOEVERMANS, MARK	227,213
56	CONNORS, JIMMY	224,319
57	KRICKSTEIN, AARON	224,005
58	CARATTI, CRISTIANO	223,273
59	MULLER, GARY	211,242
60	WASHINGTON, MALIVAI	208,208
61	CURREN, KEVIN	199,111
62	BOETSCH, ARNAUD	197,844
63	CARBONELL, TOMAS	197,363
64	LEACH, RICK	195,639
65	SANTORO, FABRICE	195,527
66	STOLTENBERG, JASON	195,459
67	GALBRAITH, PATRICK	190,549
68	MUSTER, THOMAS	189,840
69	BERGSTROM, CHRISTIAN	188,469
70	RIGLEWSKI, UDO	188,101
71	WARDER, LAURIE	186,346
72	GOMEZ, ANDRES	181,740
73	PEREZ-ROLDAN, GUILLERMO	180,995
74	YZAGA, JAIME	179,190
75	ONCINS, JAIME	179,027
76	KULTI, NICKLAS	177,517
77	GUNNARSSON, JAN	175,017
78	JENSEN, LUKE	175,006
79	ELTINGH, JACCO	174,884
80	JAITE, MARTIN	172,827
81	DELAITRE, OLIVIER	172,292
82	MATTAR, LUIZ	171,228
83	JELEN, ERIC	167,782
84	MANSDORF, AMOS	166,408
85	PIOLINE, CEDRIC	165,850
86	PUGH, JIM	165,219
87	LARSSON, MAGNUS	160,700
88	LAVALLE, LEONARDO	160,412
89	NIJSSEN, TOM	160,120
90	AGENOR, RONALD	159,725
91	KUHNEN, PATRIK	158,549
92	SUK, CYRIL	158,156
93	LUNDGREN, PETER	157,044
94	DE LA PENA, HORACIO	156,194
95	RAOUX, GUILLAUME	155,962
96	FROMBERG, RICHARD	153,194
97	FURLAN, RENZO	152,515
98	FLEURIAN, JEAN-PHILIPPE	151,671
99	MRONZ, ALEXANDER	151,292
100	ZIVOJINOVIC, SLOBODAN	150,361